Active
Second Edition

LISTENING
TEACHER'S MANUAL

STEVEN BROWN
DOROLYN SMITH

CAMBRIDGE UNIVERSITY PRESS
Cambridge, New York, Melbourne, Madrid, Cape Town, Singapore, São Paulo, Delhi

Cambridge University Press
32 Avenue of the Americas, New York, NY 10013-2473

www.cambridge.org
Information on this title: www.cambridge.org/9780521678148

First published 2007
3rd printing 2009

Printed in Hong Kong, China, by Golden Cup Printing Company, Limited

A catalog record for this book is available from the British Library

ISBN 978-0-521-67813-1 student's book and self-study audio CD
ISBN 978-0-521-67814-8 teacher's manual and audio CD
ISBN 978-0-521-67815-5 CDs (audio)

Art direction and book design: Adventure House, NYC
Layout services: Page Designs International
Audio production: Full House, NYC
Illustrations: William Waitzman

Contents

Teaching notes

Additional notes

Testing program

Plan of the book

Unit	Listening tasks	Listening skills	Speaking	Pronunciation
Before you begin **Learn how to listen.** pages 2–5	**1** Could you repeat that? **2** Types of listening	Classroom language Main idea Details Inference		
1 **Meeting people** pages 6–9	**1** How about you? **2** Around the world	Details Main idea Details	**Getting to know you** Taking a survey to find out about classmates	Rising intonation of questions
2 **Families** pages 10–13	**1** Family photos **2** Family ties	Main idea Details Details	**My family** Sharing information about a family member	-s endings in verbs
3 **Numbers** pages 14–17	**1** On the phone **2** Team scores	Main idea Details Main idea Details	**Numbers, numbers** Finding the correct number	Syllable stress in numbers
4 **Let's eat!** pages 18–21	**1** What would you like? **2** This looks great!	Details Inference Details	**The Food Game** Playing a board game	Intonation of *Wh-* questions
Expansion 1 **Thailand** pages 22–23	Information and an authentic student interview about food			
5 **Free time** pages 24–27	**1** How often? **2** What's popular?	Details Main idea Details	**My free time** Talking about free-time activities	Sentence stress
6 **Great outfit!** pages 28–31	**1** Choosing an outfit **2** The meaning of colors	Main idea Inference Main idea Details	**Find the differences.** Comparing two pictures	Contractions for *is* and *is not*
7 **In the house** pages 32–35	**1** Where does it go? **2** Where's the heater?	Inference Details Main idea Details	**My room** Drawing and describing rooms	Plural -s endings
8 **Time** pages 36–39	**1** Changing plans **2** Time and cultures	Details Main idea Details	**Making plans** Making weekend plans with your classmates	Reduction of *want to* and *have to*
Expansion 2 **Kuwait** pages 40–41	Information and an authentic student interview about clothing styles			

Unit	Listening tasks	Listening skills	Speaking	Pronunciation
9 Movies pages 42–45	1 **What's playing?** 2 **Film critics**	Inference Main idea Inference	**My favorite movie** Describing your favorite movie	Contractions for *is* and *are*
10 A typical day pages 46–49	1 **What's your schedule?** 2 **Daily schedules**	Main idea Details Main idea Details	**The perfect schedule** Describing your perfect schedule	Linked sounds
11 Locations pages 50–53	1 **Where is it?** 2 **Find the treasure.**	Main idea Inference Main idea Details	**Map it!** Drawing and describing a map	Stress for clarification
12 Gifts (pages 54–57	1 **Gift-giving occasions** 2 **Gifts and cultures**	Main idea Inference Main idea Details	**Gift exchange** Figuring out gifts for different occasions	Intonation with names
Expansion 3 **Italy** pages 58–59	Information and an authentic student interview about university life			
13 Part-time jobs pages 60–63	1 **What's the job?** 2 **Job interviews**	Inference Details Details Inference	**My ideal job** Figuring out what job features are important	Syllable stress
14 Celebrations pages 64–67	1 **Fireworks, food, and fun** 2 **Celebration time**	Details Main idea Details	**Holiday memories** Comparing holiday memories	Reduction of *Did you* and *What did you*
15 Inventions pages 68–71	1 **What's the invention?** 2 **What's it for?**	Inference Details Main idea Inference	**Thank you, Mr. Robot!** Designing chores for a robot	*can* and *can't*
16 Folktales pages 72–75	1 **The farmer and his sons** 2 **The stonecutter**	Main idea Details Main idea Inference	**Once upon a time ...** Telling a story	Sentence rhythm using pauses
Expansion 4 **India** pages 76–77	Information and an authentic student interview about a festival			

To the teacher

Active Listening, Second Edition is a fully updated and revised edition of the popular three-level listening series for adult and young adult learners of North American English. Each level offers students 16 engaging, task-based units, each built around a topic, function, or grammatical theme. Grounded in the theory that learners are more successful listeners when they activate their prior knowledge of a topic, the series gives students a frame of reference to make predictions about what they will hear. Through a careful balance of activities, students learn to listen for main ideas, to listen for details, and to listen and make inferences.

Active Listening, Second Edition Level 1 is intended for high-beginning to low-intermediate students. It can be used as a main text for listening classes or as a component in speaking or integrated-skills classes.

The second edition differs from the first in a number of ways. In recent years, there has been a greater emphasis on the role of vocabulary and pronunciation in the field of second language acquisition. To reflect this emphasis, the second edition provides a more refined vocabulary syllabus and a more extensive preview of words. The final section of each unit has also been expanded to provide a full-page speaking activity, including pronunciation practice. In addition, the Listening tasks in each unit have been expanded. Students listen to the same input twice, each time listening for a different purpose and focusing on a listening skill appropriate for that purpose. Other changes in the second edition include the systematic integration of cultural information. Most units contain interesting cultural information in the listening tasks, and a new, two-page Expansion unit, containing cultural information about a country or region of the world and an authentic student interview, has been added after every four units to review and extend the language and topics of the previous units. Each unit also has a Self-study page, accompanied by an audio CD, that can be used for self-study or homework.

ABOUT THE BOOK

The book includes 16 core units and four expansion units. Each core unit has four parts: **Warming up**, two main **Listening tasks**, and **Your turn to talk**, a speaking activity for pairs or small groups. The four **Expansion** units present cultural information related to the unit themes. In addition, there is an introductory lesson called **Before you begin**. This lesson introduces students to helpful learning strategies and types of listening.

The units can be taught in the order presented or out of sequence to follow the themes of the class or another book it is supplementing. In general, the tasks in the second half of the book are more challenging than those in the first, and language from earlier units is recycled as the book progresses.

Unit organization

Each unit begins with an activity called **Warming up**. This activity, usually done in pairs, serves two purposes: It reminds students of what they already know about the topic, and it previews common vocabulary used in the unit. When they do the warming up activity, students use their prior knowledge, or "schema," about the topic, vocabulary, and structures, as well as learn new vocabulary and phrases that are connected to the theme of the unit. The combination of the two approaches makes the listening tasks that follow easier.

Listening task 1 and **Listening task 2** are the major listening exercises. Each task has two parts. The students work with the same input in both parts of the task, but they listen for different reasons each time. The tasks are balanced to include a variety of listening skills, which are identified in a box to the left of each listening exercise. Because *Active Listening* features a task-based approach, students should do the activities as they listen, rather than wait until they have finished listening to a particular segment. To make this easier, writing is kept to a minimum. In most cases, students check boxes, number items, circle answers, or write only words or short phrases.

Your turn to talk, the final section of each unit, is a short, fluency-oriented speaking task done in pairs or small groups. First, students *prepare* for the speaking activity by gathering ideas and thinking about the topic. Next, they *practice* a pronunciation point. Finally, they *speak* to their classmates as they exchange information or opinions.

The two-page **Expansion** unit after every four units features listening activities that provide general cultural information about a country or region of the world and an authentic interview with a person from that place. The tasks focus on the same listening skills as the core units and recycle the themes and topics of the preceding four units.

The **Self-study** page reviews language, vocabulary, and themes from the unit and provides personalization exercises. It can be used for homework or for additional listening practice in class.

Hints and techniques

■ Be sure to do the **Warming up** section for each unit. This preview can help students develop useful learning strategies. It also helps students to be more successful listeners, which, in turn, motivates and encourages them.

■ Try to play a particular segment only one or two times. If students are still having difficulty, try telling them the answers. Then play the audio again and let them experience understanding what they heard previously.

■ If some students find listening very difficult, have them do the task in pairs, helping each other as necessary. The **Teacher's Manual**, described in the box in the next column, contains additional ideas.

■ Some students may not be used to active learning. Those students may be confused by your instructions since they are used to a more passive role. Explaining activities verbally is usually the least effective way to give instructions. It is better to demonstrate. For example, read the instructions as briefly as possible (e.g., "Listen. Number the

pictures."). Then play the first part of the audio program. Stop the recording and elicit the correct answer from the students. Those who weren't sure what to do will quickly understand. The same techniques work for **Warming up** and **Your turn to talk**. Lead one pair or group through the first step of the task. As the other students watch, they will quickly see what they are supposed to do.

Active Listening, Second Edition Level 1 is accompanied by a Teacher's Manual that contains step-by-step teaching notes with key words highlighted, optional speaking activities and listening strategies, photocopiable unit quizzes for each Student's Book unit, and two complete photocopiable tests with audio CD.

HOW STUDENTS LEARN TO LISTEN

Many students find listening to be one of the most difficult skills in English. The following explains some of the ideas incorporated into the book to make students become more effective listeners. *Active Listening, Second Edition* Level 1 is designed to help students make real and rapid progress. Recent research into teaching listening and its related receptive skill, reading, has given insights into how successful students learn foreign or second languages.

Bottom-up vs. top-down processing: a brick-wall analogy

To understand what our students are going through as they learn to listen or read, consider the "bottom-up vs. top-down processing" distinction. The distinction is based on the ways students process and attempt to understand what they read or hear. With bottom-up processing, students start with the component parts: words, grammar, and the like. Top-down processing is the opposite. Students start from their background knowledge.

This might be better understood by means of a metaphor. Imagine a brick wall. If you are standing at the bottom looking at the wall brick by brick, you can easily see the details. It is difficult, however, to get an overall view of the wall. And, if you come to a missing brick (e.g., an unknown word or unfamiliar structure), you're stuck. If, on the other hand, you're sitting on the top of the wall, you can easily see the landscape. Of course, because of distance, you'll miss some details.

Students, particularly those with years of "classroom English" but little experience in really using the language, try to listen from the "bottom up."

They attempt to piece the meaning together, word by word. It is difficult for us, as native and advanced non-native English users, to experience what students go through. However, try reading the following *from right to left.*

> word one ,slowly English process you When to easy is it ,now doing are you as ,time a at .word individual each of meaning the catch understand to difficult very is it ,However .passage the of meaning overall the

You were probably able to understand the paragraph:

> When you process English slowly, one word at a time, as you are doing now, it is easy to catch the meaning of each individual word. However, it is very difficult to understand the overall meaning of the passage.

While reading, however, it is likely you felt the frustration of bottom-up processing; you had to get each individual part before you could make sense of it. This is similar to what our students experience – and they're having to wrestle the meaning in a foreign language. Of course, this is an ineffective way to listen since it takes too long. While students are still trying to make sense of what has been said, the speaker keeps going. The students get lost.

Although their processing strategy makes listening difficult, students do come to class with certain strengths. From their years of English study, most have a relatively large, if passive, vocabulary. They also often have a solid receptive knowledge of English grammar. We shouldn't neglect the years of life

experience; our students bring with them a wealth of background knowledge on many topics. These three strengths – vocabulary, grammar, and life experience – can be the tools for effective listening.

The **Warming up** activities in *Active Listening* build on those strengths. By engaging the students in active, meaningful prelistening tasks, students integrate bottom-up and top-down processing. They start from meaning, but, in the process of doing the task, use vocabulary and structures (grammar) connected with the task, topic, or function. The result is an integrated listening strategy.

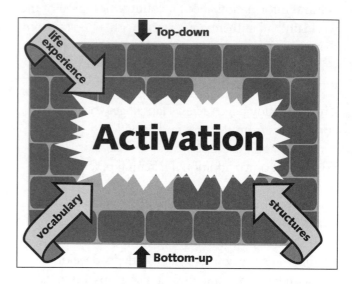

Types of listening

A second factor that is essential in creating effective listeners is exposing them to a variety of types of listening. Many students have only had experience with listening for literal comprehension. While listening for details, or specific information, is an important skill, it represents only one type. We have attempted to reach a balance in the book in order to give students experience with – and an understanding of – listening for the main idea, or gist, and listening and making inferences. Students usually are quick to understand the idea of listening for the main idea. They can easily imagine having to catch the general meaning of something they hear. Inference – listening "between the lines" – can be more difficult.

Take the following examples (from the introductory unit, **Before you begin**). The students hear the following conversation:

Paul: Hello?

Kate: Hi, Paul. This is Kate.

Paul: Oh, hi. How are you feeling? Are you still sick?

Kate: No, I feel better, thanks. I'm going to school tomorrow. What's the homework for English class?

Paul: The homework? Just a minute. . . . OK, here it is. Read pages twenty-three and twenty-four.

Kate: Twenty-three and twenty-four? OK. Thanks. See you tomorrow.

Paul: Yeah, see you tomorrow. Bye.

Students listening for the main idea, or gist, can easily identify "school" as the main topic of conversation, even though Kate and Paul also discuss the fact that Kate has been feeling sick. They are also able to pick out the specific information, or details; in this case, the page numbers for homework. To help students understand the idea of inference – listening "between the lines" – ask them whether or not both students went to school today. Even though neither speaker directly says that Kate was absent, students can understand that Kate was sick and did not go to class. Students come to understand that what they are listening for is just as important as what they are listening to.

Many of these ideas are helpful in understanding the listening process, but they should not be seen as rigid models. We need to remember that listening is actually very complex. A student listening for gist or inference may, for example, get the clues from catching a couple of specific bits of information.

Remember that although listeners need practice in listening, they also need more: They need to learn *how* to listen. They need different types of listening strategies and tasks. They need to learn to preview. Our students need exposure to it all. When students get the exposure they need, they build their listening skills. They become active listeners.

Steven Brown
Dorolyn Smith

Before you begin

Learn how to listen.

Overview

This preliminary unit introduces students to classroom language and types of listening. Students first read a letter from the authors about how to be an effective listener. Then in the **Listening tasks**, they learn useful classroom language and are introduced to the three types of listening skills in the *Active Listening* course: listening for the main idea, listening for details, and listening and making inferences.

Focus		Estimated time
Learn how to listen.	From the people who wrote this book	10–15 minutes
Listening task 1 **Could you repeat that?**	A Classroom language B Listen	20–25 minutes
Listening task 2 **Types of listening**	A Main idea D Main idea B Details E Details C Inference F Inference	20–25 minutes

---

page 2

Learn how to listen.

1. Explain to students that this letter, from the people who wrote this book, is about how to be a better listener.

2. Read the letter aloud as students read along silently. For lower-level classes, pause after each sentence to give students time to think about the meaning.

3. Have students go back and underline the most important ideas in the letter:

   • Think about what you are listening to.
   • Think about what you are listening for.
   • When you don't understand, ask.

4. Have students close their books and try to say the main ideas. Tell them that they don't have to use the same words as in the letter; rather, they can use their own words. This exercise can also be done in the students' first language.

5. To wrap up, elicit additional ways that students can be active listeners in this class (for example, predicting what they will hear, writing down new vocabulary, etc.).

Listening strategy

Places to hear English
Have students work in pairs to brainstorm as many places as they can where they can hear or practice English in their town or city. Then combine pairs and have them compare their ideas. Elicit students' ideas and list them on the board. Encourage students to visit as many places as they can by the end of the course.

---

page 3

Listening task 1
Could you repeat that?

A Classroom language

1. Point out to students that the purpose of this exercise is to get them thinking about the topic of this *Listening task* – classroom language. Read the instructions aloud. Divide the class into pairs and give students time to complete the sentences.

2. Ask for volunteers to say the complete sentences aloud. The aim here is to share ideas, so it is not necessary to comment on the sentences or correct them at this stage. Tell students that they will check their answers when they do Exercise B.

B 🖸 Listen (CD 1, track 2)

1. Read the instructions aloud. Play the audio program once or twice. Pause between items to give students time to complete their answers.

2. Check answers with the whole class and write the correct answers on the board.

Answers

1. Could you repeat that?
2. Once more, please.
3. How do you spell (that)?
4. How do you say (that) in English?

3. To wrap up, have students close their books. Then in pairs, have them try to remember and say each sentence.

Note

• In addition to the classroom language presented on page 3, you may want to teach the expression *Excuse me*. Some students may have learned this as an apology (meaning the same as *I'm sorry*) or as a way of interrupting politely (*Excuse me. Can I ask a question?*). Explain that *Excuse me?* as a question is also often used to ask someone to repeat something.

Optional speaking activity

More classroom language
Have students work in groups to write down other examples of classroom language that they know.

Call on groups to read their sentences aloud and write them on the board, correcting any mistakes.

Possible answers
• Could you say that again, please?
• How do you pronounce this word?
• What does _____ mean?
• I don't understand what to do.
• I can't hear the recording.
• Could you play the recording again, please?
• Can you speak more slowly, please?
• Excuse me. I have a question.
• I'm sorry, I don't know.

You can use this list and the sentences in the Student's Book to compile a handout of classroom language and give a copy to every student.

page 4

Listening task 2
Types of listening

A 🖸 Main idea (CD 1, track 3)

1. Give students time to look at the pictures and say what they see. Read the instructions aloud.

2. Play the audio program and give students time to complete the answer.

3. Check the answer by asking for a volunteer to say the correct answer.

4. Ask students to say any words or phrases they heard on the audio program that relate to the answer *dinner*. Make sure students understand that although the words *after class* were mentioned in the conversation, the main idea of the conversation is *dinner*.

5. To wrap up, have students read the information under the pictures.

B 🖸 Details (CD 1, track 3)

1. Give students time to look at the pictures and say what they see. Read the instructions aloud.

2. Play the audio program.

3. To check the answer, ask for a volunteer to say the correct food.

Answer

pizza

4. To wrap up, have students read the sentences under the pictures.

C 🖸 Inference (CD 1, track 3)

1. Read the instructions aloud.

2. Play the audio program.

3. To check the answer, ask for a volunteer to say *yes* or *no*.

Answer

yes

4. To wrap up, have students read the information at the bottom of the page.

Inference dialog

The idea of making inferences, or listening "between the lines," may be new to your students. If students have difficulty understanding the concept, try the following exercise.

Write the following on the board:

Does B mean . . . ?
1. Don't answer it.
2. Please answer it.
3. I want to call someone.

Then read the following aloud to students:

Listen to this conversation. What does B mean?
A: The phone's ringing.
B: I'm in the kitchen.

Call on students to give you the answer and to say what words in the conversation gave them the hints.

Answer

2, B means that A should answer the phone

Explain that in the conversation, B does not directly ask A to answer the phone, but students can infer the meaning.

This example will help students understand that making inferences involves thinking about the meaning that is present, even though specific words are not used.

---

page 5

Listening task 2
Types of listening

D–F 💿 Main idea, Details, Inference

(CD 1, track 4)

1. Explain to students that, once again, they are going to practice three skills:

   • listening for the main idea
   • listening for details
   • listening and making inferences

2. Read the instructions aloud. Tell students you are going to play the audio program three times. Explain that you will pause before each exercise to give them time to read the instructions and look at the pictures; you will also pause after each exercise to give them time to complete their answers.

3. Play the audio program, pausing between each exercise. For lower-level classes, stop the audio program to read the instructions for each exercise aloud.

4. Check answers with the whole class. If necessary, play the audio program again.

Answers

school; 23 and 24; no

5. To wrap up, call on a student to read the conclusion on the bottom of page 5 aloud, which summarizes this introduction to the listening skills students will be using throughout the book.

Listening in English

Hand out a copy of the "Listening in English" worksheet on page 5 of this Teacher's Manual to each student. Read through the statements with the class, explaining any new vocabulary.

Give students time to complete Exercise A.

When they finish Exercise A, divide the class into pairs and have students do Exercise B. Circulate while students are working to monitor their progress.

When pairs finish, have them do Exercise C.

To wrap up, ask for a few volunteers to share their suggestions for Exercise C with the class. Make a list of the suggestions on the board and discuss them. Ask:

• *Have you tried any of these ideas? If so, how did they work?*
• *Which ideas are most useful to you?*

Use students' suggestions to make a list of useful ways to improve listening. Hand out the list to the class, or put it on a poster for students to refer to throughout the course.

Listening in English

A Read these statements about listening in English. Check (✓) *true* or *false*.

	true	false
1. I don't understand well when people speak fast.	☐	☐
2. There are some accents I don't understand.	☐	☐
3. There are some slang expressions I don't understand.	☐	☐
4. It's difficult to understand people in noisy places.	☐	☐
5. It's difficult to understand when I can't see the person who is talking.	☐	☐
6. When I hear a word I don't know, I stop listening.	☐	☐
7. I have problems listening because of grammar.	☐	☐
8. I have problems listening because of vocabulary.	☐	☐
9. I try to understand every word I hear.	☐	☐

B Work with a partner. Compare your answers from Exercise A. Then choose three areas from Exercise A that you would like to improve. Can your partner suggest ways to help you?

C Write three things you can do in this class to improve your listening skills. Then tell the class.

1. _____

_____

_____

2. _____

_____

_____

3. _____

_____

_____

Meeting people

Overview

In this unit, students learn about introductions and greetings. In **Warming up**, students learn and practice phrases they can use to introduce themselves and get to know each other. In the **Listening tasks**, students practice listening for the main idea and details as they hear people introduce themselves and talk about greetings around the world. They also learn cultural information about greetings in different countries. In **Your turn to talk**, students use the new language to get to know their classmates, and learn and practice rising intonation of questions.

	Focus	Estimated time
Warming up	**Introductions –** *It's nice to meet you. By the way, my name's . . .* *I don't think we've met.* **Personal information –** *What's your name?* *Where are you from?* *Are you a/an . . . ?* *Do you like . . . ?* *What kind of . . . do you like?* *I really like . . .*	10–15 minutes
Listening task 1 **How about you?**	A Details B Main idea	20–25 minutes
Listening task 2 **Around the world**	A Details B Details	20–25 minutes
Your turn to talk **Getting to know you**	• Taking a survey to find out about classmates • Rising intonation of questions	10–20 minutes

---

page 6

Warming up

A

1. Give students time to look at the picture and read over the sentences and conversation in the boxes.

2. Read the instructions aloud. Read the sentences in the box aloud and have students listen and repeat, or call on individual students to listen and repeat. To clarify *pop music,* ask students for examples of pop music groups or songs that they know.

3. Divide the class into pairs and give students time to complete the exercise.

4. Check answers by taking the part of Brad and calling on a student to be Sun Hee, or call on two students to take the parts and read the conversation aloud.

Answers

Yes, I do. I love it.
I really like pop music.
I'm Sun Hee. It's nice to meet you, Brad.
Yes, I am. I'm studying art.

B

1. Read the instructions aloud.

2. Read questions 1 through 3 aloud and have students listen and repeat. Elicit possible ways to complete questions 4 and 5, and write them on the board, for example:

   • *Do you like jazz?*
   • *What kind of music do you like?*
   • *Do you like sports?*
   • *What kinds of movies do you like?*

3. Give students time to complete the exercise. Circulate while students are working to monitor their progress and offer help as necessary.

4. To wrap up, ask for a few volunteers to read their answers aloud. Write the answers on the board.

C

1. Read the instructions aloud.

2. Divide the class into pairs and give students time to complete the exercise. Circulate while students are working and offer help as necessary. Encourage students to introduce themselves to others in the class using the questions and their answers from Exercise B.

3. To wrap up, call on a few students to speak about themselves (for example, *My name's Miki. I'm from Japan. I'm a student. I like . . .*). For lower-level classes, have students read their sentences aloud. For higher-level classes, have students try to speak without referring to what they have written.

Listening strategy

Anticipating common patterns
Every language has common patterns. One way students can become better listeners is to anticipate and recognize these patterns. For example, in a listening exercise about introductions, we expect to hear phrases such as:

• *Hello, I'm Sue.*
• *John, this is Mary.*
• *It's nice to meet you.*
• *I don't think we've met.*

Anticipating the phrases that are likely to be used prepares students to listen.

Before doing *Listening task 1* with students, tell them to imagine they are going to introduce themselves at a party. Elicit phrases people use to introduce themselves in English, and write the phrases on the board.

After you finish *Listening task 1,* have students refer back to the board and say which phrases they heard.

---

page 7

Listening task 1
How about you?

A Details (CD 1, track 5)

1. Explain to students that they are going to hear two separate conversations at a party. You can introduce the two people in the picture as Kent and Lisa, the

first speakers students will hear. Have students predict the questions the speakers will ask.

2. Read the instructions aloud.

3. Play the audio program once or twice. If necessary, pause between items to give students time to complete their answers. For lower-level classes, have students raise their hands when they hear the question.

4. Check answers with the whole class after each conversation. Alternatively, play both conversations before checking answers.

Answers

Kent and Lisa	Lisa and Carlos
1. a	1. a
2. a	2. b
3. b	3. b
	4. a

B Main idea (CD 1, track 6)

1. Tell students to imagine that they are at the same party and have just met Lisa.

2. Read the instructions aloud. Make sure students understand that in this exercise, they should imagine they are talking to Lisa, and must choose the answer to the questions they hear.

3. Before they listen, have students read the answers and predict the possible questions or sentences that could precede them in a conversation. For example, before *Yes, I'm having fun, too,* they might hear:

   • *I'm having a great time. How about you?*
   • *This is a great party, isn't it?*

4. Play the audio program. If necessary, pause between items to give students time to complete their answers.

5. Check answers by reading aloud Lisa's part in the audio script (page 136 of this Teacher's Manual), and calling on students to say the answers.

Answers

1. Yes, I'm having fun, too.	4. I'm a student.
2. I'm (*student's name*).	5. Yes, I do.
3. I'm from (*student's hometown*).	6. Yes, I do.

6. To personalize the exercise, read Lisa's part again and call on students to answer the questions about themselves.

Meeting people in my culture
Listening task 1 presents common North American party conversations. You may want to address these points:

- Typically, people circulate and talk to each other for short periods of time.
- First topics of conversation include the event (*This is a really nice party.*), the music, the food and drinks, the weather, and things they have in common (*I play tennis, too.*).
- People generally speak for a short time before introducing themselves.

Ask students to compare these cultural norms with norms in their own cultures, for example:

- *In your culture, are these good topics to talk about when you meet people for the first time?*
- *What other topics are OK?*
- *What topics are not OK?*

To wrap up, have students list similarities and differences between greetings in their own cultures and North American culture.

---

page 8

Listening task 2
Around the world
A 💿 Details (CD 1, track 7)

1. Have students look at the pictures and the words that explain the types of greetings. Read the names of the countries aloud to model pronunciation. Have students predict which countries use which greetings.

2. Read the instructions aloud. If necessary, explain *to greet* (to welcome someone, to say "Hello").

3. Play the audio program once or twice. If necessary, pause between items to give students time to complete their answers.

4. Have students compare answers in pairs. Then check answers with the whole class.

Answers

1. a bow: Japan and South Korea
2. a hug: Brazil and Russia
3. the *salaam*: Jordan and Saudi Arabia
4. the *namaste* or *wai*: India and Thailand

Notes

- These greetings represent average cultural practices, but there may be some people in the countries listed who do not behave this way. If you have students in the class from these or other countries, ask them to share additional information about greetings in their cultures.

- Like other languages, English uses loan words for things from different cultures. *Salaam* is an Arabic word, *namaste* is a Sanskrit word, and *wai* is a Thai word. These words are used in English to describe practices from other cultures.

B 💿 Details (CD 1, track 7)

1. Read the instructions aloud. Give students time to read the statements. If students think they remember the answers, have them do the exercise and then listen to check their answers.

2. Play the audio program. If necessary, pause between items to give students time to complete their answers.

3. Check answers by reading each statement and having students raise their hands for *true* or *false*. Have students correct the false statements.

Answers

1. true	2. true	3. false	4. false

4. To wrap up, ask students which greetings are used in their cultures and what other greetings they use. Have students demonstrate how they greet people in their cultures.

Listen again!
This activity extends *Listening task 2* by having students extract more information from the audio program.

Write the following on the board:

1. *In Japan, when you bow, you don't . . .*
2. *In Brazil, when you hug, you usually give . . .*
3. *To give a* salaam, *first touch your heart, then . . .*
4. *To do the* wai, *you put your hands together . . .*

Tell students they are going to listen again for more details about the greetings. This time they will listen for *how* the greetings are performed.

Play the audio program again and have students make notes about what they hear. Then have them compare answers in pairs.

Check answers with the whole class, explaining any new vocabulary.

Answers

1. In Japan, when you bow, you don't look directly at the other person's eyes.
2. In Brazil, when you hug, you usually give the person a light kiss on the cheek, too.
3. To give a *salaam,* first touch your heart, then your forehead. Then move your hands up and away from your head.
4. To do the *wai,* you put your hands together high in front of your chest and bow slightly.

To wrap up, have students stand and demonstrate the greetings in pairs.

---

page 9

Your turn to talk
Getting to know you

A Prepare

1. Tell students they are going to ask and answer questions to get to know their classmates.

2. Read the instructions aloud. For lower-level classes, elicit two or three possible ways to finish each survey question and write them on the board for students' reference. Tell students that in this exercise, they just need to complete the questions. They will fill in the column on the right with their classmates' names when they do Exercise C.

3. Give students time to complete the survey questions. Circulate while students are working and offer help as necessary.

4. To wrap up, ask for volunteers to share their questions with the class. Write any useful vocabulary on the board.

B Practice

Exercise 1 (CD 1, track 8)

1. Read the instructions aloud. Play the audio program once without stopping so students can listen.

2. Play the audio program again, pausing between items for the class to repeat. Draw students' attention to the arrows on the page that show the rising intonation at the end of the questions. Use

your hands to demonstrate the rising intonation as students repeat the questions. You could also have students use their own hands to show the rising intonation.

Exercise 2 (CD 1, track 9)

1. Read the instructions aloud. Play the audio program once or twice. If necessary, pause between items to give students time to complete their answers.

2. Have students compare answers in pairs. Then play the audio program again and have them listen and check their answers.

3. Check answers by calling on individual students to say *Do you* or *Are you.*

Answers

a. Do you	c. Are you	e. Do you
b. Are you	d. Do you	f. Are you

4. For further practice, play the audio program again and pause between items so students can repeat the sentences using the correct intonation.

C Speak

1. Read the instructions aloud. To help students get started, model some of the questions with individual students, for example:

T: *Do you live near here?*
S1: *No, I don't.*
T: *Thank you.* [Ask another student.] *Do you live near here?*
S2: *Yes, I do.*
T: *What's your name?*

As the student answers, hold up your book and write the student's name in the survey chart.

2. Have students move around the class to complete the exercise. To extend the practice, have students collect two "yes" answers, or one "yes" and one "no" answer for each question.

3. To wrap up, ask students to share some things they learned about their classmates (for example, *Manuel lives near the school. Hussein likes soccer. Olga is from Russia.*).

Unit 1 Self-study	*Student's Book page 84*
Unit 1 Quiz	*Teacher's Manual page 82*

Families

Overview

In this unit, students listen to descriptions of families. In **Warming up**, students learn and practice vocabulary to talk about family relationships. In the **Listening tasks**, students practice listening for the main idea and details as they hear people describe their families, what their family members are like, and what they do. In **Your turn to talk**, students talk about their own families, and learn and practice the pronunciation of -s endings in verbs.

Focus		Estimated time
Warming up	**Family members** – *aunt, brother, cousins, daughter, father, granddaughter, grandfather, grandmother, grandson, husband, mother, nephew, niece, sister, son, uncle, wife*	10–15 minutes
Listening task 1 **Family photos**	A Main idea B Details	20–25 minutes
Listening task 2 **Family ties**	A Details B Details	20–25 minutes
Your turn to talk **My family**	• Sharing information about a family member • Pronunciation of -s endings in verbs	10–20 minutes

---

page 10

Warming up

A

1. Explain that the collection of pictures on page 10 is called a *family tree*; it is a visual way of showing how family members are related.

2. Read the instructions aloud. Read the words in the box aloud and have students listen and repeat.

3. Divide the class into pairs and give students time to complete the exercise. Circulate while students are working to monitor their progress and offer help as necessary.

4. Check answers by having students form complete sentences (for example, *Jack and Helen are husband and wife.*) and write the sentences on the board. Explain any unknown vocabulary.

Answers

a. Nicole / Ben	f. Helen / Ben
b. Ben / Ashley	g. Jack / Helen
c. Emma / Ashley	h. Helen / Tom
d. Jack / Maria	i. Brian / Ashley
e. Jack / Emma	

Note

• Point out that *cousins* is the plural form (*Emma and Ashley are cousins,* but *Ashley is Emma's cousin*).

B

1. Read the instructions aloud.

2. Have students close their books and give them time to do the exercise. Circulate while students are working to monitor their progress.

C

1. Read the instructions aloud.

2. Have students compare answers with their partners from Exercise A. In addition to checking the total number of words, you can have students check each other's spelling of the words.

3. To wrap up, have students close their books again and say the words they remember from the exercise.

Notes

• If students have studied family vocabulary before and have a good understanding of the vocabulary on page 10, you may want to add some or all of the following words:

great-grandmother/grandfather/grandparents: your grandparents' mother and father are your great-grandparents; their parents are your great-great-grandparents

half brother/sister: a blood relation; one parent is the same, the other is different

mother-/father-/daughter-/son-in-law: family relations by marriage (for example, your mother-in-law is your wife's or husband's mother; your son-in-law is your daughter's husband)

only child: a person with no brothers or sisters

relatives: a group of related family members (Note that the singular *relative* may be used to describe any family member.)

siblings: brothers and sisters

stepmother/father/brother/sister/daughter/son: not a blood relation; the relationship occurs through marriage (for example, your father remarries, so his wife is your stepmother and her children are your stepbrothers and stepsisters)

- Unlike some languages, English does not have separate nouns to indicate birth order of brothers and sisters. Instead, *older/oldest* or *younger/youngest* are used to explain the relationship (for example, *She's my younger sister.*).

Listening strategy

Word association

Associating new words with words or information students already know can help them learn and retain new vocabulary.

Divide the class into groups of four or five students. Tell each group to choose a secretary to write down the group's ideas.

Choose one of the family vocabulary words on page 10 and write it on the board (for example, *mother*).

Next, give groups a three-minute time limit. Tell students that they are going to race against each other to list as many words as they can think of associated with the word on the board. In the end, the group with the most words wins.

Individual students will have different associations. For example, for *mother*, students may think of *tall, good singer, doctor,* etc. This provides an opportunity for students to learn personal information about each other. Have groups look at their lists of words and ask questions such as: *Is your mother a good singer? Whose mother is a doctor? How tall is your mother?*

To wrap up, ask for volunteers to share something they learned about a classmate with the class.

---

page 11

Listening task 1
Family photos

Additional vocabulary from the audio script

cute: handsome or pretty (used for children)
picnic: outdoor meal
Grandma and Grandpa: grandmother and grandfather (casual)
kid: child (casual)
into music: really enjoys music; is interested in music

A Main idea (CD 1, track 10)

1. Have students look at the pictures and try to guess the people's relationships.

2. Read the instructions aloud.

3. Play the audio program once or twice. If necessary, pause between items to give students time to complete their answers.

4. Check answers by having students raise their hands for *a* or *b*. For lower-level classes, ask for volunteers to say what words gave them the answers.

Answers

1. a	2. a	3. b	4. b

5. To wrap up, ask students to say what family vocabulary they remember from the *Listening task*. Write the vocabulary on the board.

B Details (CD 1, track 10)

1. Read the instructions aloud. If students think they remember the answers, have them do the exercise and then listen to check their answers.

2. Play the audio program. If necessary, pause between items to give students time to complete their answers.

3. Check answers by asking for volunteers to read the complete sentences aloud.

Answers

1. The woman likes to take them to eat *pizza*.
2. His parents live *far away*.
3. The picture was taken at her *mother's* birthday party.
4. The granddaughter *likes* school.

Culture notes

• Generations ago, North American families tended to live closer together, but today, families in North America tend to be more mobile. Young adults frequently move away from home for education or career changes.

• In North American society, it is not as common as in some cultures for elderly family members to live with their adult children or grandchildren. While there are exceptions, elderly family members generally live in their own homes, in retirement communities, or in other specialized institutions.

Optional speaking activity

Family snapshots
Have students bring pictures of their own families to class. Alternatively, have students draw their own family trees in class.

Divide the class into pairs, and have students take turns showing their pictures and saying as much as they can about each family member, for example:

• the person's name
• where the person lives
• how often they see the person

Bring in some of your own pictures or draw your own family tree and use it to model the activity. Students are probably interested in your life outside school, and sharing information about yourself will help them feel more comfortable about sharing their own lives.

---

page 12

Listening task 2
Family ties

A 🔘 Details (CD 1, track 11)

1. Read the instructions aloud. Explain that the picture shows a family at the park. Have students work in pairs to try and predict the family members' relationships.

2. Play the audio program. If necessary, pause between items to give students time to complete their answers.

3. Check answers with the whole class.

Answers

1. daughter	3. brother	5. wife
2. nephew	4. father	6. mother

4. To wrap up, have students try to name the people in the picture based on what they heard.

B 🔘 Details (CD 1, track 11)

1. Read the instructions aloud. If students think they remember the answers, have them do the exercise and then listen to check their answers.

2. Play the audio program. If necessary, pause between items to give students time to complete their answers.

3. Check answers by reading the statements and having students raise their hands for *true* or *false*. Have students correct the false statements.

Answers

1. true	3. false	5. true
2. true	4. false	6. true

Optional speaking activity

You know what they say . . .
Write some or all of the following proverbs on the board and explain them to the class. Ask students to say whether they agree with the proverbs. Then have them think of proverbs about families from their own cultures. You can have students share their proverbs in groups, or ask volunteers to share with the whole class.

Point out to students that these proverbs are often used in conversation to remark on other people's behavior or familiar situations, and are often preceded by phrases such as *Well, you know what they say . . .* and *As the saying goes, ...*

Blood is thicker than water.: Connections between family members are stronger than connections between friends.
Like father, like son. and **The apple never falls far from the tree.**: Children behave like their parents.
There's a black sheep in every flock.: Every family has one member who has done something wrong or who behaves badly.
There's no place like home. and **Home is where the heart is.**: Your home is always the most comfortable and appropriate place for you.

Your turn to talk
My family

A Prepare

1. Tell students they are going to talk with their classmates about a family member.

2. Read the instructions aloud.

3. Give students time to complete the exercise. Circulate while students are working and offer help as necessary.

B Practice

Exercise 1 💿 (CD 1, track 12)

1. Read the instructions aloud. Play the audio program once without stopping so students can listen.

2. Play the audio program again, pausing between items for the class to repeat.

Exercise 2 💿 (CD 1, track 13)

1. Read the instructions aloud. Have students work alone or in pairs to do the exercise. Encourage students to say the words quietly to themselves before they write them in the chart. You can have students try covering their ears to better hear the /z/ sound, or put their hands on their throats to feel the vibration.

2. Play the audio program once or twice and have students listen to check their answers. For lower-level classes, pause between items and have students listen and repeat.

Answers		
/s/	/z/	/ɪz/
sleeps	plays	exercises
works	studies	teaches

C Speak

Exercise 1

1. Read the instructions aloud. Read the example sentences aloud or call on individual students to read them. Remind students to use the correct pronunciation of the -s endings in the verbs.

2. Divide the class into pairs and give students time to complete the exercise. Circulate while students are working and offer help as necessary.

Exercise 2

1. Read the instructions aloud.

2. Have pairs combine to make groups of four. Give groups time to complete the exercise. Circulate while students are working to monitor their progress. Make a note of any difficulties students have to address later.

Optional speaking activity

Me, too!
Have students brainstorm a list of questions they can ask about someone's family and write them on the board, for example:

• *How many brothers and sisters do you have?*
• *Do you have a younger/older brother?*
• *Do your grandparents live with you?*
• *How old are your parents?*

Have students move around the room and ask their classmates questions. They can use the questions on the board or their own questions.

Tell them that they should try to find one thing that is the same about their own family and a classmate's family (for example, the same number of brothers, parents of the same ages, etc.).

Explain that once they find something in common with one classmate, they should move on and talk to other classmates.

Variation: Once a student finds a partner with something in common, the two students form a pair and go together to find a third person who has the same thing in common. They then look for a fourth, and so on. The group with the most students wins.

Unit 2 Self-study	Student's Book page 85
Unit 2 Quiz	Teacher's Manual page 83

Numbers

Overview

In this unit, students listen to information including numbers. In **Warming up**, students learn and practice numbers from zero to one hundred. In the **Listening tasks**, students practice listening for the main idea and details as they hear people talk about phone numbers and sports scores. In **Your turn to talk**, students practice saying numbers, and learn and practice word stress in numbers ending in *-ty* and *-teen*.

	Focus	Estimated time
Warming up	**Numbers** – *zero to one hundred*	10–15 minutes
Listening task 1 **On the phone**	A Main idea B Details	20–25 minutes
Listening task 2 **Team scores**	A Main idea B Details	20–25 minutes
Your turn to talk **Numbers, numbers**	• Finding the correct number • Syllable stress in numbers	10–20 minutes

page 14

Warming up

A

1. Before students start the exercise, check their understanding of the numbers by writing some random numbers from zero to one hundred on the board and calling on students to say them aloud. Correct any mistakes and review or teach numbers as necessary.

2. Read the instructions aloud.

3. Divide the class into pairs and give students time to complete the exercise. Circulate while students are working to monitor their progress.

4. As a fun wrap-up activity, have students stand in a circle and try to count as quickly as they can by even numbers, odd numbers, fives, etc.

B

1. Read the instructions aloud. Read the example numbers aloud or call on individual students to read them.

2. Give students time to complete the exercise. Circulate while students are working to monitor their progress and offer help as necessary.

Notes

• You may want to draw students' attention to the use of *zero* in the examples. Point out that *zero* is usually pronounced "oh" in strings of numbers, although *zero* is sometimes used for extra clarity or emphasis.

• If students do not wish to give their phone numbers or birthdays to the whole class, tell them to invent a phone number or birthday.

C

1. Read the instructions aloud. Model the exercise with a student, for example:

   T: *When is your birthday?*
   S: *My birthday is ten, twenty-three, nineteen eighty-seven.*

   As the student answers, hold up your book and circle the numbers in the number game.

2. Have students work with their partners from Exercise A. Circulate while students are working to monitor their progress.

3. Have students check each other's games. Then ask for volunteers to say how many correct answers they had.

page 15

Listening task 1

On the phone

Additional vocabulary from the audio script

directory assistance: the service that informs customers of phone numbers

city code/area code: set of numbers that you must use before the main number when you want to telephone someone outside your local area

A **Details** (CD 1, track 14)

1. Give students time to look at the pictures and read the names of the places. Ask students to raise their hands if they have visited any of the places.

2. Read the instructions aloud. Read the possible answers aloud to model pronunciation.

3. Explain to students that they do not need to know all of the vocabulary for the names of the places; they just need to listen for the relevant words.

4. Play the audio program once or twice. If necessary, pause between items to give students time to complete their answers.

5. Check answers by reading the answer choices aloud and having students raise their hands for the correct answers.

Answers

1. Park Hyatt
2. American Chamber of Commerce
3. National Tourism Organization
4. Blue Jays Baseball Team Ticket Office
5. American Center Library
6. Colombia Airlines

Note

• Item 4 of this *Listening task* lists the name of the Maple Leafs hockey team from Toronto, Canada. Explain to students that the plural of *leaf* is *leaves,* and that the name of the hockey team is an exception.

B **Details** (CD 1, track 14)

1. Read the instructions aloud.

2. Play the audio program. If necessary, pause between items to give students time to complete their answers.

3. Check answers by asking for volunteers to write the correct answers on the board. Correct any mistakes; then call on students to read the numbers aloud.

Answers

1. 02-9241-1234
2. 11-5180-3804
3. 7299-496-499
4. 1-888-654-6529
5. 03-3436-0901
6. 5283-5500

Note

• In English, the hyphen (-) in phone numbers is not spoken. Rather, when saying numbers, people pause after sets of numbers (for example, after the area code and after the first three digits).

Listening task 2
Team scores

> **Additional vocabulary from the audio script**
>
> **It was Team X against Team Y.:** Team X played Team Y.
>
> Ways to talk about sports victories:
> - **Team X won.**
> - **Team X beat Team Y.**
> - **Team X over Team Y (92 to 90).**
> - **Team X (losing team) went down, 92 to 90.**

A Main idea (CD 1, track 15)

1. Give students time to look at the chart. Explain that this is a scoreboard for a basketball tournament. Read the team names aloud to model pronunciation.

2. Read the instructions aloud. Tell students that in this exercise, they should just listen and write the first letter of the winning team's name in each circle. They will fill in the scores when they do Exercise B.

3. Play the audio program once or twice. If necessary, pause between items to give students time to complete their answers.

4. Have students compare answers in pairs. Then check answers with the whole class.

Answers

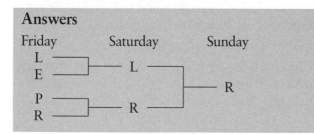

Friday   Saturday   Sunday

L
E
P
R
L
R
R

B Details (CD 1, track 15)

1. Read the instructions aloud. If necessary, explain the meaning of *score* (the number of points each team gets in a game).

2. Play the audio program. If necessary, pause between items to give students time to complete their answers.

3. Have students compare answers in pairs. Then check answers by asking students to read the numbers aloud while you write the correct answers on the board.

Answers

1. Lions 94, Hawks 68
2. Eagles 103, Tigers 99
3. Panthers 87, Bears 73
4. Rockets 72, Comets 65
5. Lions 92, Eagles 80
6. Rockets 107, Panthers 86
7. Rockets 109, Lions 98

Optional speaking activity

Fast math
Divide the class into groups of three or four students.

Hand out one copy of the "Fast math" worksheet below to each group or copy the worksheet onto the board.

Before groups start, check that they know the mathematical terms *plus, minus,* and *times.* If necessary, do a couple of simple calculations with the class on the board to make sure students understand the terms.

Tell each group to choose a quizmaster. The quizmaster first reads the answer aloud and then reads the two problems. The other students in the group write the problems down. When everyone is ready, the teams race to see who can find the correct problem first.

Fast Math

You are the quizmaster. Read the answers. Then read both problems. Your partners will write down the problems. Teams will then race to find out which problem is correct.

Math words
- **+** plus
- **−** minus
- **×** times

	Answers	Problems		
a.	25	16 + 7	or	11 + 14*
b.	89	34 − 45	or	62 + 27*
c.	107	63 + 44*	or	46 + 51
d.	317	444 − 127*	or	318 − 63
e.	121	187 − 66*	or	193 − 82
f.	128	11 × 3	or	8 × 16*
g.	104	77 + 82	or	238 − 134*

*correct problem

© Cambridge University Press 2007   **Photocopiable**

Your turn to talk
Numbers, numbers

A Prepare

1. Tell students they are going to practice saying and listening to numbers with their classmates.

2. Read the instructions aloud.

3. Give students time to complete the exercise. Circulate while students are working to monitor their progress.

B Practice

Exercise 1 (CD 1, track 16)

1. Read the instructions aloud. Play the audio program once without stopping so students can listen.

2. Play the audio program again, pausing between items for the class to repeat. Draw students' attention to the stress on the first syllable in numbers ending in -*ty,* and on the last syllable in numbers ending in -*teen.* Point out that in English, stressed syllables are said with a higher pitch and last longer in time than unstressed syllables.

3. For further practice, give each student a rubber band. Have students hold their hands in front of them, palms facing away from them and with the rubber band looped around each thumb. Tell them that when they say the stressed syllable (for example, **nine**ty or nine**teen**), they should stretch the rubber band by moving their thumbs apart. (This idea comes from *Clear Speech,* third edition, by Judy Gilbert, Cambridge University Press, 2005.)

Exercise 2 (CD 1, track 17)

1. Read the instructions aloud. Before you play the audio program, have students work in pairs to say the numbers aloud. Circulate and check that they are using the correct stress.

2. Play the audio program once or twice. If necessary, pause between items to give students time to complete their answers.

3. Check answers by calling on students to say the correct numbers while you write them on the board.

Answers		
a. 13	c. 40	e. 80
b. 17	d. 19	f. 16

C Speak

1. Read the instructions aloud. Read the example sentence aloud and have a student read the example response.

2. Divide the class into pairs. Have students sit or stand back to back, or prop up a book between them so they don't accidentally see their partner's book. Circulate while students are working and make a note of any difficulties to address later.

3. Have pairs check their answers by comparing their Student's Books.

Culture notes

• In many cultures, people have superstitions about certain numbers. For example, in the U.S. and in the U.K., thirteen is an unlucky number. In the U.S., seven is a lucky number. Ask students what numbers are lucky or unlucky in their cultures and if they know why.

• In North American English *a hundred* is often used to mean a lot or many. Parents may tell children, "I've told you a hundred times not to do that!" Of course, they don't literally mean a hundred times. Ask students if the number *one hundred* is used in this way in their cultures or if they have any other special numbers.

| Unit 3 Self-study | Student's Book page 86 |
| Unit 3 Quiz | Teacher's Manual page 84 |

Let's eat!

Overview

In this unit, students listen to conversations about food. In **Warming up**, students learn and practice names for common foods. In the **Listening tasks**, students practice listening for details and inference as they hear people order meals and talk about food. In **Your turn to talk**, students practice talking about their favorite foods, and learn and practice the intonation of questions.

	Focus	Estimated time
Warming up	**Foods** – *bananas, beef, bread, broccoli, cheese, chicken, lemons, melons, milk, mushrooms, pasta, shrimp, tomatoes, yogurt*	10–15 minutes
Listening task 1 **What would you like?**	A Details B Details	20–25 minutes
Listening task 2 **This looks great!**	A Inference B Details	20–25 minutes
Your turn to talk **The Food Game**	• Playing a board game • Intonation of *Wh-* questions	10–20 minutes

page 18

Warming up

A

1. Give students time to look at the picture and say what they see. Ask them to name any foods they like or dislike, the foods they have eaten today, and the ones they would like to eat.

2. Read the instructions aloud. Read the words in the box aloud and have students listen and repeat.

3. Divide the class into pairs and give students time to complete the exercise. Circulate while students are working to monitor their progress and offer help as necessary.

4. Check answers by saying the numbers and calling on students to say the words aloud. For lower-level classes, do the exercise with the whole class. Point to items in the picture and ask, *What do you call this in English?*

Answers

1. beef	5. mushrooms	9. lemons
2. shrimp	6. broccoli	10. pasta
3. cheese	7. tomatoes	11. bread
4. milk	8. melons	12. chicken

B

1. Read the instructions aloud.

2. Have students work with their partners from Exercise A. Circulate while students are working and offer help as necessary. Tell students they can use a separate piece of paper if they need more space.

Possible answers
apples, cabbage, cake, cookies, eggs, fish, ham, oranges, potatoes, pork, rice, steak

3. To extend the practice, have students change partners and take turns reading their words, adding any new words to their lists. For higher-level classes, have students put the food vocabulary into groups, for example:

• meat and fish
• bread and grains
• dairy
• fruit
• vegetables
• healthy/unhealthy foods
• breakfast/dinner foods

Listening strategy

Visualization

Visualizing, or making a mental image of new vocabulary, can help students recognize and remember new words when they hear them.

After students finish the exercises on page 18, have them close their books. Tell them you are going to say some vocabulary for various foods. When students hear the words, they should try to imagine what each food looks like and picture each food in their minds. You can expand the activity by having students imagine the smell or taste of each food, too.

Read the words from the box on page 18 slowly, one at a time, pausing between each word to give students time to imagine the food. You may also want to add some of the foods students will hear in *Listening tasks 1* and *2* (*soup, burger, sushi, coffee, ice cream, pizza*) to preview the vocabulary.

Tell students they can use this strategy when they do the *Listening tasks,* and that it is especially helpful when listening for details.

Optional speaking activity

Quick food review

Have students close their books and try to remember the food vocabulary they have just learned.

To do this as a game, divide the class into teams of four and try one of the following options:

- Have teams choose a secretary to write the group's ideas. Give students a one-minute time limit. Team members race to say as many of the words as they remember and list them in alphabetical order. The team with the most words in the correct order wins.

- Have teams race to be the first to say foods in the following categories:
  - *a food that begins with the letter b/c/m, etc.*
  - *a vegetable/a fruit/a kind of meat*
  - *a food that is green/red/white*

  The first team to say a correct answer gets a point. The team with the most points in the end wins.

- In higher-level classes, teams can play the game on their own. Team members take turns giving each other hints and guessing the foods on page 18. For example:

  A: *These are yellow and they taste very sour.*
  B: *Are they lemons?*

---

page 19

Listening task 1
What would you like?

Additional vocabulary from the audio script

watch the fat: be careful not to eat too much fat
count calories: be careful of the food you eat so you don't gain weight
garden salad: a green salad made mostly of lettuce with a variety of other vegetables

A Details (CD 1, track 18)

1. Give students time to look at the pictures. Read the names of the items and the answer choices aloud and have students listen and repeat.

2. Read the instructions aloud.

3. Play the audio program once or twice. If necessary, pause between items to give students time to complete their answers.

4. Check answers by playing the role of a server in a restaurant. Ask students, *What kind of soup/drink/toppings/salad would you like?* and have them say the correct responses.

Answers

1. French onion
2. Large
3. ketchup, lettuce, mushrooms, mustard, onions, pickles, tomatoes (everything except cheese)
4. pasta salad

Optional speaking activity

Waiter!
Write the following dialog on the board:

A: *What would you like?*
B: *I'll have* soup*, please.*
A: *What kind of* soup *would you like?*
B: *What kind do you have?*
A: *French onion* or *vegetable.*
B: *I'll have* French onion.

First, have students listen and repeat the dialog after you. Then have them practice in pairs.

When students can say the dialog smoothly, have them substitute the underlined words with other foods. For lower-level classes, write some substitution options on the board for students to choose from (for example, *ice cream, salad, cake, pizza, tea*).

B 💿 Details (CD 1, track 18)

1. Read the instructions aloud.

2. Play the audio program. If necessary, pause between items to give students time to complete their answers.

3. Check answers by asking for volunteers to read the complete sentences aloud.

Answers

1. The woman doesn't like *vegetables*.
2. Active Lemon Light has *no flavor*.
3. The man thinks cheese *has too much fat*.
4. She doesn't like *tomatoes*.

---

page 20

Listening task 2
This looks great!

Additional vocabulary from the audio script

Let's check out the menu.: Let's look at the menu and see what's on it.
salsa: a spicy sauce usually made with tomatoes and hot peppers and used to top Mexican food, meat, etc.
I'm starving.: I'm really hungry.
to overdo it: to have too much

A 💿 Inference (CD 1, track 19)

1. Give students time to look at the pictures and say what they see. Ask them to say how often they eat the foods pictured.

2. As this is the first inference exercise in the book, you may want to spend some time reviewing this type of exercise. Refer students back to pages 4 and 5. (Inference was introduced in *Before you begin.*) Remind students they will not hear the exact words; they need to listen for hints in the conversation. To help them prepare, ask students to think of one or two words they might use

to talk about each item. Words might be food flavors (chocolate, vanilla), ingredients (toppings on the pizza), or things that go with the food or drink (cream and sugar with coffee). Stop the recording after the first item to make sure students understand what to do.

3. Read the instructions aloud. Explain to students that first they just need to decide which food people are talking about. They will write the hints that helped them get the answers when they do Exercise B. Make sure students understand that there is one item that the speakers do not mention.

4. Play the audio program. If necessary, pause between items to give students time to complete their answers.

5. To check answers, hold up your book. Point to each picture, say the name of the food, and have students tell you the number.

Answers

1. ice cream	3. sushi	5. fish
2. pizza	4. burritos	6. coffee

B 💿 Details (CD 1, track 19)

1. Read the instructions aloud. If students think they can remember the words, have them do the exercise and then listen to check their answers.

2. Play the audio program, pausing between items to give students time to complete their answers.

3. Check answers by saying the numbers and calling on individual students to say the foods. For lower-level classes, play the audio program again after checking answers so that students can listen for any words they missed.

Answers

1. dessert, chocolate, vanilla
2. toppings (mushrooms, black olives, green peppers, extra cheese), a slice
3. Asia center, rice, sticky, raw fish
4. chicken, beef, hot sauce, salsa, spicy
5. with lemon, bones, ocean
6. pot, cream and sugar, black

Culture note

• Asian food has enjoyed a recent boom in North America. In most North American cities, food from many countries is readily available in restaurants and supermarkets. Asian cuisine is very popular on restaurant menus, and Asian dishes are served in many university cafeterias.

Your turn to talk
The Food Game

A Prepare

1. Tell students they are going to play a game about food with their classmates.

2. Read the topics on the game board aloud. Explain any unknown vocabulary.

3. Read the instructions aloud. Ask for a volunteer to read the example sentence aloud. For lower-level classes, elicit one example for each topic. Explain to students that in this exercise, they just need to think about their responses; they do not have to write anything.

4. Give students time to complete the exercise. Circulate while students are working and offer help as necessary.

B Practice

Exercise 1 (CD 1, track 20)

1. Read the instructions aloud. Play the audio program once without stopping so students can listen.

2. Play the audio program again, pausing between items for the class to repeat. Draw students' attention to the arrows on the page that show the falling intonation at the end of the questions. Use your hands to demonstrate the falling intonation as students repeat the questions. You could also have students use their own hands to show the falling intonation.

Exercise 2 (CD 1, track 21)

1. Read the instructions aloud. Play the audio program once or twice. If necessary, pause between items to give students time to complete their answers.

2. Check answers by having students say *What, When,* or *Where.*

Answers

a. What	c. What	e. When
b. Where	d. When	f. Where

C Speak

1. Divide the class into groups of four. Have each student choose a marker. They can use erasers, pen caps, etc. Tell each group to open one of their Student's Books to page 21 and place it where all group members can see it.

2. Make sure each group has a coin. Tell students to choose which side of the coin will represent *heads* and which side will represent *tails.*

3. Read the instructions aloud. Make sure all students put their markers on "Start."

4. Remind students that the questions are all *Wh-* questions, so they should use falling intonation.

5. Give students ten to fifteen minutes to play the game. Circulate while students are playing to monitor their progress and offer help as necessary. Make a note of any difficulties to address later.

Optional speaking activity

It's not a match!
Hand out one copy of the following "It's not a match!" worksheet to each student or copy the worksheet onto the board. Read the sentences with the whole class to make sure students understand them.

Give students time to write down their answers.

Next, divide the class into groups of four to eight students and have them take turns sharing their answers.

Each student in the group who has an answer that is different from all the others gets a point. When they finish, the student with the most points in the group wins.

It's not a match!

Name . . . .

1. a vegetable that is not green
2. a food that costs a lot of money
3. something you have eaten but never want to eat again
4. a food you have never eaten but would like to try
5. a food that's good to eat on a cold day
6. something you eat in a restaurant but never eat at home
7. a food that smells good
8. a food that smells bad
9. a food that has a short season (something you can eat only for a short time each year)
10. a food you eat for the holidays

© Cambridge University Press 2007   **Photocopiable**

Unit 4 Self-study	*Student's Book page 87*
Unit 4 Quiz	*Teacher's Manual page 85*

Thailand

Overview

In this **Expansion** unit, students listen to general information about Thailand. In the **Listening tasks**, students practice listening for the main idea and details as they hear people talk about Thai greetings, people, and food. They also learn cultural information about Thailand as they listen to an authentic interview with a Thai student about two popular Thai dishes.

Focus		Estimated time
Listening task 1 **Information**	A Main idea B Details	20–25 minutes
Listening task 2 **Food**	A Details B Details	20–25 minutes

---

page 22

Listening task 1

Information

Note

• Before you start this unit, write the titles of the previous four units on the board or elicit them from students (*Meeting people, Families, Numbers, Let's eat!*). Tell students that this *Expansion* unit features some of the topics and vocabulary from these units. It presents general information about Thailand and a more in-depth look at Thai culture based on an authentic interview with a student from Thailand. Give students time to look over the language and listening skills in Units 1 through 4.

A Main idea (CD 1, track 22)

1. Ask students where Thailand is located (Southeast Asia). You may want to bring a world map to class and have students find Thailand on the map. Ask students if anyone has traveled to Thailand and, if so, what it was like.

2. If you have students from Thailand, ask them to say a few things they think are special about their country. If you are teaching a class of Thai students, have students brainstorm what Thailand is known for around the world.

3. Give students time to look at the picture and say what they see. Write a list of key words and phrases on the board.

   Possible answers
   Bangkok, bus, city street, cars, taxi, traffic, truck

Note

• The photo shows a *tuk tuk,* a type of open-air taxi used in cities in Thailand.

4. Read the instructions aloud. This is a good time to review the types of listening skills introduced in *Before you begin* on pages 4 and 5 (Main idea, Details, Inference). Point out to students that in this exercise they are listening for the main idea. This means that they don't need to understand everything they hear, just the general meaning.

5. Play the audio program once or twice. If necessary, pause between items to give students time to complete their answers.

6. Check answers by calling on students to say the correct answers. For lower-level classes, ask for volunteers to say what words helped them get the answers.

Answers			
1. b	2. b	3. a	4. b

B 💿 Details (CD 1, track 22)

1. Read the instructions aloud. Point out to students that this time they are listening for details. Before you play the audio program, give students time to read the sentences and predict which ones are true and false.

2. Play the audio program. If necessary, pause between items to give students time to complete their answers.

3. Check answers by reading the statements and having students raise their hands for *true* and *false*. Have students correct the false statements.

Answers

1. false	2. true	3. false	4. true

Additional listening practice

Numbers review
Write the following chart on the board:

People in Thailand who	Percentage
are Thai	
are Chinese	
are Malay	
live with parents, brothers, and sisters	
live in bigger families	

Play the audio program again and have students complete the chart.

Check answers with the whole class.

Answers
75%
11%
3.5%
50%
30%

If students had difficulty with item 3 of the audio program, remind them that the stress is on the first syllable in numbers that end in -*ty* and on the last syllable for numbers that end in -*teen*.

page 23

Listening task 2
Food

A 💿 Details (CD 1, track 23)

1. Give students time to look at the pictures. Read the names of the ingredients aloud and have students listen and repeat. Ask if anyone has eaten Thai food and, if so, whether they liked it. If you have Thai students in your class, you could ask them to say which dish they like better – Thai green curry or pad Thai – and why.

2. Read the instructions aloud. Remind students that in this exercise, they will be listening for details. Make sure students understand that there are two items for each dish that the speaker does not mention.

3. Play the audio program once or twice. If necessary, pause between items to give students time to complete their answers.

4. Have students compare answers in pairs. Then check answers by calling on students to list the ingredients for each dish.

Answers

1. garlic, chicken, coconut milk, basil leaves, hot peppers
2. bean sprouts, peanuts, noodles, green onions, shrimp

B 💿 Details (CD 1, track 23)

1. Read the instructions aloud. If students think they remember the answers, have them do the exercise and then listen to check their answers.

2. Play the audio program. If necessary, pause between items to give students time to complete their answers.

3. Check answers by asking for volunteers to read the complete sentences aloud.

Answers

1. a. Thai people eat curry with *rice*.
   b. The most popular Thai dish *is* spicy.
2. a. The woman prefers pad Thai in *Thailand*.
   b. Thai dishes *are not* always spicy.

Free time

Overview

In this unit, students listen to conversations about free-time activities. In **Warming up**, students learn and practice frequency adverbs and vocabulary to talk about what they do in their free time. In the **Listening tasks**, students practice listening for the main idea and details as they hear people talk about free-time activities. They also learn cultural information about popular free-time activities in the U.S. In **Your turn to talk**, students talk about their own activities, and learn and practice the stress on important words in sentences.

	Focus	Estimated time
Warming up	**Frequency adverbs** – *always, often, sometimes, hardly ever, never* **Free-time activities** – *go out for lunch, go to a club, go to the movies, play sports, visit relatives, watch TV* **Time phrases** – *in the morning/afternoon, on vacation, on weekends/Saturday night*	10–15 minutes
Listening task 1 **How often?**	A Details B Details	20–25 minutes
Listening task 2 **What's popular?**	A Main idea B Details	20–25 minutes
Your turn to talk **My free time**	• Talking about free-time activities • Sentence stress	10–20 minutes

---

page 24

Warming up

A

1. Give students time to look at the chart. Read the frequency adverbs aloud and have students listen and repeat. Draw students' attention to the timeline that depicts the frequency adverbs. Point out that frequency adverbs are used to express how much or how often something happens, in this case, how often people do free-time activities. For further clarification of frequency adverbs, write the following on the board:

   always: every day
   often: three or four times a week
   sometimes: once or twice a month
   hardly ever: once every six months
   never: at no time

2. Give students time to read the questions in the chart. For lower-level classes, write the following on the board:

   A: *How often do you go out for lunch?*
   B: *Sometimes. I like to go out for lunch on weekends.*

Take the part of A and call on a student to be B. Then assign students the roles of A and B and have them practice the dialog in pairs before they do the exercise. For higher-level classes, encourage the Student Bs to give longer answers (one or two sentences), rather than just answering "often" or "never."

3. Read the instructions aloud.

4. Give students time to complete the exercise. Circulate while students are working to monitor their progress. Make a note of any difficulties and go over them with the whole class when students have finished Exercise A.

B

1. Read the instructions aloud.

2. Have students work alone or in pairs to do the exercise. Tell them they do not have to write complete sentences, just words or phrases. Circulate while students are working to monitor their progress and offer help as necessary.

3. Check answers by asking for volunteers to say the activities they wrote. Write any useful words and phrases on the board.

C

1. Read the instructions aloud.

2. Have students walk around the class and share their answers from Exercise B with their classmates. Tell students to make a note of any activities they have in common with other classmates. For lower-level classes, write the following dialog on the board for students' reference:

   A: *What do you do in your free time?*
   B: *I read and play the piano.*

3. To wrap up, ask for volunteers to say which activities they have in common with their classmates (for example, *Mari and I both go out for lunch often.*). Alternatively, read the activities aloud and have students raise their hands if they do them. Make a list on the board of the five most popular activities in the class.

Listening strategy

Listener awareness
Each time students listen, they need to know why they are listening. To help them think about this skill, it is useful to refer to real-world situations. For example, have students work in pairs to answer this question: *In your own language, what kinds of things do you listen to every day?*

Possible answers
• the evening news on TV
• the weather report on the radio in the morning
• people talking to each other on the train

After students list the things they listen to, have them write down the type of information they listen for in each case. For example, in the weather report, they may listen for the temperature or whether it's going to rain.

Point out to students that *what* they listen to affects *how* they listen. For example:

• In the evening news, they don't need to listen to every word but to the most important words and phrases, or the **main idea** of a news story.
• In the weather report, they are listening for specific numbers (20 degrees) and words (rain). They are listening for **details**.

• When they listen to people talking on the train, they may be able to guess whether the people are friends, strangers, classmates, or co-workers without actually hearing the people say those words. They are listening and making an **inference**.

Remind students to think about their purpose for listening when they are listening in English.

---

page 25

Listening task 1
How often?

Additional vocabulary from the audio script

on the big screen: in the movie theater
student union: a building on a college or university campus that usually contains restaurants, a bookstore, an ATM, meeting rooms, student club offices, etc.

A Details (CD 1, track 24)

1. Give students time to read the sentences silently to familiarize themselves with the topics.

2. Read the instructions aloud.

3. Play the audio program once or twice. If necessary, pause between items to give students time to complete their answers.

4. Check answers by asking for volunteers to read the complete sentences aloud.

Answers		
1. hardly ever	3. always	5. often
2. sometimes	4. never	6. always

B Details (CD 1, track 24)

1. Read the instructions aloud. If students think they remember the answers, have them do the exercise and then listen to check their answers.

2. Play the audio program. If necessary, pause between items to give students time to complete their answers.

3. Check answers by asking for volunteers to read the complete sentences aloud.

----

page 26

Listening task 2
What's popular?

A 🔘 **Main idea** (CD 1, track 25)

1. Give students time to look at the picture. Ask:

   • *Where do you think these people are from?*
   • *What are they doing?*
   • *How often do you think they do this activity?*

2. Read the phrases in the box aloud and have students listen and repeat. Explain any unknown vocabulary. Have students work in pairs to guess the top five ways people in the U.S. spend their free time. Ask for volunteers to share their guesses with the whole class. You can have students write their guesses on a separate piece of paper and then listen and check whether they were correct.

3. Read the instructions aloud.

4. Play the audio program once or twice. If necessary, pause between items to give students time to complete their answers.

5. Have students compare answers in pairs. Then ask for volunteers to say which activity is the most popular, the second most popular, etc.

Answers

1. watching TV or DVDs	6. going to the
2. staying home with family	movies or a play
3. resting or relaxing	7. eating out
4. reading	8. playing a sport
5. getting together	or exercising
with friends	9. other

B 🔘 **Details** (CD 1, track 25)

1. Read the instructions aloud. If students think they remember the answers, have them do the exercise and then listen to check their answers.

2. Play the audio program. If necessary, pause between items to give students time to complete their answers.

3. Check answers by calling on individual students. Write the correct answers on the board.

Source: *The Gallup Organization*

4. To wrap up, ask students to guess what the "other" activities might be.

Optional speaking activity

Our class

Divide the class into groups of three or four students. Give each group one question about free-time activities, for example:

• *How do you spend your free time on weekends?*
• *What sports do you like to watch on TV?*
• *Do you prefer watching movies in the theater or at home?*
• *What's your favorite thing to do on a rainy day?*
• *Where do you usually go when you get together with friends?*

For higher-level classes, have students write their own questions.

Have groups go around the class and ask their question to their classmates, writing down each classmate's response. Since students are working in groups to ask the same question, it is important to remind them that they should only answer the same question once to avoid repeat answers in the survey. Before students start, teach them the sentence *I've already answered that question.*

To wrap up, have students work together to enter their findings on a poster. They can tally and list the three most popular answers for each question on the poster, then put the poster on the wall for the class to see.

Culture notes

• While watching movies is still a popular pastime in the U.S., more Americans are choosing to stay at home and watch DVDs on TV rather than go out to a movie theater. One poll found that 73 percent of 1,000 people surveyed preferred to watch movies at home rather than at theaters. Another survey found that 48 percent of Americans were going to theaters less often than they were five years ago.

• American football is the most popular spectator sport in the U.S. (Baseball is the second.) The National Football League (NFL) consists of 33 professional teams located in major cities across the U.S. Each team plays 16 games between early September and the end of December. The two best teams meet at the championship tournament – called the *Super Bowl* – near the end of January.

---

page 27

Your turn to talk
My free time

A Prepare

1. Tell students that they are going to talk with their classmates about the free-time activities they like and don't like doing.

2. Read the instructions aloud. Read the example answers aloud and make sure students know that they should write two activities they like and one activity they dislike doing.

3. Give students time to complete the exercise. Circulate while students are working and offer help as necessary.

B Practice

Exercise 1 (CD 1, track 26)

1. Read the instructions aloud. Play the audio program once without stopping so students can listen.

2. Play the audio program again, pausing between items for the class to repeat. To help students hear the stress, have them clap their hands or tap their desks when they say the stressed words. Explain that stressed words in sentences are usually the important words that carry the meaning of the sentence (nouns, verbs, adjectives, and adverbs). Smaller words like conjunctions, prepositions, articles, and pronouns are not usually stressed.

Exercise 2 (CD 1, track 27)

1. Read the instructions aloud.

2. Have students work alone or in pairs to do the exercise. Encourage students to say the sentences aloud before they circle the stressed words.

3. Play the audio program and have students listen to check their answers. For lower-level classes, pause between items and have students listen and repeat.

4. Check answers by calling on individual students to repeat the sentences with the correct stress.

Answers

a. days, home	d. visiting relatives
b. sports, friends	e. swimming, class
c. watching TV	f. studying alone

C Speak

1. Read the instructions aloud. Read the first example sentence and have two students read the example responses. Model another example using a sentence about yourself and have students guess the activity you dislike (for example, *I like reading, but I don't like playing sports.*).

2. Divide the class into groups of three students and have them complete the exercise. Circulate while students are working and make a note of any difficulties to address later.

3. To wrap up, ask for volunteers to share one thing they learned about how their classmates spend their free time (for example, *I learned that Tanya likes going to the movies, but she doesn't like studying.*).

Optional speaking activity

Memory chain game
Have students sit or stand in a circle. If you have a large class, make several small circles of eight or nine students.

Join the circle and start the activity by saying one thing you like to do in your free time (for example, *I like reading.*). Tell students to think of an activity they like doing. They can choose activities they wrote about in Exercise A or new ones.

Ask the student to your left to first tell about you and then to tell about himself or herself (for example, *Mr./Ms. X likes reading, and I like listening to music.*). The next student on the left tells about you, then about the second speaker, and adds a sentence about himself or herself. See how long students can keep the chain going.

Variation: For higher-level classes, have students say one activity they like and one they dislike (for example, *I like swimming, but I don't like staying home.*).

This is a good opportunity to review and practice the third-person *-s* endings in verbs that students learned in Unit 2 (page 13).

Unit 5 Self-study	*Student's Book page 88*
Unit 5 Quiz	*Teacher's Manual page 86*

Great outfit!

Overview

In this unit, students listen to conversations about clothing. In **Warming up**, students learn and practice vocabulary to talk about clothing and patterns. In the **Listening tasks**, students practice listening for the main idea, details, and inference as they hear people talk about clothing, colors, and patterns. They also learn cultural information about the meanings of colors in different cultures. In **Your turn to talk**, students practice describing clothing, and learn and practice the pronunciation of the contractions for *is* and *is not*.

	Focus	Estimated time
Warming up	**Clothing** – *blouse, boots, cap, dress, jacket, pants, sandals, shirt, shoes, shorts, skirt, sneakers, socks, suit, sweater, T-shirt, tie* **Patterns** – *checks, plaid, solid, stripes*	10–15 minutes
Listening task 1 **Choosing an outfit**	A Main idea B Inference	20–25 minutes
Listening task 2 **The meaning of colors**	A Main idea B Details	20–25 minutes
Your turn to talk **Find the differences.**	• Comparing two pictures • Pronunciation of the contractions for *is* and *is not*	10–20 minutes

---

page 28

Warming up

A

1. Give students time to look at the pictures. Read the words in the box aloud and have students listen and try to find the items in the pictures. Write the following questions on the board:

   Which person's style is most similar to your style? Why?
   Which items of clothing would you wear? Which ones wouldn't you wear?

   Divide the class into pairs and have them discuss the questions.

2. Read the instructions aloud. If necessary, explain *outfit* (a set of matching clothes worn for a particular occasion or activity).

3. Give pairs time to complete the activity. Circulate while students are working to monitor their progress and offer help as necessary. For lower-level classes, check vocabulary by pointing to items in the picture and asking, *What do you call this in English?*

4. Draw students' attention to the vocabulary for patterns (*checks, plaid, solid, stripes*) and have students repeat the words after you. Demonstrate the meaning of the words by pointing to items of your own or students' clothing as examples. You may want to teach these expressions:

   • *It has stripes. It's a striped tie.*
   • *It has checks. It's a checked shirt.*

   For higher-level classes, teach additional words for clothing patterns using what students are wearing or pictures from magazines (for example, *flowers/floral, paisley, polka dots, spots/spotted*).

Answers

1. jacket	5. blouse	9. sweater	13. cap
2. dress	6. suit	10. T-shirt	14. tie
3. socks	7. skirt	11. shorts	15. shirt
4. shoes	8. sandals	12. sneakers	16. pants

Notes

• Students may be unfamiliar with the style of suit shown in the picture. Explain that suits may be casual or formal, and that they may be worn by both men and women. The term *suit* refers to a matching jacket and pants/skirt.

- The difference between checks and plaid is that checks usually have squares of the same size, whereas plaid has overlapping squares of different sizes. Also, plaid usually has several colors.

B

1. Read the instructions aloud.

2. Have students work alone or stay with their partners from Exercise A to do the exercise. Circulate while students are working and offer help as necessary. Tell them that they can write on a separate piece of paper if they need more space.

   Possible answers
   bag, belt, gloves, hat, pajamas, raincoat, scarf, tennis shoes, vest

C

1. Read the instructions aloud.

2. Have students work with their partners from Exercise A. Circulate while students are working and make a note of any difficulties to address later.

3. Ask for volunteers to share their words with the class. Write the words on the board and read them aloud to model correct pronunciation.

Listening strategy

Predicting
Having students predict the information they are going to hear before they listen can build students' interest and confidence while they listen.

Before you do the *Listening tasks,* give students time to read the title at the top of the page. Have them look at the pictures and predict what they will hear.

For example, before *Listening task 1,* have students try to guess which items the woman will wear to the party.

For *Listening task 2,* have students predict the meanings of the colors and in what countries the colors have those meanings.

Students can also write their predictions and check if they were correct when they do the *Listening tasks.* Encourage students to use prediction before beginning any of the *Listening tasks.*

---

page 29

Listening task 1
Choosing an outfit

Additional vocabulary from the audio script

sleeves: the part of clothing that covers some or all of the arm; short sleeves cover the upper arm and long sleeves cover the entire arm
really in right now: very popular at this time
fancy: decorative or complicated

A Main idea (CD 2, track 1)

1. Elicit a few words or phrases to describe each item of clothing in the picture (for example, the kind of clothing it is, the color, or the style).

2. Read the instructions aloud. Make sure students understand that there are two items that the speakers do not mention.

3. Play the audio program once or twice. If necessary, pause between items to give students time to complete their answers.

4. To check answers, say the numbers and have students describe the correct items of clothing (for example, *the light blue dress with the white stripe*).

Answers
1. light blue dress with the white stripe
2. blue and green plaid skirt
3. yellow blouse with flowers
4. white blouse
5. blue sweater
6. plaid cap

B Inference (CD 2, track 1)

1. Read the instructions aloud. Remind students that this is an inference exercise. Erica doesn't directly say whether or not she likes Megan's choices, so students have to listen "between the lines."

2. If students think they remember the answers, have them do the exercise and then listen to check their answers.

3. Play the audio program. If necessary, pause between items to give students time to complete their answers.

4. Check answers by asking for volunteers to form complete sentences (for example, *Erica doesn't like the dress.*).

Optional speaking activity

Back-to-back
Divide the class into pairs.

Have partners stand face-to-face. Tell students that they have one minute to study what their partner is wearing. They should try to remember even small details about their partner's clothing style, patterns, jewelry, etc.

After the time limit has passed, tell students to stand back-to-back with their partners. Students take turns saying everything they remember about what their partner is wearing. Students can confirm or correct each other's descriptions.

Have students change partners a few times so they have a chance to describe several different types of clothing.

---

page 30

Listening task 2
The meaning of colors

Additional vocabulary from the audio script

loyalty: faithfulness, truth
purity: cleanliness, goodness
funeral: ceremony honoring someone who has recently died

A 🔘 Main idea (CD 2, track 2)

1. Have students look at the picture on the page. Ask:

   • *What country do you think this woman is from?*
   • *Why do you think she is wearing a red dress?*
   • *What do you think the color red means in this culture?*

2. Give students time to read the colors and the words in the right-hand column aloud. Explain the meaning of any unknown words. Have students work in pairs to predict what each color means.

3. Read the instructions aloud.

4. Play the audio program once or twice. If necessary, pause between items to give students time to complete their answers.

---

5. Check answers by asking for volunteers to form complete sentences (for example, *For some people, blue means loyalty. Some people believe white means death.*).

B 🔘 Details (CD 2, track 2)

1. Read the instructions aloud. If students think they remember the answers, have them do the exercise and then listen to check their answers.

2. Play the audio program. If necessary, pause between items to give students time to complete their answers.

3. Check answers by asking for volunteers to read the complete sentences aloud.

---

page 31

Your turn to talk
Find the differences.

A Prepare

1. Tell students that they are going to work with a classmate to find differences between two pictures.

2. Read the instructions aloud. Assign students A and B roles and make sure students are looking at the correct page before they begin. (Student A should look at page 31, and Student B should look at page 78.)

3. Give students time to study their own pictures and try to predict the things that could be different in their partner's picture (for example, the item of clothing, the color, or the pattern). For lower-level classes, remind students that they can look at page 28 for help with the clothing words.

B Practice

Exercise 1 🔘 (CD 2, track 3)

1. Read the instructions aloud. Play the audio program once without stopping so students can listen.

2. Play the audio program again, pausing between items for the class to repeat. Draw students' attention to the pronunciation of the contractions for *is* and *is not*.

Exercise 2 🔘 (CD 2, track 4)

1. Read the instructions aloud. Play the audio program once or twice. If necessary, pause between items to give students time to complete their answers.

2. Check answers by asking for volunteers to say *is* or *is not*. For lower-level classes, play the audio program again after checking answers and have students repeat the sentences.

Answers

a. is not	c. is	e. is
b. is	d. is not	f. is not

C Speak

Exercise 1

1. Read the instructions aloud. Then read the example sentence aloud and have a student read the example response.

2. Divide the class into pairs. Make sure each pair has one Student A and one Student B. Have students sit or stand back-to-back, or prop up a book between them so they don't accidentally see their partner's book.

3. Tell students that they should try to find at least twelve differences between the two pictures. Give students time to complete the exercise. Circulate while students are working and make a note of any difficulties to address later.

4. Have students check answers in pairs by comparing their Student's Books.

Exercise 2

1. Read the instructions aloud.

2. To check answers, write the following chart on the board:

	page 31	page 78
Father		
Mother		
Girl		
Boy		

3. Say each of the family members one by one and ask students to say the differences they found between the two pictures. Write (or have students write) the differences in the chart.

Answers

	page 31	page 78
Father		
shirt	long-sleeved	short-sleeved
tie	none	striped
pants	brown	white
shoes	sandals	leather shoes
Mother		
dress/skirt	flowered	black
jacket	none	purple
sandals	white	black
Girl		
backpack	green	blue
shirt	plaid	flowered
pants	shorts	jeans
Boy		
T-shirt	striped	solid
glasses	wearing glasses	not wearing glasses
cap	none	black and purple

Optional speaking activity

Who am I talking about?
Tell students that you are going to describe the clothing of someone in the class. Ask them to listen and identify who you are talking about (for example, *This person is wearing a striped blue T-shirt and red jeans.*).

When students know the answer, they should call out the name of the person.

If students guess the wrong person, continue with another hint (for example, *The person is also wearing white sneakers.*).

Continue until you have described, and the class has successfully guessed, several students. (You could also include yourself in the activity.)

For higher-level classes, model one or two examples and then have students work in pairs or small groups to describe what their classmates are wearing.

Unit 6 Self-study	*Student's Book page 89*
Unit 6 Quiz	*Teacher's Manual page 87*

In the house

Overview

In this unit, students listen to descriptions of rooms in a house. In **Warming up**, students learn and practice prepositions of place and vocabulary to talk about household furnishings. In the **Listening tasks**, students practice listening for the main idea, details, and inference as they hear people talk about where to put furniture in a room. They also learn cultural information about how homes are heated in different countries. In **Your turn to talk**, students practice describing their rooms, and learn and practice the pronunciation of the plural -s endings.

Focus		Estimated time
Warming up	**Prepositions of place** – *between, in, next to, on, under* **Parts of a room** – *ceiling, floor, wall* **Household furnishings** – *bookshelf, calendar, chair, coffee table, couch, curtains, fishbowl, rug, TV, TV stand, vase, windows*	10–15 minutes
Listening task 1 Where does it go?	A Inference B Details	20–25 minutes
Listening task 2 Where's the heater?	A Main idea B Details	20–25 minutes
Your turn to talk My room	• Drawing and describing rooms • Pronunciation of plural -s endings	10–20 minutes

----

page 32

Warming up

A

1. Give students time to look at the pictures. Read the words in the box aloud and have students listen and repeat.

2. Read the instructions aloud. Have students work alone or in pairs to complete the exercise.

3. Check answers by calling on students to form complete sentences (for example, *The ball is in the box.*).

Answers

1. on	3. between	5. next to
2. in	4. under	

4. For further practice, have students make sentences about their own possessions or objects in the room (for example, *My notebook is on the desk.*).

B

1. Tell students they are going to look for mistakes in the picture of the room. Elicit a few of the mistakes in the picture and write them on the board (for example, *The chair is on the ceiling.*).

2. Read the words in the box at the bottom of the page aloud and have students listen and repeat. Use the picture to point out any unknown vocabulary. For lower-level classes, check students' understanding of the vocabulary by pointing to items in the picture one by one and asking, *What do you call this in English?*

3. Read the instructions aloud. Tell students there are eight mistakes in the picture. Give them one minute to look at the picture and find as many as they can. For lower-level classes, have students make brief notes about the mistakes they find. This will prepare them to speak when they do Exercise C.

C

1. Read the instructions aloud. Model the exercise by covering the picture in your own book and saying one or two mistakes from the picture. You can use the example sentences from the bottom of the page.

2. Divide the class into pairs and give students time to complete the exercise. Circulate while students are working to monitor their progress. Have students write the mistakes on a separate piece of paper.

3. Check answers by calling on students to form complete sentences, as in the examples on the bottom of page 32.

Answers

- *There's a chair/The chair is* on the ceiling.
- *There's a TV/The TV is* under the TV stand.
- *There's a dog/The dog is* under the rug. (*There's a rug/The rug is* on top of the dog.)
- *There's a shoe/The shoe is* in the vase.
- *There are some curtains/The curtains are* between the windows.
- *There's a cat/The cat is* in the fishbowl.
- *There's a calendar/The calendar is* on the floor.

Notes

- The word *couch* is used here. Students may have learned the word *sofa* before. Point out that *couch* and *sofa* have the same meaning.

- Students may be confused by the expression *on the ceiling*. Point out that the preposition *on* (and not *under*) is used with *the ceiling*, as well as with *the wall* and *the floor*.

Listening strategy

Taking a tour
One way to help students understand descriptions of places is to have them imagine walking through a place.

Have students close their eyes and listen as you slowly describe a room. It could be a room in your own home or a room at the school (for example, the library). Describe the details of the room, including the locations of the furnishings, using the prepositions students have learned. Tell students to imagine the place as you describe it and to try to picture each item you describe.

When you finish, have students work in pairs to repeat the description from memory.

---

page 33

Listening task 1
Where does it go?

Additional vocabulary from the audio script

Let's get in and out of here.: Let's finish shopping quickly.
go ahead: do that (buy the furniture)
Whoa!: exclamation used to express surprise
Come on.: Let's do it.

A 💿 Inference (CD 2, track 5)

1. Have students look at the picture and describe the location of each object in the room using the prepositions of location on page 32.

2. Read the words at the top of the page aloud and have students listen and repeat.

3. Read the instructions aloud. Explain to students that in this exercise, they will need to make inferences. They will not hear the names of the objects. Instead, they will hear descriptions from which they can guess the object the speakers are talking about. Have students work in pairs to predict two or three words the speakers might use to describe each object. For example, for *couch* they might hear *comfortable, soft, blue*, etc.

4. Play the audio program once or twice. If necessary, pause between items to give students time to complete their answers.

5. Check answers by asking the class, *What are they going to buy?* For higher-level classes, have students say what words gave them the answers.

Answers

couch, curtains, DVD player, lamp, picture, plant

B 💿 Details (CD 2, track 5)

1. Read the instructions aloud. Have students guess which furnishings from Exercise A might go in each blank space. Ask questions such as:

- *What will they put next to the clock?*
- *What might go under the TV?*

2. Play the audio program. If necessary, pause between items to give students time to complete their answers.

3. Have students compare answers in pairs by describing the location of each object (for example, *They're going to put the couch under the window.*). Then check answers with the whole class.

Answers

1. under the window
2. on the little table between the bookshelf and the armchair
3. on the big window
4. next to the vase on the coffee table
5. under the TV
6. on the wall next to the clock

Culture note

• In North America, it is common for young adults to leave their parents' home after graduating from high school. While working or attending college, young adults often share an apartment or house with one or more roommates to save money. Roommates share expenses such as rent, utilities, food, and furniture. The two men in the dialog could be university students or young working adults.

Optional speaking activity

Changing places
Collect a group of ten to twelve small objects (dictionaries, pens, notebooks, coins, etc.) and arrange them on a table in front of the class. Make sure that all students can see the objects. For large classes, divide the class into groups of six to eight students, and have each group member contribute one personal item (see above suggestions) to use for the activity.

Review the prepositions of location on page 32 of the Student's Book (*between, in, next to, on, under*) by placing the objects in various positions and asking students to say where they are, for example:

T: *Where is the pencil?*
S1: *The pencil is next to the notebook.*
T: *What is on the notebook?*
S2: *The eraser is on the notebook.*

Give students one minute to silently study the objects and try to remember where they are. Tell students they should think about how they will describe the locations, as well as try to remember them.

After the time limit has passed, ask students to close their eyes while you rearrange the items.

Have students look at the new arrangement and work in pairs to say what has changed. To help students form correct sentences, write example sentences on the board (for example, *The eraser is next to the cell phone. It was next to the pencil.*).

To wrap up, ask for volunteers to say the changes they remembered and write the sentences on the board.

----

page 34

Listening task 2
Where's the heater?

Additional vocabulary from the audio script

fortunately: luckily
tiles: thin, flat, usually square pieces used for covering floors, walls, or roofs
pipes: tubes through which liquids or gases can flow

A Main idea (CD 2, track 6)

1. Give students time to look at the pictures. Point out that number 1 has been done for them as an example.

2. Read (or have students read) the names of the countries aloud. You may want to bring a world map to class and have students find the countries on the map.

3. Read the instructions aloud.

4. Have students work in pairs to guess where the heater is in each picture. Tell them that they should describe the heater's location in words using the prepositions on page 32. Demonstrate by looking at picture number 2 and saying, *Maybe it's under the rug* or *I think it's next to the table.*

5. Play the audio program once or twice. If necessary, pause between items to give students time to complete their answers.

6. Check answers with the whole class. Hold up your book and point to the locations. Then ask for volunteers to describe the locations.

Note

• Naturally, various types of heaters are used in each of these countries. Those included in this exercise are examples of one type.

B Details (CD 2, track 6)

1. Read the instructions aloud. If students think they remember the answers, have them do the exercise and then listen to check their answers.

2. Play the audio program. If necessary, pause between items to give students time to complete their answers.

3. Check answers by asking students to form complete sentences (for example, *The woman visited Syria.*).

---

page 35

Your turn to talk
My room

A Prepare

1. Tell students they are going to draw their favorite room and describe it to a classmate.

2. Read the instructions aloud. Tell students to choose a room they can draw and describe easily. Tell them that they do not need to draw very well; they can just draw simple shapes and label them. To demonstrate, draw the following on the board:

 DVD player   plant

3. Give students a five-minute time limit to complete the exercise so they can pace themselves as they draw. Circulate while students are working to monitor their progress.

B Practice

Exercise 1 (CD 2, track 7)

1. Read the instructions aloud. Play the audio program once without stopping so students can listen. Point out that these are singular (one) and plural (more than one) noun endings.

2. Play the audio program again, pausing between items for the class to repeat. Draw students' attention to the different pronunciation of the *-s* endings of the nouns.

Exercise 2 (CD 2, track 8)

1. Read the instructions aloud.

2. Have students work alone or in pairs to do the exercise. Encourage students to say the words aloud before they write them in the chart.

3. Play the audio program and have students listen to check their answers. For lower-level classes, pause between items and have students listen and repeat.

C Speak

1. Read the instructions aloud. Call on a student to read the example description aloud. For lower-level classes, review the prepositions and vocabulary on page 32 before students do the exercise.

2. Divide the class into pairs and have students sit or stand back-to-back, or prop up a book between them so they don't accidentally see their partner's drawing. Tell pairs to decide who will describe and who will listen and draw first.

3. Give students time to complete the exercise. Circulate while students are working and offer help as necessary.

4. Have students check answers by comparing their pictures. If there are any differences, tell them to describe the differences to their partner (for example, *In my picture, the chair is next to the desk. In your picture, the chair is next to the bookshelf.*).

Unit 7 Self-study	*Student's Book page 90*
Unit 7 Quiz	*Teacher's Manual page 88*

Overview

In this unit, students listen to conversations about time and making plans. In **Warming up**, students learn and practice language used to tell time. In the **Listening tasks**, students practice listening for the main idea and details as they hear people talk about changing plans. They also learn cultural information about how time is viewed in different cultures. In **Your turn to talk**, students practice making plans and setting times to do things; they also learn and practice the reduced pronunciation of *want to* and *have to*.

	Focus	Estimated time
Warming up	**Time** – *(two) o'clock, (one)-fifteen, (three) forty-five, at night, in the morning/afternoon/evening,* A.M., P.M., *midnight, noon, a quarter after (one), a quarter to (four)*	10–15 minutes
Listening task 1 **Changing plans**	A Details B Details	20–25 minutes
Listening task 2 **Time and cultures**	A Main idea B Details	20–25 minutes
Your turn to talk **Making plans**	• Making weekend plans with your classmates • Reduction of *want to* and *have to*	10–20 minutes

page 36

Warming up

A

1. Have students read the time expressions silently. Alternatively, call on individual students to read the time expressions aloud.

2. Read the instructions.

3. Divide the class into pairs and give students time to complete the exercise. Circulate while students are working to monitor their progress and offer help as necessary.

4. Check answers by reading the time expressions and having students say the matching expressions from the box.

Answers

1. d	4. c	7. i
2. g	5. a	8. b
3. h	6. f	9. e

5. For further practice, use a large wall clock or draw a picture of a clock face on the board. Set the clock hands and call on students to say what time it is. Change the clock several times to have students practice saying several different time expressions.

B

1. Read the instructions aloud. Before students start, model the exercise by saying a few time expressions and asking for volunteers to say the same times in a different way.

2. Have students work with their partners from Exercise A. Circulate while students are working to monitor their progress and offer help as necessary.

3. For further practice, call on individual students and ask some simple questions about their daily routines, for example:

   • *What time did you get up this morning?*
   • *When do you usually have lunch?*
   • *What time does this class start?*

---

page 37

Listening task 1
Changing plans

Additional vocabulary from the audio script

make-up day: a day when a student can take a test that he or she missed during class

A **Details** (CD 2, track 9)

1. Give students time to look at the pictures and read the information.

2. Read the instructions aloud. Draw students' attention to the example in number 1. Make sure students understand that they should cross out the incorrect information and write the correct information.

3. Play the audio program once or twice. If necessary, pause between items to give students time to complete their answers.

4. Check answers by asking questions and having students give the correct new information, for example:

T: *Where are they going to meet?*
S1: *At Museum Café.*
T: *What time are they going to meet?*
S2: *At six-fifteen.*

Answers

1. ~~7:30 Hayes Hall~~	6:15 Museum Café
2. CA39 Taipei ~~6:10~~	8:00
3. ~~12:00 Bangkok Café~~	12:15 The Plaza
4. ~~Monday 10:00~~ English test	Wednesday 8:15

B **Details** (CD 2, track 9)

1. Read the instructions aloud. If students think they remember the answers, have them do the exercise and then listen to check their answers.

2. Play the audio program. If necessary, pause between items to give students time to complete their answers.

3. Check answers by asking for volunteers to read the complete sentences aloud. For lower-level classes, play the audio program again. Pause after each item and ask for volunteers to say what words gave them the answer.

Answers

1. a	2. b	3. a	4. b

Culture note

• In North America, changing social plans is not considered rude, as long as advance notice is given. When plans need to be changed, people generally just give a short apology.

Optional speaking activity

Tomorrow's schedule
Have students talk about their personal schedules for the next day.

To demonstrate, write your own schedule on the board, for example:

A.M.
7:30 – *wake up*
8:25 – *take the train to school*
9:15 – *teach English class*
12:30 – *meet friend for lunch*

Tell students about your schedule and write an example sentence on the board (for example, *Tomorrow I'll wake up at seven-thirty in the morning.*).

Give students five minutes to write their own schedules for tomorrow.

When students finish, divide the class into pairs and have students tell a partner what they will do tomorrow and at what time.

To wrap up, ask for volunteers to share one interesting thing about their partner's schedule (for example, *My partner will wake up at five o'clock tomorrow morning.*).

- -

page 38

Listening task 2

Time and cultures

Additional vocabulary from the audio script

speaking of (time): "speaking of (topic)" is an expression used to give an example of something related to the topic

show up: arrive

A 💿 Main idea (CD 2, track 10)

1. Have students work in pairs to describe the pictures. Ask:
   - *What's happening in this picture?*
   - *What's the problem?*

2. Read the instructions aloud. Make sure students understand that there is one picture the speakers do not mention.

3. Play the audio program once or twice. If necessary, pause between items to give students time to complete their answers.

4. To check answers, hold up your book, point to each picture, and have students tell you the number. For higher-level classes, ask students to describe the correct picture. For lower-level classes, ask for volunteers to say what words gave them the answers. Write the words on the board. Then play the audio program again.

Answers

(*top row*) 2, 4, X
(*bottom row*) 3, 1

Note

- The situations in *Listening task 2* reflect general attitudes toward time in various cultures. You may want to point out to students the importance of following local time practices when traveling to other countries in order to avoid misunderstandings.

B 💿 Details (CD 2, track 10)

1. Read the instructions aloud. If students think they remember the answers, have them do the exercise and then listen to check their answers.

2. Play the audio program. If necessary, pause between items to give students time to complete their answers.

3. Check answers by asking for volunteers to read the complete sentences aloud.

Answers

1. a. 7:30	3. a. 9:00
b. 9:30	b. 12:00
2. a. 7:00	4. a. 10:17
b. 7:10	b. 10:17

4. To extend the cultural discussion, ask students to tell you about time in their own cultures. Ask for volunteers to say what they think would happen in their culture in each of the situations described in *Listening task 2*.

Optional speaking activity

Our time

Have the class brainstorm a list of eight to ten survey questions about time like the ones in *Listening task 2*. Write the questions on the board, for example:

1. *What time do you arrive at a class that starts at 9:00 A.M.?*
2. *What time do you arrive at a party that starts at 8:00 P.M.?*
3. *What do you do if you are going to be late to meet a friend?*

Have students write down all of the questions on a separate piece of paper.

Next, have students go around the class and interview their classmates using the questions they brainstormed. Tell them that they should interview at least three classmates and write down each classmate's name and answers to the questions.

When they have finished interviewing, divide the class into groups of four or five students. Tell groups to compare their survey answers and tally their responses. Groups might look for differences between men and women, among different age groups, etc.

To wrap up, ask for volunteers from each group to share what they learned about the different attitudes among their classmates toward time.

---

page 39

Your turn to talk
Making plans

A Prepare

1. Tell students that they are going to talk with their classmates about their weekend plans.

2. Read the instructions aloud. Read the example activities aloud and have students listen and repeat.

3. Give students time to complete the exercise. Circulate while students are working to monitor their progress and offer help as necessary.

B Practice

Exercise 1 (CD 2, track 11)

1. Read the instructions aloud. Play the audio program once without stopping so students can listen.

2. Play the audio program again, pausing between items for the class to repeat. Draw students' attention to the reduced pronunciation of *want to* and *have to*.

Exercise 2 (CD 2, track 12)

1. Read the instructions aloud.

2. Play the audio program once or twice. If necessary, pause between items to give students time to complete their answers.

3. Have students compare answers in pairs. Then check answers with the whole class by calling on individual students to say *want to* or *have to*.

Answers		
a. want to	c. have to	e. have to
b. want to	d. want to	f. have to

4. For further practice, play the audio program again, pausing between items so students can repeat.

Note

• Remind students not to write reductions; that is, they should not write *wanna* or *hafta* as these are only spoken forms. The forms *want to* and *have to* should always be used when writing.

C Speak

Exercise 1

1. Before students do the exercise, review the time expressions presented on page 36. Read a few of the expressions and call on students to say them in another way.

2. Write the following dialogs on the board and have students practice them in pairs:

> A: *Do you want to go to the movies on Wednesday?*
> B: *Sure. What time?*
> A: *How about eight o'clock?*
> B: *OK.*
>
> A: *Do you want to go to the movies on Wednesday?*
> B: *Sorry. I have to study on Wednesday night.*
> A: *OK. Maybe some other time.*

3. Read the instructions aloud. Make sure each pair has a coin. Tell students to choose which side of the coin will represent *heads* and which side will represent *tails*.

4. Divide the class into pairs and give students time to complete the exercise. Circulate while students are working to monitor their progress and offer help as necessary.

Exercise 2

1. Read the instructions aloud.

2. Have students move around the room to complete the exercise. Tell them that they should speak to five different classmates. Circulate while students are working and offer help as necessary. Make a note of any difficulties to address later.

3. To wrap up, ask for volunteers to say which classmates accepted their invitations and what plans they made.

Unit 8 Self-study	*Student's Book page 91*
Unit 8 Quiz	*Teacher's Manual page 89*
Test 1, Units 1–8	*Teacher's Manual page 111*

Kuwait

Overview

In this **Expansion** unit, students listen to general information about Kuwait. In the **Listening tasks**, students practice listening for the main idea and details as they hear people talk about traditional and modern Kuwaiti customs. They also learn cultural information about Kuwait as they listen to an authentic interview with a Kuwaiti student about women's clothing styles.

	Focus	Estimated time
Listening task 1 **Information**	A Main idea B Details	20–25 minutes
Listening task 2 **Clothing styles**	A Main idea B Details	20–25 minutes

----

page 40

Listening task 1
Information

Note

• Before you start this unit, write the titles of the previous four units on the board or elicit them from students (*Free time, Great outfit!, In the house, Time*). Tell students that this *Expansion* unit features some of the topics and vocabulary from these units. It presents general information about Kuwait and a more in-depth look at Kuwaiti culture based on an authentic interview with a student from Kuwait. Give students time to look over the language and listening skills in Units 5 through 8.

A Main idea (CD 2, track 13)

1. Ask students where Kuwait is located (the Middle East). You may want to bring a world map to class and have students find Kuwait on the map. Ask students to say anything they know about the country of Kuwait, its culture, or its people.

2. Have students look at the pictures and make inferences about Kuwait and Kuwaiti culture. Ask, *What can you guess about Kuwait from looking at these pictures?*

   Possible answers
   • Kuwaiti cities have some Western businesses.
   • Some Kuwaitis speak/understand English.
   • Sports are/soccer is popular.

   • People drink tea/coffee.
   • Kuwait is an Arab country. (Men wear Arab dress.)

3. Read the instructions aloud. This is a good time to review the types of listening skills introduced in *Before you begin* on pages 4 and 5 (Main idea, Details, Inference). Point out to students that in this exercise they are listening for the main idea. This means that they don't need to understand everything they hear, just the general meaning. Make sure students understand that there is one picture that the speakers do not mention.

4. Play the audio program once or twice. If necessary, pause between items to give students time to complete their answers.

5. Check answers with the whole class.

Answers
(*top row*) 2, 1, 3
(*bottom row*) 4, X

Culture note
• Tea and coffee play a large role in Kuwaiti hospitality. Usually when a guest enters a house, office, or even some stores, the host offers him or her a cup of tea or coffee. In more traditional areas of the country, it is considered impolite to refuse the host's offer of tea or coffee.

B 💿 Details (CD 2, track 13)

1. Read the instructions aloud. If students think they remember the answers, have them do the exercise and then listen to check their answers.

2. Play the audio program. If necessary, pause between items to give students time to complete their answers.

3. Check answers by having students read the complete sentences aloud.

Answers

1. a   2. a   3. b   4. a

Additional listening practice

Details, details
This activity extends *Listening task 1* by having students answer additional questions about the audio program.

Write the following questions on the board:

1. *What is the capital of Kuwait?*
2. *What are the shopping hours in the afternoon?*
3. *When do women and children visit the coffee shops?*
4. *What water sports are popular in Kuwait?*

Play the audio program, pausing between items to give students time to complete their answers.

When you have played all four items, have students compare answers in pairs.

Then check answers with the whole class.

Answers

1. Kuwait City
2. 4:30 to 9:00 P.M.
3. in the mornings and afternoons
4. swimming, wind surfing, water skiing

---

page 41

Listening task 2
Clothing styles

A 💿 Main idea (CD 2, track 14)

1. Read the instructions aloud. Give students time to look at the pictures and say what they see. Point out that *hijab* (a head scarf) and *abaya* (a long, black coat) are Arabic words.

Note

• In this exercise, the word *Islamic* refers to traditional clothing commonly worn in Islamic countries. If necessary, explain to students that Islamic countries follow the religion of Islam. People who follow Islam are called Muslim. Here, *Western* refers to the style of clothing in North America, Latin America, Europe, and Australia/New Zealand.

2. Play the audio program once or twice. If necessary, pause between items to give students time to complete their answers.

3. Have students compare answers in pairs. Then check answers with the whole class.

Answers

1. both   2. Islamic   3. Western   4. both

B 💿 Details (CD 2, track 14)

1. Read the instructions aloud. If students think they remember the answers, have them do the exercise and then listen to check their answers.

2. Play the audio program. If necessary, pause between items to give students time to complete their answers.

3. Check answers by asking for volunteers to say the complete sentences aloud.

Answers

1. In Kuwait, *55* percent of the people come from other countries.
2. The *abaya* has wide *sleeves*.
3. Women enjoy wearing expensive scarves and *jewelry*.
4. It *is* common for a Kuwaiti woman to wear two styles on the same day.

4. *Listening task 2* provides a good opportunity to review some of the clothing vocabulary presented in Unit 6 (page 28). Ask students to tell you the items of clothing they heard in *Listening task 2*.

Possible answers
scarf, coat, dresses, suits, skirts, blouses

Movies

Overview

In this unit, students listen to movie scenes and conversations about movies. In **Warming up**, students learn and practice vocabulary to talk about types of movies and their content. In the **Listening tasks**, students practice listening for the main idea and inference as they hear scenes from movies and listen to people talking about movies. In **Your turn to talk**, students talk about their favorite movies, and learn and practice the pronunciation of the contractions for *is* and *are*.

	Focus	Estimated time
Warming up	**Movie types** – *action, comedy, horror, musical, romance, science fiction* **Movie content** – *car chases, dancing, fights, good jokes, love stories, robots, romances, scary scenes, silly situations, singing, space travel, special effects, vampires*	10–15 minutes
Listening task 1 **What's playing?**	A Inference B Main idea	20–25 minutes
Listening task 2 **Film critics**	A Inference B Inference	20–25 minutes
Your turn to talk **My favorite movie**	• Describing your favorite movie • Pronunciation of contractions for *is* and *are*	10–20 minutes

----

page 42

Warming up

A

1. Call on students to read the labels on the pictures aloud. Ask them to say whether they have seen any movies recently and, if so, what types of movies they saw.

2. Read the instructions aloud. Read the words in the box aloud and have students listen and repeat.

3. Divide the class into pairs and give students time to complete the exercise. Circulate while students are working to monitor their progress. Rather than explain unknown vocabulary at this stage, you may want to encourage students to make guesses. Tell them that you will go over the meaning of all of the words as a whole class.

4. To check answers, write the six movie types on the board. Then call on students to come to the board and write the words from the box under the appropriate heading.

Answers

1. romance: love stories, romances
2. comedy: good jokes, silly situations
3. science fiction: robots, space travel
4. action: car chases, fights
5. musical: dancing, singing
6. horror: scary scenes, vampires

Note

• The preceding answers are the most typical. However, students may suggest other combinations of answers. For example, it is possible to have romances in a musical. If students put words in other categories, accept the answers but ask students to explain their reasons.

5. To wrap up, explain any unknown vocabulary using the pictures of the movie scenes or other examples from movies students know.

B

1. Read the instructions aloud.

2. Have students work alone, in pairs, or in groups to do the exercise. Tell them that they can use a separate piece of paper if they need more space.

3. Call on students to say their words while you list them on the board, modeling the correct pronunciation.

Possible answers
actor, aliens, director, documentary, drama, ghost, slapstick, soundtrack, star

C

1. Divide the class into pairs. If students are already paired, have them work with their partners from Exercise B.

2. Model the exercise by first telling the class what kind of movie you like best and why (for example, *I like comedies because I enjoy good jokes. I like to laugh at silly situations. My favorite comedy is . . .*).

3. Read the instructions aloud and give students time to complete the exercise. Encourage them to say why they like the type of movie and, if they have a favorite movie, what it is.

4. To wrap up, call on individual students to share their partner's favorite type of movie and the reasons.

Listening strategy

Focus on inference
As the *Listening tasks* in this unit involve several inference exercises, this is a good opportunity to help students focus on developing their skills in listening "between the lines."

Remind students that when they *infer* something in a conversation, it means they understand the meaning without the other person saying it directly.

To give an example using movies, choose a movie currently playing in the theater. Ask students to listen to the following statements and say whether they think you like or dislike the movie:

• *I've already seen* [movie title] *twice, and I'm going again tonight.* (liked it)
• *You haven't seen* [movie title] *yet? I can't believe it!* (liked it)
• *Yeah, I saw* [movie title], *unfortunately.* (didn't like it)
• *How was* [movie title]? [*sarcastically*] *Well, it was . . . um . . . interesting, I guess.* (didn't like it)

Point out to students that they can guess the meaning without your saying directly whether you liked it or not.

To wrap up, have students think of alternative ways to express whether they liked or disliked a movie. Have them share their ideas with the class.

----

page 43

Listening task 1
What's playing?

Additional vocabulary from the audio script

Oops!: an expression used when a person makes a mistake (for example, drops something or falls down)
Ouch!: an expression used when a person gets hurt or injured
starship: a spaceship

A Inference (CD 2, track 15)

1. Give students time to look at the picture. Ask:
   • *Where are these people? How do you know?*
   • *What do you think they are talking about?*

2. Read the instructions aloud. Make sure students understand that there is one type of movie that the speakers do not mention.

3. Play the audio program once or twice. If necessary, pause between items to give students time to complete their answers.

4. Check answers by saying the numbers and asking students to tell you the kind of movie. For lower-level classes, ask for volunteers to say which words and phrases helped them get the answers.

Answers
1. romance	3. comedy	5. action
2. horror	4. science fiction	

B Main idea (CD 2, track 15)

1. Read the instructions aloud. If students think they remember the answers, have them do the exercise and then listen to check their answers.

2. Play the audio program. If necessary, pause between items to give students time to complete their answers.

3. Check answers by asking for volunteers to read the complete sentences aloud.

4. To wrap up, review the skill of making inferences by asking for volunteers to say what words and phrases helped them get the answers.

Optional speaking activity

Movies I know

Have students brainstorm a list of popular movies they know and write the list on the board.

Divide the class into pairs. Tell students to choose a movie from the list on the board. It should be a movie that they have seen but that their partner has not seen.

Tell pairs to take turns describing one movie from the list to their partners. They can describe the type of movie, the characters, and the events in the movie, as well as their opinions of the movie. For lower-level students, write some sentences on the board to help them, for example:

_____ *is a horror movie. It's about* _____. *It's very scary.*

_____ *is an action movie. It's about* _____. *There are car chases and fights in this movie.*

To wrap up, ask for volunteers to read their movie descriptions for the class. You can have them omit the title so the class can try to guess the movie.

---

page 44

Listening task 2
Film critics

Additional vocabulary from the audio script

astronauts: people who travel into space
stupid: in this case, the story is stupid; it doesn't make sense
boring: not interesting

---

nightclub: a place that is open in the evening where people can go to dance and see musical performances
violent: containing lots of fighting
Skip this movie.: Don't go to this movie.
awful: not good, terrible

A **Inference** (CD 2, track 16)

1. Give students time to read the movie titles and predict what types of movies they are.

2. Read the instructions aloud. If necessary explain *film critic* (someone who writes or talks about his or her opinions of movies).

3. Play the audio program once or twice. If necessary, pause between items to give students time to complete their answers.

4. Have students compare answers in pairs. Then check answers with the whole class by calling on volunteers to say the type of movie.

B **Inference** (CD 2, track 16)

1. Read the instructions aloud. Make sure students understand that the smile ☺ means "likes" and the frown ☹ means "dislikes."

2. If students think they remember the answers, have them do the exercise and then listen to check their answers.

3. Play the audio program. If necessary, pause between items to give students time to complete their answers.

4. Check answers by asking for volunteers to say complete sentences (for example, *Mark likes/doesn't like* _____. or *Anna likes/doesn't like* _____.).

Culture notes

- Many countries have motion picture rating systems to indicate the nature and appropriateness of the movie content for moviegoers or the public. In some places (e.g. Australia), the country's government decides on ratings; in other countries (e.g. the U.S.), it is done by industry organizations with no official government status. You may see some of the following ratings on DVD rentals:

  G – General Audience
  PG – Parental Guidance
  PG-13 – Some material may be inappropriate for children under 13.
  R – Restricted – Under 17 requires accompanying parent or adult guardian.
  NC-17 – No one 17 and under admitted

- Here are a few movie-related slang expressions:

  to catch a flick: to go and see a movie
  movie buff: someone who loves movies and watches a lot of them
  on the big/silver screen: in the movie theater (as opposed to on TV)

---

page 45

Your turn to talk
My favorite movie

A Prepare

1. Tell students that they are going to talk with their classmates about their favorite movies.

2. Read the instructions aloud. Tell students that they can refer to the vocabulary on page 42 to help them.

3. Give students time to complete the exercise. Circulate while students are working and offer help as necessary.

B Practice

Exercise 1 (CD 2, track 17)

1. Read the instructions aloud. Play the audio program once without stopping so students can listen.

2. Play the audio program again, pausing between items for the class to repeat. Explain that in speech, contractions are more common than the full forms. Even if students choose to say the full forms themselves, they should get used to hearing the contractions, since that is what native speakers will use most often.

Exercise 2 (CD 2, track 18)

1. Read the instructions aloud.

2. Play the audio program once or twice. If necessary, pause between items to give students time to complete their answers.

3. Check answers by asking for volunteers to say *is* or *are*.

Answers		
a. is	c. is	e. are
b. are	d. are	f. is

4. For further practice, play the audio program again pausing between items for students to repeat the sentences.

C Speak

1. Read the instructions aloud.

2. Divide the class into pairs and give students time to complete the exercise. Circulate while students are working to monitor their progress. Make a note of any difficulties to address later.

3. To wrap up, ask for volunteers to tell the class about their partner's favorite movie. In large classes, students could work in groups of four to six while you circulate and listen.

> **Optional speaking activity**
>
> *The best movies of all time*
> Divide the class into groups of four to six students.
>
> Tell each group to choose a spokesperson who will share the group's ideas with the class.
>
> Give groups ten minutes to brainstorm and write a list of the five best movies of all time.
>
> As they discuss, encourage students to explain their choices using the vocabulary from page 42 of the Student's Book (for example, *I think* Star Wars *is the best science fiction movie of all time. The special effects are great.*).
>
> When the groups finish, call on the spokespeople to present their group's list and explain why they chose those movies.

Unit 9 Self-study	*Student's Book page 92*
Unit 9 Quiz	*Teacher's Manual page 90*

A typical day

Overview

In this unit, students listen to conversations about schedules and daily routines. In **Warming up**, students learn and practice sequence words and vocabulary to talk about typical daily activities. In the **Listening tasks**, students practice listening for the main idea and details as they hear people talk about things they do every day and the times they do them. They also learn cultural information about the daily routines of people around the world. In **Your turn to talk**, students talk about their daily schedules, and learn and practice the pronunciation of linked sounds.

	Focus	Estimated time
Warming up	**Daily activities** – *check e-mail, eat breakfast, eat dinner, eat lunch, exercise, go to school or work, have a cup of coffee, listen to the radio, read the newspaper, study, take a bath or shower, take a break* **Sequence words** – *first, then, next, after that, finally*	10–15 minutes
Listening task 1 **What's your schedule?**	A Main idea B Details	20–25 minutes
Listening task 2 **Daily schedules**	A Main idea B Details	20–25 minutes
Your turn to talk **The perfect schedule**	• Describing your perfect schedule • Pronunciation of linked sounds	10–20 minutes

---

page 46

Warming up

A

1. Give students time to look at the picture and say what they see. Ask:

   • *What is the woman doing?*
   • *What time of day do you think this is?*
   • *Do you ever start your day like this?*

2. Read the instructions aloud.

3. Read the words and phrases in the box aloud. Have students match them to the activities in the picture, where possible. Explain any unknown vocabulary.

4. Give students time to complete the exercise. Circulate while students are working to monitor their progress.

5. Have students compare answers in pairs. Then ask for volunteers to report what their partners do on a typical day.

6. For further practice, ask students to say other things they do during a typical day. List any new vocabulary on the board.

B

1. Read the instructions aloud. To model the exercise, share your own typical day with the class using the words and phrases in the box (for example, *I get up at 6:30 A.M. First, I have a cup of coffee. Then . . .*). For lower-level classes, write your daily activities in order on the board so students can refer to them while you speak. You may also want to give students a few minutes to make some notes about their own daily routines before they begin working.

2. Divide the class into pairs and give students time to complete the exercise. Circulate while students are working to monitor their progress.

3. To wrap up, ask for volunteers to share their daily routines with the class.

Using the body and the mind
A fun way to practice new words, especially actions such as daily routines, is to have students act out or mime the activities, charades-style. The physical movement will help students remember the vocabulary when they listen.

Divide the class into groups of four students. Each student in the group chooses one of the daily activities from page 46 and acts it out. The other group members guess what it is.

Groups continue until they have acted out all of the activities.

Variation: For higher-level classes, have students act out two or three activities in sequence. When group members guess, they should use the sequence words (for example, *First, you check e-mail. Then you exercise . . .*).

Note

• If students are shy about acting out the activities, try demonstrating a few of them yourself before students start. You can also have students work in pairs rather than groups to help them feel more comfortable.

Chain game: Every morning
Have students stand or sit in a circle. If you have a large class, make several small circles of eight or nine

Join the circle and start the activity by stating one activity you do every morning (for example, *Every morning, I eat breakfast.*). Tell students to think of an activity they do every morning.

Ask the student to your left to repeat, *Every morning I eat breakfast* and then to add another activity (for example, *Then I read the newspaper.*) The next student on the left repeats the first two activities and adds another one. See how long students can keep the chain going.

To wrap up, point out to students that hearing the vocabulary repeated several times helped them to remember a long chain of events.

---

page 47

Listening task 1
What's your schedule?

Additional vocabulary from the audio script

economics: the study of money and finance
on campus: at the university
specialty: something someone does well or is especially good at
That settles it.: It's decided.

A Main idea (CD 2, track 19)

1. Ask the class if anyone has ever lived with a roommate and, if so, what the experience was like.

Culture note

• North American university students and young people often share apartments or houses. Roommates share the rent and the bills. It is an economical way to live and allows them to enjoy independence and living with their peers.

2. Have students work in pairs to predict some of the words and phrases from the conversation that might give them the answers. For example, for *university classes* they might hear *I'm taking _____, studying, teacher, classmates,* etc.

3. Read the instructions aloud.

4. Play the audio program once or twice. If necessary, pause between items to give students time to complete their answers.

5. Check answers by asking for volunteers to complete the sentence (for example, *They're talking about _____.*).

Answers

1. university classes	4. the library
2. breakfast	5. dinner
3. exercising	6. evenings

B Details (CD 2, track 19)

1. Read the instructions aloud. If students think they remember the answers, have them do the exercise and then listen to check their answers.

2. Play the audio program. If necessary, pause between items to give students time to complete their answers.

3. Check answers by calling on students to read the complete sentences aloud.

Answers

1. b   2. b   3. a   4. b   5. a   6. b

Optional speaking activity

Roommates

Tell students to imagine that they are going to look for a roommate to share an apartment.

With the whole class, brainstorm a list of interview questions they might ask to find out if someone would be a good roommate, and write them on the board, for example:

- *What do you do?*
- *What time do you usually get up?*
- *What do you do in the evenings?*
- *Do you like to cook?*

Divide the class into pairs. Have students interview their partners and then decide if they would be good roommates.

To wrap up, ask pairs to say why they think they would or would not be good roommates.

---

page 48

Listening task 2
Daily schedules

Additional vocabulary from the audio script

customers: people who come into a shop or restaurant to buy something

a nap: a short sleep, usually in the afternoon

A Main idea (CD 2, track 20)

1. Read the instructions aloud and give students time to read the phrases under each picture. Have students work in pairs to predict the activities each person does. Make sure students understand that there is one activity that each speaker does not mention.

2. Play the audio program once or twice. If necessary, pause between items to give students time to complete their answers.

---

3. Check answers by calling on students to say what each person does (for example *Alex Chan drinks tea, checks e-mail, . . .*). For lower-level classes, play the audio program again to allow students to check any answers they missed.

Answers

1. drinks tea, checks e-mail, eats lunch
2. eats breakfast, meets friends, watches TV
3. cleans, takes a break, takes the bus home
4. goes to work, eats lunch, meets friends

B Details (CD 2, track 20)

1. Read the instructions aloud. If students think they remember the answers, have them do the exercise and then listen to check their answers.

2. Play the audio program. If necessary, pause between items to give students time to complete their answers.

3. Check answers by calling on students to read the complete sentences aloud. This is a good opportunity to review the pronunciation of the third-person -*s* endings in verbs from Unit 2 (page 13).

Answers

1. a. 6:15	3. a. 4:30
b. 8:30	b. 8:30
c. 5:30	c. 10:00
2. a. 8:30, 9:00	4. a. 8:00
b. 10:30	b. 12:30, 3:30
c. 4:30	c. 7:30

Optional speaking activity

Find someone who . . .

Have students look at the activities in the box on page 46 of the Student's Book.

Ask for volunteers to say the activities, adding a time phrase to each one. Write the sentences on the board, for example:

. . . check e-mail in the morning.
. . . eat breakfast at 7 A.M.

Tell students that they are going to try to find someone in the class who does one of the activities at the time written on the board. Review the question form *Do you . . . ?*

---

48   Unit 10 A typical day

Have students move around the room and ask each other questions about the activities (for example, *Do you check your e-mail in the morning? Do you eat breakfast at 7 A.M.?* etc.).

Explain that when a classmate answers "yes," students should make a note of the person's name and the activity, then ask someone else a different question.

If a classmate answers "no," students ask the classmate another question until they get a "yes" answer or have asked all the questions. Then they move on to someone else.

To wrap up, ask for volunteers to report which classmates answered "yes." Remind them to use the third-person *-s* ending when they answer (for example, *Maria checks e-mail in the morning.*).

For higher-level classes, encourage students to ask a follow-up question to extend the conversation (for example, *How many e-mails do you get each day? What do you eat for breakfast?*).

---

page 49

Your turn to talk
The perfect schedule

A Prepare

1. Tell students that they are going to imagine and talk about their perfect schedule. Give them an example of your perfect schedule (for example, *In my perfect schedule, I get up at nine o'clock. Then I go jogging in the park . . .*).

2. Read the instructions aloud. Remind students that they can refer to the vocabulary on page 46 to help them.

3. Give students time to complete the exercise. Circulate while students are working to monitor their progress.

B Practice

Exercise 1 (CD 2, track 21)

1. Read the instructions aloud. Play the audio program once without stopping so students can listen.

2. Play the audio program again, pausing between items for the class to repeat. Draw students' attention to the linking lines between the consonants and vowels. Explain that when a

consonant at the end of a word is followed by a vowel at the beginning of the next word, the two sounds are linked. Say the linked words in the examples and have students listen and repeat, for example:

T: *gets up*
Ss: *gets up*
T: *up at*
Ss: *up at*

Exercise 2 (CD 2, track 22)

1. Read the instructions aloud.

2. Have students work alone or in pairs to complete the exercise. Circulate while students are working to monitor their progress and offer help as necessary.

3. Play the audio program and have students listen and check their answers.

Answers

a. works until	d. wakes up at eleven
b. goes out	e. drinks a cup of
c. takes a	f. uses a computer at

4. To wrap up, write the sentences on the board and ask for volunteers to come to the board and draw linking lines in the appropriate places. Then play the audio program again and have students repeat the sentences quietly, focusing on the linking sounds.

C Speak

Exercise 1

1. Read the instructions aloud. Then read the example sentence aloud and have two students read the example responses.

2. Divide the class into pairs and give students time to complete the exercise. Circulate while students are working and check that they are using the phrases and linking sounds appropriately.

Exercise 2

Call on individual students to tell the class about their partner's schedule. In large classes, have students say one sentence about their partner.

| Unit 10 Self-study | Student's Book page 93 |
| Unit 10 Quiz | Teacher's Manual page 91 |

Locations

Overview

In this unit, students listen to people describe locations and give and receive directions. In **Warming up**, students learn and practice vocabulary for giving directions and describing locations in a shopping mall. In the **Listening tasks**, students practice listening for the main idea, details, and inference as they hear people talk about locations in a zoo and about how to play a video game. In **Your turn to talk**, students practice giving and receiving directions, and learn and practice using stress for clarification.

Focus		Estimated time
Warming up	**Locations and directions** – *across from, around the corner from, between, go across, go straight, next to, on the left, on the right, turn left, turn right* **Mall locations** – *aquarium, arcade, bank, café, clothing store, entrance, food court, Internet café, movie theater, pet store, restaurant, restrooms, tower, toy store*	10–15 minutes
Listening task 1 Where is it?	A Main idea B Inference	20–25 minutes
Listening task 2 Find the treasure.	A Main idea B Details	20–25 minutes
Your turn to talk Map it!	• Giving and receiving directions • Using stress for clarification	10–20 minutes

---

page 50

Warming up

A

1. Give students time to look at the map. For lower-level classes, read the names of the places on the map and have students point to them in their Student's Books.

2. Read the instructions aloud.

3. Read the prepositions of location in the box aloud (*across from, between, next to, around the corner from, on the right, on the left*) and have students listen and repeat. Review the meanings of the prepositions of location. You can do this by drawing a simple map on the board to demonstrate the locations.

4. Divide the class into pairs and give students time to complete the exercise. Circulate while students are working to monitor their progress. Make a note of any difficulties to address later.

5. Check answers with the whole class.

Answers

1. the tower	4. the movie theater/the tower
2. the Internet café	5. the arcade
3. the pet store	6. the restaurant

6. For further practice, ask students a few more questions about the map, for example:

   • *Where is the arcade?*
   • *Is the restaurant across from the entrance or next to the entrance?*

Culture notes

• Students may be familiar with Internet cafés (cafés with computers where people can go and pay a fee to use the Internet).

• A food court is an area, usually in a shopping mall, that has many small self-service restaurants offering a variety of food types.

B

1. Read the instructions aloud. Read the phrases in the box aloud and have students listen and repeat.

2. Have students work alone or in pairs to do the exercise.

3. Check answers with the whole class.

Answers	
1. go straight	3. turn left
2. turn right	4. go across

C

1. Read the instructions aloud. Read the example sentences aloud and have a student read the example response. For lower-level classes, do one or two more examples before students start the exercise.

2. Have students work with their partners from Exercise A. Circulate while students are working and offer help as necessary.

3. To wrap up, call on a few students to give directions using the map while the rest of the students listen and guess the place. Alternatively, give the directions yourself and have students raise their hands when they know the answer. Give shorter directions for lower-level classes, and longer ones for higher-level classes. This could also be played as a team game, with teams winning points for correct answers.

Optional speaking activity

Focusing on specific words
Think of a location near your school. Choose a place that most students will know (for example, a coffee shop, the library, etc.).

Tell students you are going to give them directions to a place nearby and that they should just listen for the words and phrases they learned on page 50 of the Student's Book.

Have students listen as you give simple verbal directions to the place. As students listen, have them note the direction words they hear. You can also have them point right, left, or straight ahead as appropriate to add a physical component to the activity. When you finish, ask for volunteers to say the direction words they heard.

To wrap up, say the directions again and have students guess the place.

---

page 51

Listening task 1
Where is it?

Additional vocabulary from the audio script

reptiles: cold-blooded animals that have scales and lay eggs (for example, crocodiles, snakes, lizards)
insects: small flying and crawling animals; bugs
exhibit: an object or a collection of objects displayed for the public
environment: the natural surroundings in which people, animals, and plants live (for example, land, air, water)

A **Main idea** (CD 2, track 23)

1. Give students time to look at the map. Have students identify the animals they can see in the picture. Explain any new vocabulary.

2. To help familiarize students with the map, ask students to tell you what kind of place it is (a zoo, an animal park). Ask some questions about the map and have students call out the answers, for example:

   • *Where can you see dolphins?*
   • *Where can you get information about the attractions and animals?*

3. Read the instructions aloud. Make sure students understand that there is one place on the map the speakers do not mention.

4. Play the audio program once or twice. If necessary, pause between items to give students time to complete their answers.

5. Check answers by asking the class, *Where's Monkey Mountain?* etc. Encourage students to describe the locations using the vocabulary from page 50. For lower-level classes, play the audio program again, item by item, so students can check any answers they missed.

Culture notes

• The term *zoology* comes from the Greek words for "animal" and "study." The term was first used in 1828 for the London Zoological Gardens, and was shortened sometime later to the abbreviation "zoo."

• The oldest existing zoo is the Vienna Zoo in Austria, founded in 1752. The first zoo founded primarily for scientific and educational reasons was the *Ménagerie du Jardin des Plantes,* founded in Paris in 1794.

Answers

1. b   2. a   3. c   4. g   5. e   6. f

B 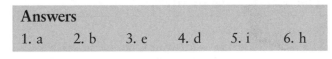 Inference (CD 2, track 23)

1. Read the instructions aloud. If students think they remember the answers, have them do the exercise and then listen to check their answers.

2. Play the audio program. If necessary, pause between items to give students time to complete their answers.

3. Check answers by asking students to form complete sentences (for example, *They both want to see the monkeys. The boy wants to see the lions.*).

Answers

1. both	3. girl	5. boy
2. boy	4. both	6. both

Optional speaking activity

A trip to Safari Park
Have students look at the Safari Park map on page 51 of the Student's Book and think about which animals and attractions they would like to see if they visited Safari Park.

Write the following dialog on the board:

A: *Excuse me, I'd like to go to _____. Can you tell me where it is/they are?*
B: *Sure. It's/They're _____.*

To model the activity, take the role of A and ask a student to take the role of B.

Divide the class into pairs. Have students take turns asking for and giving directions to the locations on the map.

To wrap up, take the part of A in the dialog and ask for volunteers to help you find a few more locations on the map.

---

page 52

Listening task 2
Find the treasure.

Additional vocabulary from the audio script

treasure: something of value (for example, money, gold, jewelry)
level: degree of difficulty in a video game
temple: a religious building

A 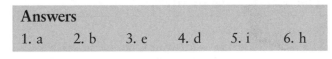 Main idea (CD 2, track 24)

1. Give students time to look at the picture and say what they see. Elicit any vocabulary that will be useful for the *Listening task* (for example, *bag of gold, banana, boat, building, lake, rock, snake, store, temple*).

2. Ask students to find the main character in the video game. Have them predict where he might go and what he might be trying to do.

3. Read the instructions aloud. If necessary, explain *treasure*. Make sure students understand that there are three places that the speakers do not mention.

4. Play the audio program once or twice. If necessary, pause between items to give students time to complete their answers. For lower-level classes, have students raise their hands when they hear a direction (*turn left/right, go straight*).

5. Check answers with the whole class.

Answers

1. a	2. b	3. e	4. d	5. i	6. h

B 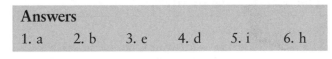 Details (CD 2, track 24)

1. Read the instructions aloud. If students think they remember the answers, have them do the exercise and then listen to check their answers.

2. Play the audio program. If necessary, pause between items to give students time to complete their answers.

3. Check answers by asking for volunteers to read the complete sentences aloud.

---

page 53

Your turn to talk

Map it!

A Prepare

1. Tell students they are going to draw maps and give their classmates directions to places near their school.

2. Read the instructions aloud. To help students with ideas, brainstorm places near your school that most students know (for example, a coffee shop, a sports center, or a movie theater).

3. To model the exercise, choose a location and draw another simple example map on the board. Ask students to tell you what to draw and where, and have them explain the directions. Point out to students that their drawings can be very simple.

4. Give students a five- to ten-minute time limit to do the exercise. Circulate while students are working and offer help as necessary.

B Practice

Exercise 1 (CD 2, track 25)

1. Read the instructions aloud. Play the audio program once without stopping so students can listen.

2. Play the audio program again, pausing between items for the class to repeat. You can add a physical element to the practice by having students tap their desks or clap on the stressed words.

Exercise 2 (CD 2, track 26)

1. Read the instructions aloud. Have students do the exercise alone or in pairs.

2. Play the audio program and have students listen and check their answers. For lower-level classes, pause between items and have students listen and repeat.

3. For further practice, have students work in pairs to make similar questions about the map on page 52 (for example, *Is the temple on the right or the left?*). Circulate while students are working and check that they are using the appropriate stress.

C Speak

1. Divide the class into groups of three. You can make groups by having students find two classmates who take the same route to get home from school, who turn the same direction (right or left) to go home when they leave school, etc.

2. Read the instructions aloud. Tell students that they can refer to the vocabulary on page 50 to help them.

3. Give students time to complete the exercise. Circulate while students are working to monitor their progress. Remind them to use the clarification questions they practiced in Exercise B(1) if they are unsure of any directions.

| **Unit 11 Self-study** | *Student's Book page 94* |
| **Unit 11 Quiz** | *Teacher's Manual page 92* |

Gifts

Overview

In this unit, students listen to conversations about giving and receiving gifts. In **Warming up**, students practice vocabulary to talk about gift-giving occasions. In the **Listening tasks**, students practice listening for the main idea, details, and inference as they hear people talk about choosing and giving gifts. They also learn cultural information about appropriate and inappropriate gifts in different cultures. In **Your turn to talk**, students role-play giving and receiving gifts, and learn and practice intonation with names.

Focus		Estimated time
Warming up	**Gift survey** – *birthday, business meeting, celebrate, wedding*	10–15 minutes
Listening task 1 **Gift-giving occasions**	A Main idea B Inference	20–25 minutes
Listening task 2 **Gifts and cultures**	A Main idea B Details	20–25 minutes
Your turn to talk **Gift exchange**	• Figuring out gifts for different occasions • Intonation with names	10–20 minutes

page 54

Warming up

A

1. Have students say what occasions they think of when they look at the items pictured on page 54.

2. Read the survey questions aloud and have students listen. Explain any new vocabulary.

3. Divide the class into pairs and give students time to complete the exercise. Circulate while students are working to monitor their progress and offer help as necessary.

4. To wrap up, ask for volunteers to share their answers with the class and list any useful words or phrases on the board.

B

1. Read the instructions aloud. Explain to students that this exercise asks for types of gifts that may be considered bad or unlucky in their culture (for example, a certain color gift, number of items, etc.). Elicit one or two examples from students before they begin the exercise.

2. Have students work alone or in pairs to do the exercise. Circulate while students are working and offer help as necessary.

3. To wrap up, ask for volunteers to share their answers. Encourage students to explain why a particular gift might have a bad meaning.

Listening strategy

Thinking about accomplishments
Students are now about three-quarters of the way through the course, so this is a good point to talk about the progress they have made so far.

Ask students to think back to the beginning of the course and how they felt about listening in English. You may want to give them time to write their thoughts in a notebook or journal. Ask guiding questions to help them, for example:

• *Before you started the course, how did you feel about listening in English?*
• *How did you feel during the first few lessons of this course? Were the exercises challenging, easy, enjoyable?*
• *How much did you feel you could understand when you listened to native speakers of English?*

Divide the class into pairs and have students share their answers with a partner.

When they finish, tell students to compare their initial feelings in the course to how they feel now when they listen to English. Ask:

• *What skills have become easier for you? Listening for the main idea, details, inference?*
• *When you do the exercises in class now, how much do you feel you understand?*

Ask for volunteers to share their answers.

To wrap up, ask students to share one thing they feel they have accomplished in the course or one activity they really enjoyed and were successful at. If they don't wish to speak, students can just think about their answers or write them down.

Stress the importance of not getting discouraged in language learning. Remind students that progress is often steady and gradual, not dramatic or sudden.

Culture note

• In North American culture, it is common for people to hold wedding and baby "showers" when someone is getting married or having a baby. Showers are usually a gathering of friends and family members who bring gifts for the couple or the new baby. Shower gifts are usually practical necessities such as household items to help the couple or the family begin their new life.

----

page 55

Listening task 1
Gift-giving occasions

Additional vocabulary from the audio script

retirement: when a person reaches the age when he or she stops working (usually around 65 years old)

gift catalog: a magazine or book with gift selections one can order for home delivery

on the court: a place where certain sports are played (for example, tennis, basketball, squash)

anniversary: an occasion when people celebrate the date a special event happened (for example, a wedding)

a dozen: twelve, usually used with flowers or food

A 🔘 Main idea (CD 3, track 1)

1. Have students work in pairs to name the items in the pictures. Do not explain unknown vocabulary

at this stage. Tell students that you will go over the vocabulary before they do Exercise B.

2. Read the instructions aloud. Make sure students understand that there are two occasions that the speakers do not mention.

3. Read the list of occasions aloud. Do not explain any unknown occasions at this point; however, reassure students that they will be able to understand the meanings when they hear the conversations on the audio program.

4. Play the audio program once or twice. If necessary, pause between items to give students time to complete their answers.

5. Check answers with the whole class.

Answers

1. retirement	3. Father's Day	5. thank you
2. graduation	4. birthday	6. anniversary

6. To wrap up, ask for volunteers to explain the meanings of the occasions, and what people might do or celebrate on each occasion.

B 🔘 Inference (CD 3, track 1)

1. Give students a chance to ask questions to clarify any unknown vocabulary in the pictures. Have students tell you the names of all the items and write the words on the board.

2. Read the instructions aloud.

3. Play the audio program. If necessary, pause between items to give students time to complete their answers.

4. Check answers by asking for volunteers to form complete sentences. Write an example sentence on the board for students to follow (for example, *He's/ She's going to buy a/an _____.*).

Answers

1. a	2. b	3. b	4. a	5. a	6. b

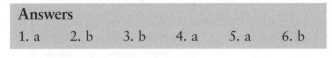

Additional listening practice

Listen again!
This activity extends *Listening task 1* by having students extract more information from the audio program.

Write the following questions on the board:

1. *What does the speaker's mother want to do after she retires?*
2. *Who is the gift for?*
3. *How often does his father play tennis?*
4. *Why does the salesclerk suggest a gift card?*
5. *Why does the woman decide not to buy a dictionary?*
6. *Why does the man buy pink roses?*

Play the audio program, pausing between items so students can listen and write their answers.

Check answers after each item, or play all six items and then check answers.

Answers

1. spend more time taking pictures/ doing photography
2. the speaker's niece
3. almost every weekend
4. because the woman doesn't know what kind of music her grandson likes
5. because the teacher probably has one already
6. because pink is his wife's favorite color

---

page 56

Listening task 2

Gifts and cultures

Additional vocabulary from the audio script

to go (to China) on business: take a business trip
lightweight: light, not heavy
handkerchiefs: small pieces of cloth carried in the pocket or purse, used as a tissue

A Main idea (CD 3, track 2)

1. Give students time to look at the pictures and say what they see. Write any new vocabulary on the board.

2. Read the instructions aloud.

3. Play the audio program once or twice. If necessary, pause between items to give students time to complete their answers.

4. Have students compare answers in pairs. They can do this after each item, or after they complete all the items.

5. Check answers with the whole class.

Answers

1. a	2. a	3. b	4. b

Note

• These cultural "rules" are, of course, generalizations, and individuals in each of the countries may act differently. Much of the information here is from *Do's and Taboos Around the World,* second edition, by Roger E. Axtell (New York: John Wiley and Sons, 1990); the case of handkerchiefs in Chinese culture is from the authors' personal experience.

B Details (CD 3, track 2)

1. Read the instructions aloud. If students think they remember the answers, have them do the exercise and then listen to check their answers.

2. Play the audio program. If necessary, pause between items to give students time to complete their answers.

3. Check answers by asking the class to raise their hands for *a* or *b.*

Answers

1. a	2. a	3. b	4. a

Optional speaking activity

In my country
This activity uses the language and context of *Listening task 2* as a prompt for students to discuss gift giving in their own cultures.

Write these phrases for gift-giving advice and suggestions on the board:

• _____ *are always a good gift.*
• *I don't think you should give . . .*
• *You should never give . . .*
• *I think _____ or _____ might be better . . .*

For lower-level classes, play the audio program for *Listening task 2* again so students can hear the phrases in context. Have students raise their hands when they hear the phrases.

Divide the class into pairs. Tell students to think of a gift-giving occasion and examples of appropriate and inappropriate gifts for that occasion in their country.

Combine pairs and have students share their ideas using the phrases on the board (for example, *For a birthday, candy is always a good gift.*).

To wrap up, ask for volunteers to share some examples of the gifts they chose.

----

page 57

Your turn to talk
Gift exchange

A Prepare

1. Tell students they are going to think of gifts they would like to give to some of their classmates.

2. Read the instructions aloud. Tell students they can refer to the pictures on page 55 to help them. You can also lead a whole-class brainstorm to elicit other occasions and gifts.

3. Give students time to complete the exercise. Circulate while students are working to monitor their progress and offer help as necessary.

B Practice

Exercise 1 (CD 3, track 3)

1. Read the instructions aloud. Play the audio program once without stopping so students can listen.

2. Play the audio program again, pausing between items for the class to repeat. Draw students' attention to the arrows that show the rising and falling intonation. Use your hands to demonstrate the intonation as students repeat the statements. You could also have students use their hands to show the rising and falling intonation.

Exercise 2 (CD 3, track 4)

1. Read the instructions aloud.

2. Play the audio program once or twice. If necessary, pause between items to give students time to complete their answers.

3. Have students compare their answers in pairs. Then play the audio program again so students can check their answers.

4. Check answers with the whole class. Have students tell you the names they hear.

Answers

a. no	c. yes (Tom)	e. no
b. yes (Kent)	d. no	f. yes (Dennis)

5. For further practice, play the audio program again and have students listen and tell you the sentences they hear. Write the sentences on the board or have a student write them. Read the sentences aloud and have students listen and repeat with the correct intonation pattern. For higher-level classes, have students prepare similar sentences of their own, using these sentences as a model.

C Speak

1. Read the instructions aloud. To model the activity, have a student stand and face you. Read the example sentence and have the student read the example response.

2. Have students move around the class to do the exercise. You can add a physical element by having students pantomime lifting the gift, handing it to their partner, reacting to the gift, etc. Circulate while students are working to monitor their progress. Make a note of any difficulties to address later.

Optional speaking activity

A gift I remember
Tell students to think of an occasion when they received a gift that was especially memorable. It could be the best gift they've ever received, the most unusual, the funniest, the most surprising, etc.

Write the following questions on the board:

• *What was the occasion?*
• *What was the gift?*
• *Who gave it to you?*
• *How did you feel when you received it?*

Model the activity by having students ask you the questions and telling them about a memorable gift that you have received.

Divide the class into groups of four students. Have group members take turns describing the occasions and gifts using the questions on the board.

For higher-level classes, have each group member ask one follow-up question for each question asked (for example, *How old were you? Where were you when you received the gift? What did you say?*).

Unit 12 Self-study	*Student's Book page 95*
Unit 12 Quiz	*Teacher's Manual page 93*

Overview

In this **Expansion** unit, students listen to general information about Italy. In the **Listening tasks,** students practice listening for the main idea and details as they hear people talk about famous Italian cities. They also learn cultural information as they listen to an authentic interview with an Italian student about what university life is like in Italy.

	Focus	Estimated time
Listening task 1 **Information**	A Main idea B Details	20–25 minutes
Listening task 2 **University life**	A Main idea B Details	20–25 minutes

---

page 58

Listening task 1
Information

Note

• Before you start this unit, write the titles of the previous four units on the board or elicit them from students (*Movies, A typical day, Locations, Gifts*). Tell students that this *Expansion* unit features some of the topics and vocabulary from these units. It presents general information about Italy and a more in-depth look at Italian culture based on an authentic interview with a student from Italy. Give students time to look over the language and listening skills in Units 9 through 12.

A  Main idea (CD 3, track 5)

1. Ask students where Italy is located (western Europe). You may want to bring a world map to class and have students find Italy on the map. Ask students if anyone has traveled to Italy and, if so, what it was like. Alternatively, ask students to say anything they know about the country of Italy, its culture, or its people.

2. Give students time to look at the pictures and say what they see. Write a list of key words and phrases on the board.

   Possible answers
   Milan: designer shop, people shopping
   Venice: river (canal), bridge, boat (the boat in the picture is called a *gondola*; the man is a *gondolier*)

   Rome: church, fountain, statues
   Florence: garden, museum, people, tourists
   Bologna: outdoor restaurant, people eating

3. Read the instructions aloud. At this stage in the course, students may already have a good understanding of the types of listening skills introduced in *Before you begin* on pages 4 and 5 (Main idea, Details, Inference). However, if you feel students would benefit from a review, the *Expansion* units provide a good opportunity to do so. Point out to students that in this exercise, they are listening for the main idea. This means that they don't need to understand everything they hear, just the general meaning. Make sure students understand that there is one picture that the speakers do not mention.

4. Play the audio program once or twice. If necessary, pause between items to give students time to complete their answers. Draw students' attention to the pronunciation of the city names. Point out that the pronunciation in English may be different from the one in students' own languages, and from the name in Italian.

5. Check answers by asking for volunteers to say the names of the cities and any words or phrases that gave them the answers. Add the words and phrases to the list on the board.

Answers
1. Rome   2. Milan   3. Florence   4. Bologna

B 🔘 Details (CD 3, track 5)

1. Read the instructions aloud. If students think they remember the answers, have them do the exercise and then listen to check their answers.

2. Play the audio program. If necessary, pause between items to give students time to complete their answers.

3. Check answers by calling on students to read the complete, correct sentences aloud.

- -

page 59

Listening task 2
University life

A 🔘 Main idea (CD 3, track 6)

1. Give students time to look at the pictures. Ask them to guess which university is in Italy and which one is in the U.S., and why they think so.

2. Give students time to read the topics. Have them predict some of the information they might learn about Italian universities and university life. Ask:

   • *Do you think students in Italy have the same school schedule as in your culture?*
   • *Do you think Italian university students have the same interests and lifestyle as students in your culture?*
   • *What might be the same or different?*

3. Read the instructions aloud. Make sure students understand that there are two topics the speakers do not mention.

4. Play the audio program once or twice. If necessary, pause between items to give students time to complete their answers.

5. Have students compare answers in pairs. Then check answers by calling on students to tell you the topics and any words or phrases that helped them get the answers.

Culture note

• Historians say that the University of Bologna in Bologna, Italy, was the first university in the Western world. It celebrated its 900th anniversary in 1988. Today the University of Bologna is the second largest university in Italy with over 100,000 students.

B 🔘 Details (CD 3, track 6)

1. Read the instructions aloud. If students think they remember the answers, have them do the exercise and then listen to check their answers.

2. Play the audio program. If necessary, pause between items to give students time to complete their answers.

3. Check answers by calling on students to read the complete sentences aloud. Write the following examples on the board for students to follow:

   Students . . . in Italy.
   Students . . . in the U.S.
   Students . . . in both Italy and the U.S.

4. To wrap up, divide the class into groups and have students list ways university life in their country is similar to and different from university life in Italy.

Part-time jobs

Overview

In this unit, students listen to people talking about part-time and temporary jobs. In **Warming up**, students learn and practice vocabulary to talk about jobs. In the **Listening tasks**, students practice listening for details and inference as they guess people's jobs and hear people interviewing for part-time jobs. In **Your turn to talk**, students practice talking about ideal jobs, and learn and practice syllable stress.

	Focus	Estimated time
Warming up	**Jobs** – *childcare worker, cleaning staff, convenience store clerk, lifeguard, porter, server, tour guide, tutor*	10–15 minutes
Listening task 1 What's the job?	A Inference B Details	20–25 minutes
Listening task 2 Job interviews	A Details B Inference	20–25 minutes
Your turn to talk My ideal job	• Figuring out what job features are important • Syllable stress	10–20 minutes

---

page 60

Warming up

A

1. Ask the class if anyone has done any of the part-time jobs pictured on the page and, if so, what the experience was like.

2. Read the instructions aloud.

3. Read the words and phrases in the box aloud and have students listen and repeat. Explain any unknown vocabulary.

4. Divide the class into pairs and give students time to complete the exercise. Circulate while students are working to monitor their progress.

5. Check answers with the whole class.

Answers

(top row) tutor, childcare worker, cleaning staff, server
(bottom row) convenience store clerk, lifeguard, porter, tour guide

Note
• A part-time job is one in which someone works less than forty hours per week (usually around twenty hours). A temporary job is one in which someone works for a short time (for example, during the summer).

Culture notes
• In the U.S., the minimum legal working age for most jobs is 16. Many high school and university students take temporary jobs or internships during their summer vacations.

• The term *server* is often used instead of *waiter* or *waitress* in North American restaurants. This allows people to have the same job title regardless of gender.

B

1. Read the instructions aloud. Tell students they can use a separate piece of paper if they need more space.

2. Have students work with their partners from Exercise A. Circulate while students are working to monitor their progress and offer help as necessary.

Possible answers
baby-sitter, carpenter, construction worker, cook, gardener, landscaper, nurse's aide, librarian, sports coach

C

1. Have students change partners.

2. Read the instructions aloud. Circulate while students are working and make a note of any difficulties to address later. If students don't know the correct word for a job, ask them to explain to you what the person does, where the person works, etc., so you (or another student) can help them with the vocabulary word.

3. Ask for volunteers to share their words with the class. List the words on the board and read them aloud to model the correct pronunciation.

Listening strategy

Guessing meaning from context
Point out to students that they can often find clues to the meaning of unknown vocabulary within the context of the conversation. Context refers to the topic about which the person is speaking or the situation or circumstances within which the conversation is taking place.

To demonstrate this concept, tell students that they are going to help you figure out the meaning of a new (nonsense) vocabulary word: *quom*.

Write the following on the board:

Every morning, I drink a cup of quom.
I usually put milk and sugar in my quom.
I just bought a new quom table for my living room.

Elicit from students that *quom* means *coffee*. Then ask them to explain how they knew.

Students are likely to say that the cues *drink . . . in the morning, milk and sugar,* and *table* gave them the answer. Point out to students that they have just figured out the meaning from the context.

Have students work in pairs to create their own examples using nonsense words. Pairs can read their sentences to the class, and classmates can guess the meaning.

Tell students that they can use this strategy anytime they listen to help them understand the meaning of unknown vocabulary.

page 61

Listening task 1
What's the job?

> **Additional vocabulary from the audio script**
>
> **a pack (of gum):** package, usually five or six pieces
> **grab (a cup of coffee):** to get (slang)
> **luggage:** suitcases (This is used as a noncount noun, for example, *I have a lot of luggage.*)
> **a nap:** a short sleep, usually in the afternoon

A ⊙ Inference (CD 3, track 7)

1. Read the instructions and the words in the box aloud. Remind students that for this exercise they need to infer who the people are talking to; that is, the job titles are not stated in the audio program – students have to figure out the answers from the conversation. Make sure students understand that there is one job title the speakers do not mention.

2. Play the audio program once or twice. If necessary, pause between items to give students time to complete their answers.

3. Check answers by asking for volunteers to say the jobs and any words or phrases that helped them get the answers.

Answers

1. a tutor	4. a porter
2. a server	5. a tour guide
3. a convenience store clerk	6. a childcare worker

B ⊙ Details (CD 3, track 7)

1. Read the instructions aloud. If students think they remember the answers, have them do the exercise and then listen to check their answers.

2. Play the audio program. If necessary, pause between items to give students time to complete their answers. For lower-level classes, have students raise their hands when they hear the answers.

3. Check answers by calling on students to read the complete sentences aloud.

Answers

1. The student has to write a *five-page* paper.
2. They're going to drink *tea.*
3. The woman is buying a *magazine.*
4. They're in room *726.*
5. The man wants to send a picture to his *cousin.*
6. Michael is a bit *tired.*

Vocabulary games

For a quick review of jobs vocabulary, have students close their books and try to remember the words they have learned so far in Unit 13 (*childcare worker, cleaning staff, convenience store clerk, lifeguard, porter, server, tour guide, tutor*).

Here are a few ways to make vocabulary review fun and active.

• Call out the first letter of one of the jobs and have students guess the job (for example, *I'm thinking of a job that begins with . . .*).

• Choose one of the jobs and give clues to describe it (for example, *This person carries luggage for guests at a hotel.*). Then have students guess the job. Ask for a volunteer to describe another job while their classmates try to guess.

• Use gestures to pantomime a couple of the jobs and have students guess the jobs from your actions. Then divide the class into pairs and have students take turns miming the rest of the jobs.

- -

page 62

Listening task 2
Job interviews

Additional vocabulary from the audio script

experience: having done the same thing, or something similar, in the past
volunteer: unpaid
intern: someone who works in a (usually unpaid) position with a company or organization in order to get experience or university course credit

A Details (CD 3, track 8)

1. Read the job titles and the job features aloud and explain any unknown vocabulary. Ask for a volunteer to describe each job and what the person does (for example, *A park ranger works outside and keeps the park clean and safe.*)

2. If necessary, explain *interview* (a formal meeting where an employer asks questions to find out if a person is suited for a job). Ask:

   • *What happens at a job interview?*
   • *What kinds of questions does the interviewer ask?*
   • *What information does the interviewee want to find out about a job?*

3. Play the audio program once or twice. If necessary, pause between items to give students time to complete their answers.

4. Check answers by calling out each category (experience required, etc.) and having students raise their hands if they checked the box.

Answers

1. experience required, part-time, volunteer
2. experience required, full-time, paid
3. no experience required, full-time, volunteer
4. experience required, part-time, paid

Culture note

• Here are ten commonly asked job interview questions:

   Tell me about yourself.
   Why did you leave your last job?
   What do you see yourself doing five/ten years from now?
   How well do you work with people? Do you prefer working alone or in teams?
   How would a good friend describe you?
   What makes you qualified for this position?
   In what ways do you think you can make a contribution to our company?
   What can you tell us about our company?
   What do you know about our competitors?
   What two or three things are most important to you in your job?

B Inference (CD 3, track 8)

1. Read the instructions aloud. If students think they remember the answers, have them do the exercise and then listen to check their answers.

2. Play the audio program. If necessary, pause between items to give students time to complete their answers.

3. Check answers by having students raise their hands for *yes* or *no*.

Answers

1. no	2. yes	3. no	4. yes

4. To wrap up, ask students to explain how they got the answers. Ask, *Why did the interviewee accept/ refuse the job?*

Answers

1. refused because the job is unpaid and he needs to make some money
2. accepted because she loves working with kids and the pay is good

3. refused because they need someone for the month of August and he has to be back in college on August 1st

4. accepted because getting paid to play tennis is a dream job for her

5. For further practice, ask students to say which of the four jobs they would prefer to do and why. You could do this as a whole-class activity, or have students work in pairs or small groups.

---

page 63

Your turn to talk
My ideal job

A Prepare

1. Tell students they are going to talk about what features are important to them in a job.

2. Read the instructions and the list of job features aloud. Explain any new vocabulary:

   responsibility: the duty of doing something or making sure that it is done properly
   routine: a fixed or regular way of doing things
   salary: a fixed, regular payment for doing a job
   uniform: special clothes for a job (for example, a police officer's uniform)

3. Give students time to complete the exercise. Circulate while students are working to monitor their progress.

B Practice

Exercise 1 (CD 3, track 9)

1. Read the instructions aloud. Have students predict which syllables in each word they think will be stressed.

2. Play the audio program once without stopping so students can listen.

3. Play the audio program again, pausing between items for the class to repeat. Add a physical element by having students clap or tap their desks on the stressed syllables.

Exercise 2 (CD 3, track 10)

1. Read the instructions aloud.

2. Play the audio program once or twice. If necessary, pause between items to give students time to complete their answers.

3. To check answers, write the words from Exercise B(2) on the board and ask for volunteers to come to the board and circle the correct syllables.

Answers
a. intern   c. salary   e. convenience
b. instructor   d. outdoors   f. alone

C Speak

Exercise 1

1. Read the instructions aloud. Read the example question and have a student read the first example answer. Then read the example question again and have a different student read the second example answer.

2. Divide the class into pairs and give students time to complete the exercise. Circulate while students are working and make a note of any difficulties to address later.

Exercise 2

1. Read the instructions aloud.

2. Have pairs combine to make groups of four. Circulate while students are working to monitor their progress. Make a note of any difficulties students have to address later.

3. To wrap up, ask for volunteers to tell the class what jobs would be good for their partner and why. In large classes, students could work in groups of four to six while you circulate and listen.

Optional speaking activity

What's my job?
Choose one of the jobs presented in the unit (for example, *server*).

Explain to the class that students can ask questions to try to find out the job you are thinking of. They can ask up to ten yes-no questions before guessing the job, for example:

Do you work in an office?
Do you work alone?
Do you have the same routine every day?

When they have guessed the job, divide the class into groups of three or four students. Group members take turns choosing a job and asking questions to try to guess their partners' jobs.

| Unit 13 Self-study | *Student's Book page 96* |
| Unit 13 Quiz | *Teacher's Manual page 94* |

Celebrations

Overview

In this unit, students listen to people talking about holidays and celebrations. In **Warming up**, students learn and practice vocabulary to talk about ways people celebrate holidays and special occasions. In the **Listening tasks**, students practice listening for the main idea and details as they hear people talk about celebrations around the world. They also learn cultural information about holidays and celebrations in several countries. In **Your turn to talk**, students practice talking about holiday memories, and learn and practice the reduced pronunciation of *Did you* and *What did you*.

	Focus	Estimated time
Warming up	**Ways people celebrate** – *do a special dance, eat special food, fly special flags, give presents, go to a parade, ring bells, watch fireworks, wear special clothes*	10–15 minutes
Listening task 1 **Fireworks, food, and fun**	A Details B Details	20–25 minutes
Listening task 2 **Celebration time**	A Main idea B Details	20–25 minutes
Your turn to talk **Holiday memories**	• Comparing holiday memories • Reduction of *Did you* and *What did you*	10–20 minutes

---

page 64

Warming up

A

1. Have students look at the pictures and try to name each of the holidays pictured (*pictured from left to right, top row:* St. Patrick's Day, Kartini Day, Bob Marley Day; *bottom row:* St. Lucia's Day, Chinese New Year, Day of the Dead). Encourage them to guess where each of the celebrations takes place.

2. Read the instructions aloud.

3. Read the phrases in the box aloud. Where possible, use the pictures to help students understand the meanings of the phrases.

4. Divide the class into pairs and give students time to complete the exercise. Tell students that they can think of holidays from their own culture or from another culture they know well.

Notes

• If students do not know the names of the holidays in English, you can have them write them in their own language. However, you may want to use

this opportunity to teach the English names for some of the holidays. Bring a calendar to class that lists international holidays. Have students find holidays from their culture and make a list of the English names.

• Some holidays are translated into English and others are not. For example, the Mexican holiday Day of the Dead is usually translated into English, while *Obon*, a similar Japanese holiday, is not.

5. Combine pairs of students to make groups of four and have them compare answers. Then ask for volunteers to share their answers with the class. Answers will vary.

B

1. Read the instructions aloud.

2. Divide the class into pairs and give students time to do the exercise. Tell them that they can use a separate piece of paper if they need more space.

3. Circulate while students are working to monitor their progress and offer help as necessary.

4. Call on students to say their answers and write the holidays on the board. Lower-level students can answer with complete sentences (for example, *People eat special food on New Year's Day.*). For higher-level classes, have students explain in general what people do to celebrate each of the holidays.

Culture note
• Here are some well-known international holidays and customs:

do a special dance: Carnaval (Brazil)
eat special food: Thanksgiving (U.S.), Ramadan (Muslim countries)
fly special flags: Children's Day (Japan)
give presents: Christmas (U.K., U.S.)
go to a parade: St. Patrick's Day (U.S.)
ring bells: New Year's Day (Japan)
watch fireworks: Independence Day (U.S.)
wear special clothes: Halloween (U.S, U.K.)

Listening strategy

Semantic mapping
Semantic mapping helps students think about the words they are likely to hear before they listen. It also helps them to associate new words with words they already know.

Draw the following diagram on the board:

winter

Valentine's Day

Winter is given as an example; however, you may choose any season.

Divide the class into groups of three or four students. Have groups copy the diagram onto a piece of paper. Tell them that they have five minutes to add one celebration to each of the remaining spokes. This may include holidays and celebrations from their own culture or from other cultures, as well as birthdays, if any group member's birthday falls during the appropriate season.

When the time limit has passed, elicit some of the answers and write them on the board.

Next, have groups add two more spokes for each celebration they have written. Give groups ten minutes to write two ways people celebrate each one. They can use the activities on page 64 or their own ideas.

To wrap up, have groups exchange diagrams with another group and compare.

page 65

Listening task 1
Fireworks, food, and fun

Additional vocabulary from the audio script

harvest: a time when plants are done growing and are ready to be collected
crown: a decoration for the head made of gold and jewels to show a high position (for example, the crown of a king or queen)
candle: a round, usually long piece of wax with a wick (piece of string) that is burned for light

A Details (CD 3, track 11)

1. Give students time to look at the calendar. If necessary, review the months of the year by reading the months aloud and having students listen and repeat. Have students work in pairs to try to think of one holiday or celebration for each month.

2. Read the names of the celebrations aloud. Ask students if they are familiar with any of the celebrations and, if so, to share any information they already know about them. Refer students to the pictures on page 64.

3. Read the instructions aloud.

4. Play the audio program once or twice. If necessary, pause between items to give students a chance to complete their answers.

5. Check answers by calling on students to form complete sentences. Write an example sentence on the board (for example, *Bob Marley Day is in February.*).

Answers
February: Bob Marley Day
March: St. Patrick's Day
April: Kartini Day
September: Moon Festival
November: Day of the Dead
December: St. Lucia's Day

B 💿 Details (CD 3, track 11)

1. Read the instructions aloud. If students think they remember the answers, have them do the exercise and then listen to check their answers.

2. Play the audio program. If necessary, pause between items to give students time to complete their answers.

3. Check answers by asking for volunteers to form complete sentences. Write an example sentence on the board (for example, *On the Day of the Dead, people visit graves.*).

Answers

1. e	2. f	3. b	4. a	5. c	6. d

Note

• Students often confuse the terms *holiday, festival, vacation,* and *day off.*

  holiday: a special day to celebrate a religious or historical event. On official holidays, people usually do not go to work. On celebrations, such as Valentine's Day and Halloween, people go to work in the U.S.

  festival: a public gathering to celebrate a holiday. Festivals often last for more than one day.

  vacation: a period of time to relax or travel for pleasure instead of going to work or school (In British and Australian English, the term *go on holiday* also means to "go on vacation.")

  day off: either a regularly scheduled day, such as Saturday and Sunday, or one day taken by an individual, when one does not go to work

----

page 66

Listening task 2
Celebration time

Additional vocabulary from the audio script

kite: a toy to fly in the air; it's made of lightweight material and has a long string (see *Kite-flying festival* picture)

bucket: a round container with an open top and a handle, often used for carrying water (see *Water festival* picture)

fancy: expensive and beautiful

contest: an event in which people compete against each other, often for a prize; a competition

A 💿 Main idea (CD 3, track 12)

1. Have students look at the pictures and try to predict what words they might hear in each description.

2. Read the instructions aloud.

3. Play the audio program once or twice. If necessary, pause between items to give students a chance to complete their answers.

4. Have students compare answers in pairs. Then check answers with the whole class.

Answers

1. Kite-flying festival	3. Carnaval
2. Water festival	4. Chinese New Year

B 💿 Details (CD 3, track 12)

1. Read the instructions aloud. If students think they remember the answers, have them do the exercise and then listen to check their answers.

2. Play the audio program. If necessary, pause between items to give students time to complete their answers.

3. Check answers by calling on students to read the complete sentences aloud.

Answers

1. Cutting strings *takes away bad luck.*
2. Pouring water *shows respect.*
3. The purpose of this holiday is *for people to have a good time.*
4. It's important to start the year *without owing money.*

Optional speaking activity

A family celebration
This activity uses the language and contexts of *Listening task 2* as a prompt for students to talk about how they celebrate holidays or celebrations with their own families.

Write the following on the board:

I celebrate this holiday with my (family members) . . .
We usually celebrate by _____ing . . .
Something special we do in my family is . . .
We wear/eat/dance . . .

Give students a few minutes to think of a holiday they would like to talk about. Then divide the class into pairs.

Have pairs take turns talking about how they celebrate the holidays they chose using the prompts on the board. Encourage students to ask each other questions to find out more information. Circulate while students are working to monitor their progress and offer help as necessary.

To wrap up, have students share something interesting they learned about their partners.

---

page 67

Your turn to talk
Holiday memories

A Prepare

1. Tell students they are going to talk about three holidays or celebrations they remember.

2. Read the instructions and the list of holidays and events aloud. Explain any unknown vocabulary.

3. Give students time to check the holidays they want to talk about and to make some notes about the holidays. Write guiding questions on the board to help them, for example:

   Where were you?
   Who was there?
   When was it?
   What happened?

4. Circulate while students are working to monitor their progress.

B Practice

Exercise 1 (CD 3, track 13)

1. Read the instructions aloud. Play the audio program once without stopping so students can listen.

2. Play the audio program again, pausing between items for the class to repeat.

Exercise 2 (CD 3, track 14)

1. Read the instructions aloud.

2. Play the audio program once or twice. If necessary, pause between items to give students time to complete their answers.

3. Have students compare answers in pairs. Then check answers by calling on individual students to say *Did you* or *What did you*.

Answers

a. What did you	d. Did you
b. What did you	e. What did you
c. Did you	f. Did you

4. For further practice, play the audio program again and pause between items so that students can listen and repeat the sentences with the reduced forms of *Did you* and *What did you*.

Note

• Remind students that the reduction of *Did you* is used in spoken English only; they should not write *Didja*.

C Speak

1. Read the instructions aloud. Then read the example sentence aloud and have a student read the example response.

2. Divide the class into groups of three and give students time to complete the exercise. Model the exercise by choosing one of the holidays in Exercise A for yourself and having students ask you about it. Remind them to practice the reduced forms of *Did you* and *What did you*. Circulate while students are working and make a note of any difficulties to address later.

3. To wrap up, ask for volunteers to share a funny or interesting event from their group's discussion.

Unit 14 Self-study	*Student's Book page 97*
Unit 14 Quiz	*Teacher's Manual page 95*

Inventions

Overview

In this unit, students listen to information about inventions. In **Warming up**, students learn and practice vocabulary to talk about inventions. In the **Listening tasks**, students practice listening for the main idea, details, and inference as they hear people talk about inventions. In **Your turn to talk**, students talk about a robot invention that can do household chores, and learn and practice the pronunciation of *can* and *can't*.

Focus		Estimated time
Warming up	**Inventions** – *calendar, chocolate bar, computer, fax machine, folding fans, mechanical clock, microwave oven, puppets* **Describing inventions** – *accurate, was/were invented 1,200 years ago, in 1885, in the 1800s*	10–15 minutes
Listening task 1 **What's the invention?**	A Inference B Details	20–25 minutes
Listening task 2 **What's it for?**	A Main idea B Inference	20–25 minutes
Your turn to talk **Thank you, Mr. Robot!**	• Designing chores for a robot • Pronunciation of *can* and *can't*	10–20 minutes

page 68

Warming up

A

1. Give students time to look at the pictures and read the Inventions Quiz. Explain any unknown vocabulary. Ask for volunteers to say which of the quiz inventions they use and how often.

2. Read the instructions aloud. Point out the different ways to talk about dates in the quiz (for example, *in 1943*; *in the 1800s*; *1,200 years ago*). Read each way aloud and have students listen and repeat.

3. Divide the class into pairs and give students time to complete the exercise. Circulate while students are working to monitor their progress.

4. Have students check their answers on page 79.

Answers		
1. England	4. Germany	7. China
2. Scotland	5. England	8. India
3. Japan	6. Mexico	

5. To wrap up, ask pairs to say how many correct answers they had.

B

1. Read the instructions aloud. Make sure students understand the meaning of the question *What inventions could you not live without?* Explain that it means "Which inventions are very important to you because you use them very often in your daily life?"

2. Model the exercise by telling students a few inventions that are very important to you and why (for example, *I couldn't live without my computer because I use it to send e-mail every day.*).

3. Have students work alone or in pairs to do the exercise. Circulate while students are working and offer help as necessary.

C

1. Read the instructions aloud.

2. Ask for volunteers to share their answers to Exercise B and write them on the board. For large classes, have students share just one or two items from their lists. When an invention is repeated, keep a tally of how many times by making check marks on the board.

3. To wrap up, make a list of the five most popular inventions mentioned by students and have a discussion about them. Ask:

- *How would your lives change without these inventions?*
- *What would you do differently?*

Note
- The information in this activity comes from a variety of sources, including *The Guinness Book of World Records*, updated every year, and *The Dictionary of Misinformation*.

Listening strategy

Listening for clues
Students often rely too much on their dictionaries. You can help students learn that they do not need to look up every new word they see or hear in the dictionary.

When students encounter a word they don't know, try giving them a series of sentences using the word. Each sentence should give a clue about the meaning. For example, they may not know the word *puppet*. Try reading the following clues for *puppet* and have students guess the meaning:

- *A puppet is a kind of doll.*
- *A puppet is often worn on the hand.*
- *A person "speaks" for the puppet.*

You can use this strategy anytime students ask for an explanation of unknown vocabulary instead of giving them the definition or a first-language translation.

Point out to students that they can also try listening for linguistic clues to figure out the meaning of unknown vocabulary in the *Listening tasks*.

- -

page 69

Listening task 1
What's the invention?

Additional vocabulary from the audio script

ancient: very old
specialty: a special dish for which a restaurant becomes well known
treat: a food, usually something sweet, that is very enjoyable and not always available
dial: a round knob that is turned to control a machine

A ⬤ Inference (CD 3, track 15)

1. Read the labels on the pictures aloud and have students listen and repeat. Ask students which inventions they think are the most useful.

2. Read the instructions aloud. Remind students that in this exercise, they will need to make inferences. They will not hear the name of the invention; they have to figure out the answer from what they hear. Have the class brainstorm some words they might hear about each invention, for example:

   badminton: *game, play, hit*
   calculator: *numbers, add*

   Accept all answers; the purpose is to build students' schema about the topic and to encourage them to predict what they will hear. Make sure students understand that there are two pictures that the speakers do not mention.

3. Play the audio program once or twice. If necessary, pause between items to give students time to complete their answers.

4. Check answers by calling on students to say the correct inventions. For higher-level classes, students can give their answers by giving clues about the invention (for example, for *ice cream* they could say, *It's cold and sweet. You eat it on a hot day.*).

Answers

1. badminton	4. ice cream cone
2. potato chips	5. paper cup
3. elevator	6. calculator

B ⬤ Details (CD 3, track 15)

1. Read the instructions aloud. If students think they remember the answers, have them do the exercise and then listen to check their answers.

2. Play the audio program. If necessary, pause between items to give students time to complete their answers.

3. Check answers by having students raise their hands for *a* or *b*.

Answers

1. b	2. a	3. b	4. a	5. b	6. b

Culture note

• Here are some popular inventions and their inventors:

Inventor	Invention	When invented
Karl Benz (Germany)	automobile	1885
Ladislao & Georg Biro (Hungary)	ball point pen	1938
George Crum (the U.S.)	potato chips	1853
Christiaan Huygens (the Netherlands)	clock	1657
Italo Marcioni (Italy)	ice-cream cone	1896
Antoine Joseph Sax (Belgium)	saxophone	1844
Dr. John Stith Pemberton (the U.S.)	Coca-cola	1886
Levi Strauss (German-born American)	blue jeans	1850

Optional speaking activity

Useful inventions
Brainstorm four or five categories of inventions with the class and write them on the board, for example:

• *things you can use to brush your teeth*
• *things that make you feel warm*
• *things that make you laugh*
• *things you use to lose weight*
• *things you can use to keep in touch with friends*

Divide the class into groups of four or five students. Tell each group to choose a secretary to write down the group's ideas.

Tell the groups that they will have one minute to list as many useful inventions as they can for each category on the board.

Announce the first category; then say, "Start!" After one minute, tell students to stop. Then call on each of the secretaries to read their group's list of inventions.

Groups score one point for each appropriate invention not listed by anyone else. The group with the most points in the end wins.

You can repeat the procedure with as many categories as you like.

page 70

Listening task 2
What's it for?

Additional vocabulary from the audio script

insects: small flying and crawling animals; bugs
mosquitoes: a type of insect that bites humans and animals and lives on their blood
bug spray: a spray used to keep insects away
mop: a tool with a long handle and a soft end for cleaning the floor
swing: a playground ride that lifts children off the ground and moves them back and forth
umbrella: something you hold over your head to keep the rain off

A ⊙ Main idea (CD 3, track 16)

1. Have students work in pairs to guess what the inventions in the pictures might be used for.

2. Play the audio program once or twice. If necessary, pause between items to give students time to complete their answers.

3. Check answers by asking students to read the complete sentences aloud.

Answers

1. People use these to block *insects*.
2. People use this to *eat* spaghetti.
3. Cats use these to *clean the floor*.
4. People use this to *sit* on the train.
5. People use this to *open* letters.
6. People use this to *hold* their cameras.

4. To wrap up, ask students to say which inventions they think are the most useful, which ones they would buy, and why.

B ⊙ Inference (CD 3, track 16)

1. Read the instructions aloud. If students think they remember the answers, have them do the exercise and then listen to check their answers.

2. Play the audio program. If necessary, pause between items to give students time to complete their answers.

3. Check answers by having students raise their hands for *yes* or *no*. Ask for volunteers to say which words or phrases helped them get the answers.

---

page 71

Your turn to talk
Thank you, Mr. Robot!

A Prepare

1. Give students time to look at the picture. Ask, *What's happening in this picture?* Elicit as many words and phrases as possible from the box next to the picture and use the picture to explain any unknown vocabulary.

2. Read the words and phrases in the box aloud and have students listen and repeat.

3. Read the instructions aloud. Make sure students understand *chore* (job, task).

4. Divide the class into pairs and give students time to complete the exercise. Circulate while students are working to monitor their progress and offer help as necessary.

B Practice

Exercise 1 (CD 3, track 17)

1. Read the instructions aloud. Play the audio program once without stopping so students can listen.

2. Play the audio program again, pausing between items for the class to repeat. Draw students' attention to the pronunciation of *can* and *can't*.

Exercise 2 (CD 3, track 18)

1. Read the instructions aloud.

2. Play the audio program once or twice. If necessary, pause between items to give students time to complete their answers.

3. Have students compare answers in pairs. Then check answers with the whole class.

4. For further practice, play the audio program and pause between items so students can repeat.

Answers

a. can	c. can	e. can't
b. can't	d. can	f. can't

C Speak

Exercise 1

1. Have students work with their partners from Exercise A. Then have pairs combine to make groups of four.

2. Read the instructions aloud. Read the example question aloud and have a student read the example response.

3. Circulate while students are working to monitor their progress. Remind them to practice the pronunciation of *can* and *can't*.

Exercise 2

1. Read the instructions aloud.

2. Ask for volunteers from the groups to talk about their robots. In large classes, each group of four could choose one robot to describe to the class.

3. To wrap up, have the whole class vote on the most useful, most unusual, and silliest robots. Higher-level classes can give reasons for their choices.

Optional speaking activity

Our own invention
Tell students that they are going to design and draw their own useful or strange invention such as those on page 70 of the Student's Book.

Brainstorm types of inventions for students to choose from and write them on the board, for example:

- *something to wake you up in the morning*
- *something to keep you cool/warm*
- *something to help you exercise without leaving the couch*

Divide the class into pairs and give pairs ten minutes to design and draw their invention. Tell them to think about the features of their invention, and what it *can* and *can't* do.

When students finish, have pairs combine and make groups of four to share their inventions.

To wrap up, ask for volunteers to share their inventions with the class.

Unit 15 Self-study	*Student's Book page 98*
Unit 15 Quiz	*Teacher's Manual page 96*

Folktales

Overview

In this unit, students listen to traditional folktales. In **Warming up**, students learn and practice vocabulary to talk about characters and events in folktales. In the **Listening tasks**, students practice listening for the main idea, details, and inference as they hear two folktales. They also learn cultural information as they hear stories from other cultures. In **Your turn to talk**, students practice telling their own stories, and learn and practice sentence rhythm using pauses.

Focus		Estimated time
Warming up	**Characters and events in folktales** – *diamonds, farmer, field, genie, gold, magic lamp, money, prince, rich man, stonecutter, stones, wheat*	10–15 minutes
Listening task 1 **The farmer and his sons**	A Main idea B Details	20–25 minutes
Listening task 2 **The stonecutter**	A Main idea B Inference	20–25 minutes
Your turn to talk **Once upon a time . . .**	• Telling a story • Sentence rhythm using pauses	10–20 minutes

page 72

Warming up

A

1. Elicit an explanation of *folktale* (a traditional story passed on in spoken form from one generation to the next). Ask students to give examples of folktales from their own culture.

2. Read the words and phrases in the box aloud. Have students listen and try to find the items in the pictures.

3. Read the instructions aloud.

4. Divide the class into pairs and give students time to complete the exercise. Circulate while students are working to monitor their progress and offer help as necessary.

5. Check answers by holding up your book, pointing to the objects in the pictures, and calling on students to say the corresponding word or phrase.

Answers

The farmer and his sons
1. farmer   3. diamonds   5. money
2. field   4. gold   6. wheat

The stonecutter
1. prince   3. magic lamp   5. stones
2. rich man   4. genie   6. stonecutter

B

1. Read the instructions aloud.

2. Have students work alone or stay in pairs to do the exercise. Remind them to look at the pictures if they need help. For lower-level classes, elicit or give an example answer from the box for all four categories: kinds of treasure, magical things, people, nature.

3. Write the four categories on the board. Check answers with the whole class and write the answers on the board under the appropriate category.

Answers

kinds of treasure: diamonds, gold, money
magical things: genie, magic lamp
people: farmer, prince, rich man, stonecutter
nature: field, stones, wheat

C

1. Read the instructions aloud.

2. Have students work with their partners from Exercise A. Circulate while students are working and offer help as necessary.

3. Check answers by asking for volunteers to say their words or phrases. Write the words on the board and explain any new vocabulary.

Possible answers
kinds of treasure: emeralds, rubies, silver
magical things: magic carpet, coin, ring, elf, unicorn
people: boy, girl, king, princess, queen
nature: flowers, river, tree

Listening strategy

Seeing progress
Sometimes it is difficult for students to recognize their own progress. When they are beginners, everything they learned was clearly new. Now, even though students' skills are improving, they may not notice their progress as much because the steps they are taking are smaller than when they were just beginning.

To help students see their progress over the term, ask them to choose a *Listening task* that they found challenging earlier in the course.

Divide the class into pairs and give students five minutes to list anything they remember about the activity (for example, the speed, the speakers, the vocabulary, what made it challenging for them).

Play the audio program and have students listen and make note of how much they understand overall.

To wrap up, ask for volunteers to share how they felt about doing the *Listening task* this time. Point out to students how much progress they have made in their general listening comprehension skills.

---

page 73

Listening task 1
The farmer and his sons

Additional vocabulary from the audio script

lazy: disliking and avoiding work
treasure: riches such as gold and jewels; something that's valuable
harvest: time when plants are done growing and are ready to be collected
townspeople: people who live in a town (an old expression)

A  **Main idea** (CD 3, track 19)

1. Divide the class into pairs. Give students time to look at the pictures and predict what the story will be about. Elicit a few guesses and write any useful vocabulary on the board. Be sure to include some key words from the story (for example, *dig, farmer, lazy, money, sell, sons, townspeople, treasure, wheat*).

2. Read the instructions aloud.

3. Play the audio program once or twice. If necessary, pause between items to give students time to complete their answers.

4. Check answers by saying the numbers and having students say the corresponding letters.

Answers					
1. b	2. e	3. a	4. c	5. f	6. d

Culture note
• "The farmer and his sons" is based on a traditional Sufi story from the Middle East. *Sufi* refers to *sufism*, a sect of Islamic religion that began in the Middle East (Persia) in the eighth century.

B **Details** (CD 3, track 19)

1. Read the instructions aloud. If students think they remember the answers, have them do the exercise and then listen to check their answers.

2. Play the audio program. If necessary, pause between items to give students time to complete their answers.

3. Check answers by asking for volunteers to read the complete sentences aloud.

Answers					
1. a	2. b	3. a	4. b	5. b	6. a

Optional speaking activity

Correct the mistakes
This activity requires students to correct mistakes in the story of the farmer and his sons. Do this activity after students have done *Listening task 1* on page 73 of the Student's Book and are familiar with the story.

Using the audio script on page 162 of this Teacher's Manual, prepare a short narrative version of the story. You may want to vary the length of the story according to the level of your students – a shorter version for lower-level classes, a longer one for higher-level classes.

In your story, make some deliberate mistakes, for example:

• *Once upon a time, a farmer and his four sons lived on a farm.*
• *The sons decided to plant some corn, and soon the fields were full of tall corn plants.*

Read the story aloud. Tell students to raise their hands each time they hear a mistake and to correct it. Alternatively, have students listen to the whole story and write down the mistakes they hear.

To wrap up, have students write or tell the story of the farmer and his sons in their own words.

----

page 74

Listening task 2
The stonecutter

> **Additional vocabulary from the audio script**
>
> **palace:** home of a king, queen, or other rich or powerful person
> **favor:** a helpful or kind act

A Main idea (CD 3, track 20)

1. Read the title of the story. Review the meaning of *stonecutter*. Give students time to look at the picture and say what they see. Ask, *What's happening in this picture?*

2. Have students cover the text at the top of the page. Tell them they will first just look at the picture and listen to the whole story before they do the exercise. This will allow them to focus on the main idea, or gist, of what happens in the story.

3. For lower-level classes, review the key vocabulary from the story (for example, *genie, magic lamp, prince*). Explain *grant a wish* (give someone something that they really want).

4. Play the audio program while students look at the picture. Ask the following questions to check students' understanding:

   • *Was the stonecutter rich?*
   • *Was he happy?*
   • *What did the genie in the lamp offer the stonecutter?*
   • *What was the stonecutter's first wish?*
   • *What happened to him in the end?*

5. Read the instructions aloud. Give students time to read the statements silently or call on students to read them aloud. If students think they remember the sequence, have them do the exercise and then listen to check their answers.

6. Play the audio program again. If necessary, pause between items to give students time to complete their answers.

7. Check answers with the whole class. Read the first statement aloud and then call on students to read the next statement in the sequence.

> **Answers**
>
> 1. The stonecutter lived with his wife in a small house. They were poor but happy.
> 2. The stonecutter found a genie in a magic lamp. He asked the genie to make him a prince.
> 3. The stonecutter was too busy, and he was tired. He asked the genie to make him a rich man.
> 4. The stonecutter saw a man building a stone house. He understood that he didn't need money and power to be happy.

Note
• "The stonecutter" is based on a Japanese folktale.

B Inference (CD 3, track 20)

1. Give students time to read the statements. Read the instructions aloud. If students think they remember the answers, have them do the exercise and then listen to check their answers.

2. Play the audio program. If necessary, pause between items to give students time to complete their answers.

3. Check answers by asking for volunteers to read the complete sentences aloud.

> **Answers**
>
> 1. The stonecutter did not want to change his job.
> 2. The stonecutter wanted to have more money.
> 3. The prince and his wife wanted to be alone.
> 4. The story means happiness is important.

4. To wrap up, tell students that folktales often contain a "message" or a lesson about life. Ask them what they think is the message of "The stonecutter." Have students work in pairs or groups to write one or two sentences about the message of the story and then share them with the class.

Possible answers
- Even rich and powerful people have problems.
- You should be happy with who you are and what you have in your life.
- Don't wish for things that may not make you happy.

----

page 75

Your turn to talk
Once upon a time . . .

A Prepare

1. Tell students they are going to create folktales and share them with their classmates. Explain that "Once upon a time . . ." is the traditional way to begin a folktale in English.

2. Read the instructions aloud.

3. Divide the class into pairs and give students time to complete the exercise. Circulate while students are working and offer help as necessary.

B Practice

Exercise 1 (CD 3, track 21)

1. Read the instructions aloud. Play the audio program once without stopping so students can listen.

2. Play the audio program again, pausing between items for the class to repeat. Point out that the comma indicates a pause in the sentence.

Exercise 2 (CD 3, track 22)

1. Read the instructions aloud.

2. Have students work alone or in pairs to do the exercise. Encourage them to read the sentences aloud a few times before they add the comma.

3. Play the audio program and have students check their answers. Then play the audio program again and pause between items so students can repeat the sentences.

Answers

a. day, a	c. working, a
b. poor, so	d. hard, the

4. For further practice, have students work in pairs to write similar sentences of their own on a separate piece of paper. Then have them exchange papers with another pair and practice saying the sentences aloud.

C Speak

1. Read the instructions aloud. Read the example sentence aloud and have a student read the example response.

2. Divide the class into groups of four and give students time to complete the exercise. Remind them to practice the pause after a comma when they tell their stories. Circulate while students are working to monitor their progress. Make a note of any difficulties to address later.

Optional speaking activity

Chain stories
Divide the class into groups of five or six students.

Tell groups that they are going to work together to create original stories. Each member of the group needs a blank piece of paper.

Brainstorm some interesting first story lines with the class and write them on the board, for example:

- *Once upon a time, there was a dark forest . . .*
- *Long, long ago, in a faraway land . . .*
- *Many years ago, in a tiny village . . .*

Tell students to write the first line of their story at the top of the page. When everyone has written the first line, tell students to pass their papers to the group member on their left.

The next person reads the first line and adds the second line of the story, then again passes the paper to the person on the left. A short time limit (thirty seconds) will help keep the pace moving.

Continue until students have received their original papers back. Then have students silently read what their classmates have written and add the last line of the story.

To wrap up, have students take turns reading their stories aloud to their group. Then ask for volunteers to share their stories with the whole class.

Unit 16 Self-study	*Student's Book page 99*
Unit 16 Quiz	*Teacher's Manual page 97*
Test 2, Units 9–16	*Teacher's Manual page 120*

Overview

In this **Expansion** unit, students listen to general information about India. In the **Listening tasks**, students practice listening for the main idea and details as they hear people talking about languages, food, inventions, and movies in India. They also learn cultural information about India as they listen to an authentic interview with an Indian student about the Indian festival Diwali.

Focus		Estimated time
Listening task 1 Information	A Main idea B Details	20–25 minutes
Listening task 2 A festival	A Main idea B Details	20–25 minutes

---

page 76

Listening task 1
Information

Note

• Before you start this unit, write the titles of the previous four units on the board or elicit them from students (*Part-time jobs, Celebrations, Inventions, Folktales*). Tell students that this *Expansion* unit features some of the topics and vocabulary from these units. It presents general information about India and a more in-depth look at Indian culture based on an authentic interview with a student from India. Give students time to look over the language and listening skills in Units 13 through 16.

> **Additional vocabulary from the audio script**
>
> **official purposes:** for government business
> **religious:** related to religion or spiritual beliefs
> **tropical:** from a hot, humid climate
> **movie industry:** movie business
> **violence:** fighting

A 🔘 **Main idea** (CD 3, track 23)

1. Ask students where India is located (southern Asia). You may want to bring a world map to class and have students find India on the map. Ask students if anyone has traveled to India and, if so, what it was like. Alternatively, ask students to say anything they know about the country of India, its culture, or its people.

2. Give students time to look at the picture and say what they see. Write a list of key words and phrases on the board.

Possible answers
• people shopping/selling things at a crowded market
• a young boy
• a woman carrying something on her head
• women wearing scarves and robes

3. Read the instructions aloud. At this stage in the course, students may already have a good understanding of the types of listening skills introduced in *Before you begin* on pages 4 and 5 (Main idea, Details, Inference). However, if you feel students would benefit from a review, the *Expansion* units provide a good opportunity to do so. Point out to students that in this exercise, they are listening for the main idea. This means that they don't need to understand everything they hear, just the general meaning.

4. Play the audio program once or twice. If necessary, pause between items to give students time to complete their answers.

5. Check answers with the whole class.

> **Answers**
>
> 1. languages
> 2. food and drinks
> 3. a scientist and inventor
> 4. movies

B 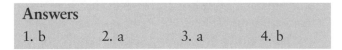 Details (CD 3, track 23)

1. Read the instructions aloud. If students think they remember the answers, have them do the exercise and then listen to check their answers.

2. Play the audio program. If necessary, pause between items to give students time to complete their answers.

3. Check answers by having students read the complete sentences aloud.

Answers

1. b	2. a	3. a	4. b

4. The items in *Listening task 1* present a good opportunity to review some of the language presented in Units 4 (*Let's eat*) and 9 (*Movies*). Ask the class if anyone has eaten Indian food and, if so, what was in the dish. Ask if anyone has seen an Indian movie and, if so, what type of movie it was.

---

page 77

Listening task 2
A festival

> **Additional vocabulary from the audio script**
>
> **look forward to:** wait for something to happen
> **legend:** a story from the past that may or may not be true
> **lord of death:** here, the (male) god of death and the afterlife
> **shiny:** something that reflects light
> **togetherness:** a close, happy relationship
> **sweets:** desserts like cookies, cakes, and candies
> **goddess of wealth:** here, the (female) god of money

A 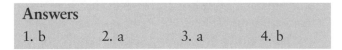 Main idea (CD 3, track 24)

1. Give students time to look at the pictures and say what they see. Ask them to guess why the lights might be important in Indian culture.

2. Have students cover the text and just listen while you play the audio program once. This will allow students to focus on the gist of the legend before they do the exercise.

3. Ask a few simple comprehension questions to check students' understanding, for example:
   - *What kind of festival is Diwali?* (a festival of light)
   - *Did the lights in the house save her husband?* (yes)
   - *How?* (by blinding the lord of death who came to get him)

4. Give students time to read the statements. Explain any unknown vocabulary.

5. Read the instructions aloud.

6. Play the audio program again. If necessary, pause between items to give students time to complete their answers.

7. Have students compare answers in pairs. If necessary, play the audio program again so students can check their answers.

8. Check answers with the whole class. Read the first statement aloud and then call on students to read the next statement in the sequence.

Answers

1. There was a woman who tried to save her husband's life by keeping away the lord of death.
2. She kept him awake all night.
3. She put her jewelry all over the house.
4. She lit many candles and lights.
5. When the lord of death came to take her husband, the lord was blinded by the lights.
6. Her husband was saved.
7. The story explains the significance of the lights and why Diwali is celebrated.

B 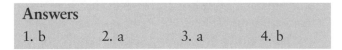 Details (CD 3, track 25)

1. Read the instructions aloud.

2. Read the list of phrases below the picture aloud and have students listen and repeat. Have students work in pairs to predict which activities Indians do to celebrate Diwali.

3. Play the audio program. If necessary, pause between items to give students time to complete their answers.

4. Check answers by asking for volunteers to say the activities.

Answers

buy new clothes, eat special food, give presents, meet relatives, set off fireworks

Activation

pages 80–81
A speaking and listening game

Introduction

Activation is a review game. The discussion questions and tasks are designed to encourage students to use the topics, vocabulary, and structures they have heard and practiced throughout the *Active Listening, Second Edition* course.

Using *Activation*

Use *Activation* as a fun, final wrap-up activity at the end of the course, or as a whole-class review before the final test (pages 120–126 of this Teacher's Manual). It is also possible to play the game more than once during the course. For example, you may wish to have students play it mid-term to review as well as to preview upcoming topics, vocabulary, and structures.

Allow at least twenty minutes of class time to play the game. Students will benefit from an opportunity to take their time, ask follow-up questions, and enjoy communicating with their classmates.

Preparation

1. Tell students that they are going to play a game with their classmates to review the topics and language they have learned so far in the *Active Listening* course.

2. Divide the class into groups of four and give students time to look through their Student's Books to review the vocabulary and topics. You can ask guiding questions and have students find the units or pages in their Student's Books, for example:

   • *In which unit did you learn the words* niece *and* nephew? (Unit 2, *Families*)
   • *On what page can you find the phone number for the American Center Library?* (page 15)

3. Have each student choose a marker. They can use coins, erasers, or similar small objects. Tell each group to open one of their Student's Books to pages 80 and 81 and place it where all group members can see it.

Playing the game

1. Read the instructions aloud. Make sure all students put their markers in the box marked "Start."

2. To make the instructions clear, demonstrate each step with one group while the other groups watch. Close your eyes and touch the *How many spaces?* box with a pencil. Then move a student's marker that many spaces. Read the game question aloud and give your response. For large classes, have one member from each group come and watch while you demonstrate with one group; then have them go back and teach their own groups how to play.

3. Give students twenty to thirty minutes to play the game. Encourage them to volunteer additional information and ask follow-up questions. Circulate while students are playing to monitor their progress and offer help as necessary.

Notes

• It is not necessary for players to complete a circuit around the board. If one group finishes early, players can continue around the board, answering questions they didn't land on before.

• If there is a question someone doesn't want or isn't able to answer, allow the student to move ahead or back one space.

• Many students will enjoy playing the game more than once. Changing groups each time keeps the information fresh and interesting.

• Point out to students that there is no reward for getting around the board more quickly than the other players; the "winners" are the ones who thoroughly practice their English!

• Because *Activation* is a fluency game, corrections are usually not appropriate while students play. However, you could make a note of errors you hear while students are playing to address later.

Self-study

Introduction
The *Self-study* material provides further practice in the listening skills, language, and topics presented in *Active Listening, Second Edition,* Student's Book 1, and offers students the opportunity to personalize the information they have learned.

Purpose of the *Self-study* pages
It is important to draw students' attention to the *Self-study* pages in the Student's Book and discuss their purpose. Explain to students that the *Self-study* pages are designed to give them extra practice in the listening skills, language, and topics they are learning in the course, as well as an opportunity to practice listening to English outside of class.

About the *Self-study* pages
There is one page of *Self-study* exercises for each of the sixteen core units in the Student's Book. Each *Self-study* page is divided into two exercises. Exercise A contains five multiple-choice items. Exercise B contains personalized questions or prompts that students respond to with their own answers.

The *Self-study* units can be found on pages 84–99 of the Student's Book, and the answer key can be found on pages 100–101. The audio program is included on a separate CD packaged in the Student's Book, and the audio script starts on page 166 of this Teacher's Manual.

Using the *Self-study* pages
The *Self-study* pages may be used as a regular homework assignment at the end of a unit, or in class for additional listening practice or review material. You can also assign particular pages as make-up work for students who have missed class, or for students who you feel need additional practice.

Preparation
Do an orientation to the *Self-study* pages in class to show students how the pages are organized and how they should use the material. Point out that the audio program is included in the back of the Student's Book. Explain to students the following procedure for doing the *Self-study* pages. Because students will work on the *Self-study* pages outside of class, you may want to prepare a handout for students explaining these procedures:

1. Look over the unit in the Student's Book to review the topics, vocabulary, and structures.

2. Read through the whole *Self-study* page before listening.

3. Play the audio program for Exercise A once and listen. Then complete the exercise when the audio program repeats.

4. Play the audio program for Exercise B and complete the exercise. If necessary, pause between items to allow time to complete the answers.

5. Use the answer key on pages 100–101 in the Student's Book to check answers.

6. If any answers were incorrect, listen again. Make a note of any questions or problems to ask about in class.

Notes
- Tell students they will not be graded on their scores for the *Self-study* pages. However, you may choose to grade students on whether or not they completed the pages.

- You can go over the *Self-study* pages at the beginning of the class as a warm-up, or at the end of the class. Have students show you their books so you can see that they have completed the assignment, and let them ask you any questions they have. If several students had problems, it may be helpful to play the exercise in class, or go over the audio script with them. However, students should be reminded that they do not need to understand every word in a conversation in order to complete the tasks.

Testing program

Quizzes

Introduction

The *Active Listening* quizzes may be used to assess students' progress and achievement in the listening skills, language, and topics presented in *Active Listening, Second Edition,* Student's Book 1. If students have been successful with the *Listening tasks* in the Student's Book, they should also be successful with the quizzes.

Purpose of the quizzes

It is important to discuss the purpose of the quizzes with your students. Explain to them that the quizzes are designed to measure their progress in the course, and to show them (and you) what material still needs to be reviewed before moving to a new unit.

About the quizzes

There is one quiz for each of the sixteen core units in the Student's Book. Each quiz has two parts and a total of ten items. The quizzes integrate the three listening skills introduced in the Student's Book – main idea, details, and inference – and use the same exercise types.

The quizzes can be found on pages 82–97 of this Teacher's Manual. The answer keys are on pages 98–99, and the audio scripts can be found on pages 100–107.

Using the quizzes

Give the appropriate quiz in class after you have completed the corresponding Student's Book unit. After scoring, you may wish to go over the items students missed with the whole class. Have students who got the correct answer say which words or phrases helped them.

Encourage students to reread *Before you begin* on pages 4 and 5 of the Student's Book to refresh their understanding of the different types of listening skills before you administer the quizzes.

In addition to using the quizzes as an evaluation tool, you may choose to use them for additional in-class study, review material, or as an extra-credit opportunity.

Preparation

1. Photocopy one quiz for each student in the class. Students should mark their answers directly on the quiz; there is no separate answer sheet for the quizzes.

2. Schedule fifteen to twenty minutes of class time for administering the quiz.

3. (Optional) Give students a few minutes to look over the Student's Book unit to review the topic, vocabulary, and structures before they take the quiz.

Administering the quizzes

1. Have students sit apart from one another. Hand out the quizzes.

2. Have students write their names, the date, and their class in the spaces provided at the top of the quiz.

3. Read the instructions for Part A aloud.

4. Play the audio program once for Part A. If necessary, pause between items to give students time to complete their answers.

5. Read the instructions for Part B aloud.

6. Play the audio program for Part B. If necessary, pause between items to give students time to complete their answers. Repeat instructions for Part C of Quiz 1.

7. Collect the quizzes to check answers, or have students check their own quizzes while you read the answers aloud.

Scoring

Assign 10 points for each correct answer on the quizzes (for example, if a student misses two questions, assign a score of 80%). Record students' scores on their quizzes, as well as on the Score Records Sheet (page 134 of this Teacher's Manual).

Quiz • Unit 1

Name: _____ Date: _____

Class: _____ Score: _____/100

A 🎧 **Listen. Imagine you are talking to these people. What is your part of the conversation? Circle the correct answers.**

1. a. Yes, I do.
   b. I like jazz.

2. a. I'm a student.
   b. No, I'm not.

3. a. Yes, I am.
   b. I live near here.

4. a. Yes, I am.
   b. Yes, I do.

5. a. I study here.
   b. I'm from Canada.

B 🎧 **Listen to the information.**

C **Are the statements true or false? Check (✓) the correct answers.**

	true	false
1. In Canada and the U.S., people kiss when they first meet.	☐	☐
2. Friends sometimes hug each other.	☐	☐
3. Hugs are more common among men.	☐	☐
4. A hug can mean both "Hello" and "Good-bye."	☐	☐
5. Children hug their teachers when they get to school.	☐	☐

© Cambridge University Press 2007 **Photocopiable**

Quiz • Unit 2

Name: _____ Date: _____

Class: _____ Score: _____/100

A 🎧 **Listen. People are talking about their families. Who are they talking about? Check (✓) the correct answers.**

1. ☐ her father
   ☐ her brother

2. ☐ his niece
   ☐ his daughter

3. ☐ her uncle
   ☐ her cousin

4. ☐ his aunt
   ☐ his wife

5. ☐ her son
   ☐ her husband

B 🎧 **Listen again. Circle the correct information.**

1. Josh and the woman play *basketball / tennis* together.

2. Carmen likes playing *video / computer* games.

3. The woman lives in *the U.S. / Australia*.

4. The picture was taken at a *cousin's / friend's* wedding.

5. The person in the picture is *playing / watching* soccer.

Quiz • Unit 3

Name: _____   Date: _____

Class: _____   Score: _____/100

A 🎧 **Listen. People are talking. Circle the correct answers.**

1. The man is at a
   a. tennis match.
   b. basketball game.

2. The man wants the phone number for a
   a. hospital.
   b. hotel.

3. The woman wants to know
   a. the man's birth date.
   b. today's date.

4. The answering machine is at
   a. a home.
   b. an office.

5. The man wants to pay by
   a. credit card.
   b. check.

B 🎧 **Listen again. Circle the correct information.**

1. The Lions scored *93 / 97* points.

2. The phone number is *555-8023 / 555-9023*.

3. The date is *2/5/87 / 12/5/87*.

4. After 6:00 P.M., call *555-6231 / 555-8321*.

5. The date is *April 17th / April 18th*.

Quiz • Unit 4

Name: _____ Date: _____

Class: _____ Score: _____/100

A 🎧 **Listen. People are talking. Circle the correct answers.**

1. The people are
   a. at home.
   b. in a restaurant.

2. The woman is going to have
   a. breakfast.
   b. lunch.

3. The people are
   a. friends.
   b. a server and a customer.

4. The woman is going to have
   a. dinner.
   b. dessert.

5. The man is
   a. at home.
   b. in a restaurant.

B 🎧 **Listen again. Check (✓) *all* of the things the people are going to have.**

1. ☐ fish   ☐ soup   ☐ a salad

2. ☐ a sandwich   ☐ coffee   ☐ milk

3. ☐ broccoli   ☐ mushrooms   ☐ onions

4. ☐ pizza   ☐ cake   ☐ coffee

5. ☐ lettuce   ☐ mayonnaise ☐ mustard

Quiz • Unit 5

Name: _____ Date: _____

Class: _____ Score: _____/100

A 🎧 **Listen. People are talking about free-time activities. What are the topics? Circle the correct answers.**

1. a. going to the movies
   b. listening to music

2. a. shopping
   b. cooking

3. a. getting together with friends
   b. visiting family

4. a. watching TV
   b. seeing movies

5. a. going out
   b. staying home

B 🎧 **Listen again. How often do the people do the activities? Check (✓) the correct answers.**

1. ☐ always
   ☐ often

2. ☐ sometimes
   ☐ hardly ever

3. ☐ always
   ☐ sometimes

4. ☐ hardly ever
   ☐ never

5. ☐ often
   ☐ sometimes

Quiz • Unit 6

Name: _____   Date: _____

Class: _____   Score: _____/100

A 🎧 Listen. Carla is telling her friend Sylvie what clothes she's planning to wear on her business trip. Check (✓) *all* of the items she's planning to wear.

1. ☐ blouse   ☐ jacket   ☐ jeans   ☐ pants   ☐ sandals   ☐ shoes

2. ☐ blouse   ☐ jacket   ☐ shirt   ☐ skirt   ☐ pants   ☐ boots

3. ☐ cap   ☐ T-shirt ☐ skirt   ☐ sneakers ☐ sweater   ☐ socks

4. ☐ blouse   ☐ dress   ☐ jacket   ☐ sandals   ☐ shoes   ☐ sweater

5. ☐ jeans   ☐ shirt   ☐ shorts   ☐ sneakers ☐ sweater   ☐ T-shirt

B 🎧 Listen again. Does Sylvie like Carla's choices? Check (✓) *yes* or *no.*

	yes	no
1.	☐	☐
2.	☐	☐
3.	☐	☐
4.	☐	☐
5.	☐	☐

Quiz • Unit 7

Name: _____ Date: _____

Class: _____ Score: _____/100

A 🎧 **Listen. What are the people looking for? Check (✓) the correct answers.**

1. ☐ a clock   ☐ a calendar   ☐ a picture

2. ☐ a vase   ☐ some flowers   ☐ a book

3. ☐ some tea   ☐ a table   ☐ a rug

4. ☐ a fishbowl   ☐ a fish   ☐ a TV

5. ☐ a heater   ☐ a couch   ☐ a sweater

B 🎧 **Listen again. Where are the objects? Circle the correct answers.**

1. a. on the wall
   b. on the coffee table

2. a. next to the bookshelf
   b. on the bookshelf

3. a. on the floor
   b. in the yard

4. a. on the floor
   b. next to the TV

5. a. between the couch and the TV stand
   b. between the coffee table and the couch

     © Cambridge University Press 2007   **Photocopiable**

Quiz • Unit 8

Name: _____   Date: _____

Class: _____   Score: _____/100

A 🎧 **Listen. Are the statements true or false? Check (✓) the correct answers.**

	true	false
1. They're going to the movies.	☐	☐
2. They're going to go to a restaurant.	☐	☐
3. They're waiting for a train.	☐	☐
4. They can get to the movie before it starts.	☐	☐
5. They're going to go shopping after the TV show.	☐	☐

B 🎧 **Listen again. Circle the correct information.**

1. The show starts at *8:00 / 8:15.*

2. The conversation starts at *11:45 / 12:30.*

3. They're going to leave at *2:15 / 2:30.*

4. The movie starts at *9:15 / 9:50.*

5. The conversation starts a little before *12:00 / 1:00.*

Quiz • Unit 9

Name: _____ Date: _____

Class: _____ Score: _____/100

A 🎧 Listen. What kinds of movies are the people talking about? Circle the correct answers.

1. a. romance
   b. science fiction

2. a. action
   b. comedy

3. a. horror
   b. musical

4. a. comedy
   b. action

5. a. romance
   b. horror

B 🎧 Listen again. Who wants to watch the movie? Check (✓) *man*, *woman*, or *both*.

	man	woman	both
1.	☐	☐	☐
2.	☐	☐	☐
3.	☐	☐	☐
4.	☐	☐	☐
5.	☐	☐	☐

Quiz • Unit 10

Name: _____   Date: _____

Class: _____   Score: _____/100

A 🎧 Listen. People are talking about their schedules. Number the activities in the correct order from 1 to 3. (There is one extra activity.)

1. ___ play sports   ___ write letters   ___ watch TV   ___ go dancing

2. ___ eat lunch   ___ drink tea   ___ watch TV   ___ read the newspaper

3. ___ write reports   ___ return phone calls   ___ take the bus   ___ check e-mail

4. ___ eat dinner   ___ go to work   ___ drink coffee   ___ take a shower

5. ___ find gifts   ___ eat dinner   ___ open gifts   ___ eat birthday cake

B 🎧 Listen again. Circle the correct information.

1. On Saturdays, he sleeps until *7:30 / 9:30.*

2. She gets home at *12:30 / 12:45.*

3. He usually answers his e-mail from *4:00 to 5:00 / 5:00 to 6:00.*

4. The kids get to school at *7:30 / 7:40.*

5. On his birthday, he gets up at *5:00 / 5:30.*

Quiz • Unit 11

Name: _____ Date: _____

Class: _____ Score: _____/100

A 🎧 **Listen. Where are the people going to go? Circle the correct answers.**

1. a. to a bookstore
   b. to a café

2. a. to the mall
   b. to a toy store

3. a. to the aquarium
   b. to City Hall

4. a. to an Indian restaurant
   b. to an Italian restaurant

5. a. to the library
   b. to an Internet café

B 🎧 **Listen again. Are the statements true or false? Check (✓) the correct answers.**

	true	false
1. The bookstore is across from the café.	☐	☐
2. The movie theater is around the corner from the toy store.	☐	☐
3. The free parking lot is behind the aquarium.	☐	☐
4. The restaurant is next to the convenience store.	☐	☐
5. The library is between the Internet café and the museum.	☐	☐

Quiz • Unit 12

Name: _____   Date: _____

Class: _____   Score: _____/100

A 🎧 **Listen. What are the occasions? Circle the correct answers.**

1. a. a birthday
   b. Father's Day

2. a. an anniversary
   b. a good-bye party

3. a. New Year's Day
   b. a graduation

4. a. an anniversary
   b. a birthday

5. a. Children's Day
   b. Father's Day

B 🎧 **Listen again. Check (✓) the correct answers.**

1. Brian is
   ☐ 40 years old.
   ☐ 50 years old.

2. The gift is from the woman's
   ☐ family.
   ☐ co-workers.

3. The gift is
   ☐ a watch.
   ☐ a camera.

4. The woman wears size
   ☐ extra small.
   ☐ medium.

5. The son
   ☐ wrote the book.
   ☐ read the book.

Quiz • Unit 13

Name: _____   Date: _____

Class: _____   Score: _____/100

A 🎧 Listen. Which jobs do the people want? Circle the correct answers.

1. a. server
   b. office worker

2. a. childcare worker
   b. cleaning staff

3. a. lifeguard
   b. tour guide

4. a. business intern
   b. camp counselor

5. a. English teacher
   b. childcare worker

B 🎧 Listen again. Circle the correct information.

1. The man thinks the job is good for him because *it's part-time / it pays very well.*

2. The woman likes working *with children / alone.*

3. The man wants to *exercise / relax* at work.

4. The woman wants to work *outside / inside.*

5. The man wants to *get experience / learn English.*

Quiz • Unit 14

Name: _____   Date: _____

Class: _____   Score: _____/100

A 🎧 **Listen. People are talking about celebrations. Check (✓) *all* of the activities they mention.**

1. Thanksgiving
   ☐ eat special food   ☐ play football   ☐ watch TV

2. Valentine's Day
   ☐ wear special clothes   ☐ send cards   ☐ eat chocolate

3. Queen's Birthday
   ☐ have a parade   ☐ take the day off from work   ☐ go skiing

4. Independence Day
   ☐ watch a parade   ☐ wear special clothes   ☐ watch fireworks

5. Teacher's Day
   ☐ give flowers   ☐ stay home from school   ☐ do homework

B 🎧 **Listen again. Circle the correct information.**

1. This year, Thanksgiving is on *November 24th / November 25th.*

2. The people are talking *two / three* weeks before Valentine's Day.

3. In Western Australia, the Queen's Birthday is in *June or July / September or October.*

4. On Independence Day in the U.S., the most popular colors for clothes are red, white, and *green / blue.*

5. Teacher's Day in Thailand is on *January 15th / January 16th.*

Quiz • Unit 15

Name: _____ Date: _____

Class: _____ Score: _____/100

A 🎧 **Listen. Which inventions are the people describing? Circle the correct answers.**

1. a. the piano
   b. the guitar

2. a. the TV
   b. the camera

3. a. the calendar
   b. the watch

4. a. the airplane
   b. movies

5. a. the home computer
   b. video games

B 🎧 **Listen again. Are the statements true or false? Check (✓) the correct answers.**

	true	false
1. The invention is from Italy.	☐	☐
2. These were first sold in 1964.	☐	☐
3. People started using the first ones more than 400 years ago.	☐	☐
4. Two American cousins invented this.	☐	☐
5. The first one of these was invented in 1958.	☐	☐

Quiz • Unit 16

Name: _____ Date: _____

Class: _____ Score: _____/100

A 🎧 **Listen to the story. What is the main idea of each part of the story? Number the statements from 1 to 5. (There is one extra statement.)**

_____ The young man asked the farmer what life in the village was like.

_____ A rich man asked the farmer what life in the village was like.

_____ The young man said his hometown was a nice place.
The farmer said the young man would be happy in the new village.

_____ A young man met an old farmer from a small village.

_____ The rich man asked to buy the farmer's home.

_____ The rich man said his hometown was not a good place.
The farmer said the rich man would be unhappy in the new village.

B 🎧 **Listen again. Circle the correct answers.**

1. The farmer grew up
   a. in the village.
   b. in another village.

2. The young man will
   a. visit the village.
   b. move to the village.

3. The young man
   a. likes his hometown.
   b. doesn't like his hometown.

4. The farmer asked the men questions because
   a. he had never traveled before.
   b. he wanted to know their personalities.

5. The meaning of this story is:
   a. People see the same place in different ways.
   b. Farmers don't give good advice.

Quiz answer key

Unit 1
A
1. b
2. b
3. a
4. b
5. a

C
1. false
2. true
3. false
4. true
5. false

Unit 2
A
1. her brother
2. his niece
3. her uncle
4. his wife
5. her son

B
1. tennis
2. computer
3. the U.S.
4. friend's
5. playing

Unit 3
A
1. b
2. a
3. a
4. b
5. b

B
1. 97
2. 555-8023
3. 12/5/87
4. 555-6231
5. April 18th

Unit 4
A
1. b
2. b
3. a
4. b
5. a

B
1. fish, a salad
2. a sandwich, coffee
3. mushrooms, onions
4. cake, coffee
5. lettuce, mustard

Unit 5
A
1. a
2. a
3. b
4. a
5. b

B
1. often
2. hardly ever
3. always
4. never
5. often

Unit 6
A
1. blouse, pants, sandals
2. jacket, pants, boots
3. T-shirt, skirt, sneakers
4. dress, jacket, shoes
5. jeans, shirt, sweater

B
1. no
2. yes
3. yes
4. no
5. yes

Unit 7
A
1. a calendar
2. a vase
3. a rug
4. a fish
5. a heater

B
1. b
2. a
3. b
4. b
5. a

Unit 8
A
1. false
2. true
3. false
4. truc
5. true

B
1. 8:00
2. 11:45
3. 2:30
4. 9:50
5. 12:00

Unit 9
A
1. b
2. b
3. a
4. b
5. a

B
1. both
2. woman
3. both
4. man
5. man

Unit 10

A

1. [1] watch TV
   [2] play sports
   [3] go dancing
2. [1] eat lunch
   [2] read the newspaper
   [3] watch TV
3. [1] return phone calls
   [2] check e-mail
   [3] take the bus
4. [1] drink coffee
   [2] take a shower
   [3] go to work
5. [1] find gifts
   [2] open gifts
   [3] eat dinner

B

1. 9:30
2. 12:45
3. 5:00 to 6:00
4. 7:30
5. 5:30

Unit 11

A

1. a
2. b
3. a
4. b
5. a

B

1. false
2. true
3. false
4. false
5. true

Unit 12

A

1. a
2. b
3. b
4. a
5. b

B

1. 40 years old
2. co-workers
3. a watch
4. medium
5. wrote the book

Unit 13

A

1. a
2. b
3. b
4. b
5. a

B

1. it's part-time
2. alone
3. exercise
4. outside
5. get experience

Unit 14

A

1. eat special food,
   watch TV
2. send cards,
   eat chocolate
3. take the day off from
   work, go skiing
4. watch a parade, wear
   special clothes, watch
   fireworks
5. give flowers, stay
   home from school,
   do homework

B

1. November 25th
2. two
3. September or October
4. blue
5. January 16th

Unit 15

A

1. a
2. a
3. b
4. a
5. b

B

1. true
2. false
3. true
4. false
5. true

Unit 16

A

1. A young man met
   an old farmer from
   a small village.
2. The young man asked
   the farmer what life in
   the village was like.
3. The young man said his
   hometown was a nice
   place. The farmer said
   the young man would be
   happy in the new village.
4. A rich man asked the
   farmer what life in the
   village was like.
5. The rich man said his
   hometown was not a
   good place. The farmer
   said the rich man would
   be unhappy in the
   new village.

B

1. a
2. b
3. a
4. b
5. a

Quiz audio scripts

Quiz • Unit 1 (TM 1 CD, track 2)

Part A Listen. Imagine you are talking to these people. What is your part of the conversation? Circle the correct answers.

1.
Woman: What kind of music do you like?

2.
Man: Are you from Mexico?

3.
Woman: Are you a student?

4.
Man: Do you like this music?

5.
Woman: Where do you study?

Part B Listen to the information.

Man: In Canada and the U.S., people shake hands when they first meet each other, but friends sometimes hug. Hugs are more common among women. They hug to say "Hello" and to say "Good-bye," too. Young children also hug their parents when they leave for school in the morning.

Quiz • Unit 2 (TM 1 CD, track 3)

Part A Listen. People are talking about their families. Who are they talking about? Check the correct answers.

1.
Woman: This is a picture of Josh. He's two years older than I am. He likes a lot of different sports – basketball, baseball, soccer, and tennis. I like tennis, too, so we often play together on weekends. It's nice to have a big brother.

2.
Man: Isn't she cute? Her name's Carmen. She's my sister's daughter. She's five years old now and just started school. She likes playing computer games. She's really smart . . . the perfect niece.

3.
Woman: This is a great picture. That's me and my mother's brother, Ted. We're in front of his house in Sydney. He moved to Australia five years ago, but he comes back to the U.S. to visit us every year. And last year, I visited him there. He's my favorite uncle.

4.
Man: This was taken at my friend's wedding last June. My wife Julie and I had a great time dancing together and seeing all of our old friends. In this picture, we're eating cake and listening to some speeches. Julie loves weddings. She always cries.

5.
Woman: This picture isn't very clear, I know, but I still like it. I took it at a soccer game. That's my son, number forty-five, in the red shirt. He's about to score a goal. I'm so proud of him.

Part B Listen again. Circle the correct information.

[Replay Quiz • Unit 2, Part A, track 3]

Quiz • Unit 3 (TM 1 CD, track 4)

Part A Listen. People are talking. Circle the correct answers.

1.
Man: And . . . Player number ninety-three has the ball. He shoots . . . he scores! And there's the buzzer! The final score for the Lions is ninety-seven points. Yes, the Lions win by just one point. What an exciting basketball game!

2.
Woman: Directory Assistance. How may I help you?
Man: Hi. Could you give me the number for Gracie Square Hospital, please?
Woman: Of course. Here's the number. It's five-five-five, eight-oh-two-three.

3.
Woman: And let's see . . . What is your birth date?
Man: My birthday?
Woman: Yes, I need your birth date. When were you born?
Man: Oh, I see. December fifth, nineteen eighty-seven. Twelve-five-eighty-seven.

4.
Woman: You have reached the office of Dr. Martin. No one is available to take your call right now, so please leave a message after the tone. If you're calling outside of regular business hours, before eight A.M. or after six P.M., please call five-five-five, six-two-three-one.

5.

Man: Can I pay with a check?

Woman: Certainly, sir. We accept checks. Do you have ID?

Man: Yes, here you are. OK, so I'll just sign it . . . here . . . and the date . . . Is today the seventeenth?

Woman: Actually, it's April eighteenth.

Man: OK. So, four-eighteen . . . Uh . . .

Part B Listen again. Circle the correct information.

[Replay Quiz • Unit 3, Part A, track 4]

Quiz • Unit 4 (TM 1 CD, track 5)

Part A Listen. People are talking. Circle the correct answers.

1.

Server: Are you ready to order?

Woman: Yes, I think I'll have the fish.

Server: OK. And would you like soup or salad with that?

Woman: Uh . . . does it come with the fish?

Server: Yes, either soup or salad comes with every meal.

Woman: OK, then I'll have a salad, please.

2.

Woman: Let's see . . . I'll have the breakfast special.

Server: I'm sorry. It's eleven o'clock, and we stopped serving breakfast at ten-thirty. But you can order from *this* menu.

Woman: Oh. Uh . . . OK. I'll have a chicken sandwich and a cup of coffee.

Server: Milk and sugar?

Woman: No, just black.

3.

Woman: What should we get on the pizza?

Man: Let's see . . . They have a lot of toppings.

Woman: I'd like some vegetables on it.

Man: OK, how about broccoli and mushrooms?

Woman: I don't really like broccoli. Let's get onions.

Man: Sure. A mushroom and onion pizza sounds good.

4.

Man: Come on in, Emily. Have a seat. Can I get you anything?

Woman: No, thanks. I just had dinner.

Man: How about a slice of lemon cake?

Woman: Well, actually, that sounds good. Sure, I'll have a piece of cake – just a small piece, please.

Man: Coffee?

Woman: Yes, please. A cup of coffee sounds great. Thanks!

5.

Woman: House of Sandwiches. Can I help you?

Man: Yeah, hi. Do you deliver?

Woman: We sure do.

Man: OK, I'd like a roast beef sandwich – with cheese, tomatoes, and lettuce.

Woman: OK. Would you like mustard or mayonnaise on that?

Man: Mustard, please.

Woman: Sure. And what's your address, please?

Man: It's . . .

Part B Listen again. Check *all* of the things the people are going to have.

[Replay Quiz • Unit 4, Part A, track 5]

Quiz • Unit 5 (TM 1 CD, track 6)

Part A Listen. People are talking about free-time activities. What are the topics? Circle the correct answers.

1.

Man: I love going to the movies. I'm interested in everything – the actors, the music . . . I go really often, maybe three or four times a month.

2.

Woman: I don't have a lot of extra money, so I don't go shopping very much. In fact, I hardly ever go shopping. I try to buy only the things I really need, like food.

3.

Man: I'm a college student, so I have a long summer vacation. Whenever I have a break from school, I always visit my relatives – my grandparents, my aunt and uncle . . . I have a really great family.

4.

Woman: A lot of people like to stay home in the evening. My roommate stays home and watches TV every night. Can you believe it? I never watch TV. I don't like most of the programs, and I can't stand all the ads. I'd much rather go out with my friends.

5.

Man: We're pretty quiet, I guess, and we both have busy jobs. So on the weekends, we often just stay home and relax. You know, watch TV, listen to music, or just talk. I like being at home.

Part B Listen again. How often do the people do the activities? Check the correct answers.

[*Replay Quiz • Unit 5, Part A, track 6*]

Quiz • Unit 6 (TM 1 CD, track 7)

Part A Listen. Carla is telling her friend Sylvie what clothes she's planning to wear on her business trip. Check *all* of the items she's planning to wear.

1.
Sylvie: So, are you ready for your trip?
Carla: No, not really. I'm packing now.
Sylvie: What are you taking?
Carla: For the plane trip, I'm going to wear my pink blouse, my new plaid pants, and brown sandals.
Sylvie: You bought plaid pants? And brown sandals? Don't you have black sandals?

2.
Carla: For the first day of meetings, I'm taking my dark blue suit – the jacket and pants. And my black boots.
Sylvie: Yeah, that's a great suit, very professional. And perfect with boots.

3.
Carla: We're going to have a company picnic on Friday. I'm going to wear my green T-shirt with my checked skirt and green sneakers. Does that sound OK?
Sylvie: Oh, yes. That's a cute outfit. And comfortable, too.

4.
Carla: For the evening, I'm taking that great little red dress. Remember it? It has a matching jacket. And I got some really nice shoes to go with the outfit.
Sylvie: That is a nice dress . . . but red for a business trip? I don't think so. Do you have something else?

5.
Carla: And for the trip home, I'm taking my black jeans, a light yellow shirt, and a yellow and white striped sweater.
Sylvie: That sounds nice. You look good in yellow.

Part B Listen again. Does Sylvie like Carla's choices? Check *yes* or *no*.

[*Replay Quiz • Unit 6, Part A, track 7*]

Quiz • Unit 7 (TM 1 CD, track 8)

Part A Listen. What are the people looking for? Check the correct answers.

1.
Man: What's today's date?
Woman: Let's see . . . Hey! Where's the calendar? It's not on the wall.
Man: Oh, I took it down last week. Uh, where did I put it?
Woman: Oh, here it is! It's on the coffee table, under the newspaper.
Man: Oh – sorry!

2.
Woman: These are beautiful flowers! Thank you so much.
Man: I'll go get something to put them in.
Woman: I think the vase is on the bookshelf.
Man: Hmm. I don't see it. Maybe it's on my desk . . .
Woman: Oh, there it is – on the floor, next to the bookshelf.
Man: Oh, yeah. You're right!

3.
Man: Hey! What happened here? The living room looks different!
Woman: Oh . . . Well, I spilled some tea on the rug. But don't worry, I washed it.
Man: Well, that's OK, then. But where is it?
Woman: It's outside, in the yard . . . drying in the sun.

4.
Woman: Brad, I have some bad news. I . . . I broke the fishbowl. I'm really sorry.
Brad: Well, don't worry about it. It wasn't a very good one. But wait – where's the fish?
Woman: Oh, he's OK. I put him in the big vase.
Brad: What vase?
Woman: That big yellow one. It's next to the TV. See? I think he likes it.

5.
Man: Ooooh, it's cold in here.
Woman: Well, you can turn on the heater.
Man: Where is it?
Woman: Right over there, between the couch and the TV stand.
Man: Thanks. Mmm . . . that feels better.

Part B Listen again. Where are the objects? Circle the correct answers.

[*Replay Quiz • Unit 7, Part A, track 8*]

Quiz • Unit 8 (TM 1 CD, track 9)

Part A Listen. Are the statements true or false? Check the correct answers.

1.
Woman: John, we're going to be late. It's seven-thirty already!
John: Relax! The show starts at eight o'clock, and it only takes fifteen minutes to get to the theater.
Woman: That's true, but the play's not at the theater! It's at the high school, downtown.
John: Oh, no. We'd better leave right now!

2.
Man: Do you have time to go out for lunch?
Woman: I have a lot of work to do. What time is it now?
Man: It's eleven forty-five. Let's go to the Mexican restaurant. The food is good, and the service is really fast. We can be back at the office by twelve-thirty.
Woman: OK, that sounds good. And I am hungry.

3.
Woman: Where's Jasmine? It's two-fifteen and we planned to meet here at two o'clock.
Man: Maybe she missed the train.
Woman: I can wait for her another fifteen minutes, but then I have to leave.
Man: OK. Let's wait until two-thirty.

4.
Man: Hey! Let's go to a movie tonight.
Woman: Are you kidding? It's already nine-fifteen.
Man: Well, there's a show at nine-fifty. We have plenty of time.
Woman: Yes, but it ends at eleven-thirty! That's too late for me.
Man: OK. Let's watch something on TV, then.

5.
Woman: What time is it now?
Man: Just a little before noon, I think.
Woman: Oh, good. There's a TV show I want to watch.
Man: What time does it end?
Woman: One-thirty, I think. Why?
Man: You said you'd go shopping with me this afternoon. Remember?
Woman: Of course . . . after my TV show.

Part B Listen again. Circle the correct information.

[*Replay Quiz • Unit 8, Part A, track 9*]

Quiz • Unit 9 (TM 1 CD, track 10)

Part A Listen. What kinds of movies are the people talking about? Circle the correct answers.

1.
Woman: There's a good movie on TV tonight.
Man: What's it called?
Woman: *No Space Too Big.* It's new.
Man: Is that a romance? Boy meets girl, boy loses girl . . . boring.
Woman: No, no. It's a science-fiction movie. I heard it has great special effects.
Man: Oh, science fiction. Well, that's OK, then.

2.
Woman: Hey, you like funny movies, don't you?
Man: Sure. Why? Is there a good one playing?
Woman: Yes, *His Bark Is Worse Than His Bite.* It's about this dentist who moves to a small town, and there's a mistake, and he gets a job as an animal doctor! Isn't that crazy?
Man: That just sounds silly. No thanks.
Woman: But I thought you liked comedies . . .
Man: With people, not animals.

3.
Woman: Guess what DVD I got! *Dracula: The Vampire Returns*!
Man: What? You're kidding.
Woman: Really. It's the new version, the modern horror story.
Man: Is it really scary?
Woman: Well, I hope so. That's why I got it.
Man: Hmm. Can I watch it with you?

4.
Man: What do you want to do tonight?
Woman: I don't know. I'm pretty tired.
Man: Why don't I get us a DVD to watch?
Woman: Hey, that sounds good.
Man: I'll get *The Big Race.* It's an action movie – with plenty of fights and car chases!
Woman: Actually, you know, I think I'll just go to bed early.

5.
Woman: What did you say this movie was called?
Man: Uh, it's called *Tea for Two.*
Woman: What's it about?
Man: Oh, it's a great love story – a real classic.
Woman: I didn't know you liked love stories.
Man: Me? I like all kinds of movies.
Woman: Me, too, except romance. I think I'll skip this one.

Part B Listen again. Who wants to watch the movie? Check *man, woman,* or *both*.

[*Replay Quiz • Unit 9, Part A, track 10*]

Quiz • Unit 10 (TM 1 CD, track 11)

Part A Listen. People are talking about their schedules. Number the activities in the correct order from 1 to 3. There is one extra activity.

1.

Man: I like to relax on Saturdays. I get up late, around nine-thirty. In the morning, I watch my favorite news program on TV. In the afternoon, I usually play soccer or basketball with some friends. In the evening, I go dancing!

2.

Woman: My job is part-time, so I finish work at twelve-thirty. I live close to the office, so I usually get home at twelve forty-five. I eat lunch, and then I read the newspaper. After that, I clean the apartment or do laundry. I usually take a break and turn on the TV. I almost never miss my favorite talk show at three o'clock.

3.

Man: My job's pretty busy. When I get to work, the first thing I do is check my phone messages and return calls. Next, I check my e-mail. I don't answer it – I don't have time in the morning. I always answer my e-mail in the afternoon, usually from five to six. At six-ten, I take the bus home.

4.

Woman: My mornings are crazy! I get up at six o'clock. First, I have a cup of coffee. Then I wake up the kids. While the kids eat their breakfast, I take a shower. Then we all get into the car and I drive the kids to school. I drop them off at seven-thirty. Then I go to work.

5.

Man: We have a great birthday tradition in my house. On my birthday, I wake up really early in the morning – around five-thirty! Then I look for my gifts. My family hides them in the living room – under the couch, behind the curtains. After I find all the gifts, it's time to open them. That's my favorite part. In the evening, we have a special dinner. No birthday cake – I don't really like cake.

Part B Listen again. Circle the correct information.

[*Replay Quiz • Unit 10, Part A, track 11*]

Quiz • Unit 11 (TM 1 CD, track 12)

Part A Listen. Where are the people going to go? Circle the correct answers.

1.

Man: I need to buy a map. Is there a bookstore around here?

Woman: Yes. Try the one on First Street.

Man: Which one?

Woman: You know, the one next to the French café.

Man: Oh, yeah. I know where that is.

2.

Woman: Excuse me. Is there a mall near here?

Man: Well, it's a little far. What do you need to buy?

Woman: I need a gift for my nephew. He's seven.

Man: Oh, well, there's a big toy store right around the corner from the movie theater – straight down this street.

Woman: Thank you.

3.

Man: Excuse me. I'm going to the aquarium. Do you know if I can park my car there?

Woman: Yes, you can, but it will cost you ten dollars.

Man: Really? Well, is there someplace cheaper?

Woman: You can park in the lot behind City Hall. It's not too far – and it's free.

Man: Oh, great. Thank you.

4.

Woman: Excuse me. I'm looking for a restaurant – someplace to get some lunch.

Man: Sure. There are lots of places around here. Do you like Indian food?

Woman: Well, . . .

Man: Or there's an Italian place.

Woman: That sounds good. Where's that?

Man: Go straight down Main Street and then turn left. You'll see the restaurant on the right, across from the convenience store.

5.

Man: Oh, no! My research paper is due tomorrow, and my computer isn't working!

Woman: Your computer's broken? Well, why don't you go to an Internet café?

Man: No, too noisy and crowded. Hey, I know! I can go to the library. Do you know how to get there from here?

Woman: Yeah. It's on Oak Street, right between the Internet café and the museum.

Part B Listen again. Are the statements true or false? Check the correct answers.

[*Replay Quiz • Unit 11, Part A, track 12*]

Quiz • Unit 12 (TM 1 CD, track 13)

Part A Listen. What are the occasions? Circle the correct answers.

1.
Erin: So, Brian, you're forty today. How does it feel?
Brian: I don't know. I don't really feel any older. It's just another day.
Erin: Here, this is for you.
Brian: Oh, you didn't have to get me anything.
Erin: Go on, open it.
Brian: Chocolates! Oh, wow! I'm going to have one right now. Here, you have one, too, Erin.

2.
Man: We're all going to miss you.
Woman: I'll come back and visit the office.
Man: And we all wish you good luck in your new job. Here. This is from all of your co-workers.
Woman: Oh, a card.
Man: We all signed it.
Woman: And a gift certificate for my favorite restaurant. Thank you, everybody. That's really nice.

3.
Grandmother: You're all finished! Congratulations!
Granddaughter: Thanks, Grandma.
Grandmother: Here. It's just a little something.
Granddaughter: Thank you. Oh, it's a watch.
Grandmother: So you won't be late for any job interviews!
Granddaughter: Grandma, I don't have any job interviews yet.
Grandmother: Well, you will very soon. Come on, put it on.
Granddaughter: Oh, it's beautiful. I love it.

4.
Man: So . . . we've been married for five years now. Can you believe it?
Woman: Five wonderful years.
Man: Here, honey. I hope you like it.
Woman: A pink sweater! But . . . it's a size extra small.
Man: Aren't you an extra small?
Woman: Well, . . . actually, sweetie, I'm a medium.
Man: Oh, sorry, honey.
Woman: That's OK. I'll just exchange it for the right size.

5.
Son: Here, Dad – for your special day.
Father: Thanks. Let's see, a book. *The Long Journey*. Huh. What's it about?
Son: Look, uh, here – on the cover.
Father: Hey! That's you! This is your book! You finally wrote your book! That's great.

Son: I couldn't have done it without you. You're the best father in the world.
Father: Well, I'm proud of you. I can't wait to read this!

Part B Listen again. Check the correct answers.
[*Replay Quiz • Unit 12, Part A, track 13*]

Quiz • Unit 13 (TM 1 CD, track 14)

Part A Listen. Which jobs do the people want? Circle the correct answers.

1.
Man: Here's a good job for me: server.
Woman: Server? That's a busy job, you know. It's not easy. You should work in an office.
Man: I can't. I don't have any office experience. A job as a server is fine.
Woman: Well, I guess you can make a lot of money.
Man: I don't care about that. I like the hours. It's just part-time, so I can still practice my music.

2.
Man: Which job are you going to apply for – childcare worker or cleaning staff?
Woman: I don't know. Childcare worker might be easier.
Man: Oh, I don't think so. I did it once. Taking care of children is really hard.
Woman: Yeah, and I prefer to work alone. I guess cleaning staff is better for me.

3.
Man: I need a summer job that will give me some exercise.
Woman: How about being a lifeguard? You like to swim.
Man: Lifeguards don't swim that much. They usually just sit.
Woman: Well, then, you could be a tour guide . . . or a porter.
Man: Tour guide is a good idea. I'd walk all day . . . and maybe practice my Spanish, too.

4.
Man: Are you really going to be a camp counselor?
Woman: Yes, I am. Why?
Man: Because my uncle needs a business intern. It's a great job. Full-time, paid . . .
Woman: No, I really want to be outside.
Man: With all the insects and animals and dirt? Don't you want to work in an office with a nice desk and chair, and a computer . . .
Woman: No, thanks. That's not for me.

5.

Woman: I heard you applied for a job!

Man: Well, sort of. It's volunteer work. I'd be helping out in an elementary school.

Woman: Oh? Doing what?

Man: Teaching English, and maybe some math and science.

Woman: Oh. And you don't mind volunteering?

Man: You know I want to be a teacher after I graduate. This way, I can get some experience. You can't get a good job without experience these days.

Part B Listen again. Circle the correct information.

[Replay Quiz • Unit 13, Part A, track 14]

Quiz • Unit 14 (TM 1 CD, track 15)

Part A Listen. People are talking about celebrations. Check *all* of the activities they mention.

1.

Man: Thanksgiving is on November twenty-fifth this year. I love Thanksgiving. I always visit my relatives, and we eat a big dinner. My grandparents cook special food – and lots of it!

Woman: What else do you do?

Man: Well, I watch football on TV with my cousins – and then we eat some more!

Woman: You just eat and watch TV?

Man: Yeah. That's why I love Thanksgiving!

2.

Woman: My favorite holiday? Valentine's Day, I guess.

Man: Why is that?

Woman: I like sending cards to my friends, and I like getting them, too. And I love the candy on Valentine's Day – especially the chocolate.

Man: I guess I know what to get you! It's in two weeks, isn't it?

Woman: Yes. February fourteenth – just two weeks from now. Don't forget!

3.

Man: I see the Queen's Birthday is on June tenth this year. That's early.

Woman: This year? Isn't it the same day every year?

Man: Not in Australia! In most states, it's the second Monday in June, but in Western Australia, it's in late September or early October.

Woman: How unusual. So how will you celebrate?

Man: Most people celebrate by not working. It's a day off. It's also the official start of the ski season – so I'm going skiing!

4.

Woman: While you're in the U.S., you *must* go to a Fourth of July celebration.

Man: Fourth of July?

Woman: Yes. It's our Independence Day. We usually go to see the parade downtown. Everyone wears red, white, and blue clothes and, then at night, we watch fireworks.

Man: It sounds like a lot of fun.

5.

Nee: Here, Ms. Johnson. These are for you.

Ms. Johnson: Why, thank you, Nee. Flowers! How lovely. Uh . . . is there any special reason?

Nee: Yes. It's January sixteenth!

Ms. Johnson: January sixteenth?

Nee: In Thailand, it's Teacher's Day – and *you* are my teacher.

Ms. Johnson: What a nice custom! What do you do on Teacher's Day?

Nee: We give flowers to our teachers, to show respect. But . . . it's a holiday, so we don't go to school on that day. *I* always do my homework.

Ms. Johnson: Homework?

Nee: Yes. I show respect to my teachers by doing their assignments.

Ms. Johnson: Well, we don't have a holiday here, but you can still do your homework!

Part B Listen again. Circle the correct information.

[Replay Quiz • Unit 14, Part A, track 15]

Quiz • Unit 15 (TM 1 CD, track 16)

Part A Listen. Which inventions are the people describing? Circle the correct answers.

1.

Man: People love listening to music, and people love making music. Most musical instruments are very old – so old that we don't know when they were invented. But one popular instrument, the piano, is more modern. It was invented in seventeen twenty in Italy.

2.

Woman: You're probably too young to remember black-and-white televisions. The first color TV was invented in nineteen oh four by a German company. But color television sets weren't sold until ninteen fifty-four. Now many families have two or three of them!

3.

Man: Today, people have clocks on their cell phones and laptop computers. People first started carrying their time with them more than four hundred years ago. The first pocket watch was made in fifteen twenty-four. Then, in sixteen seventy-five, a Dutch scientist produced a more accurate pocket watch that kept better time.

4.

Woman: Do you enjoy air travel? Then you should thank Orville and Wilbur Wright, two American brothers who flew the first airplane in 1903, more than one hundred years ago. Of course, they couldn't take any luggage with them, or enjoy movies and meals on the plane, like you can.

5.

Man: Today's video games look very different from the early ones. The very first video game was invented in nineteen fifty-eight and was called *Tennis for Two*. It was followed in nineteen sixty-two by *SpaceWar!* And in nineteen seventy-two, *Pong* became the first video game for the home computer.

Part B Listen again. Are the statements true or false? Check the correct answers.

[*Replay Quiz • Unit 15, Part A, track 16*]

Quiz • Unit 16 (TM 1 CD, track 17)

Part A Listen to the story. What is the main idea of each part of the story? Number the statements from 1 to 5. There is one extra statement.

1.

Woman: An old farmer was sitting by the side of the road near a small village. A young man walked by. "Good morning, Farmer," said the young man politely. "Do you live in that village?" "Yes, I do," replied the farmer. "I have lived there since the day I was born."

2.

Woman: The young man said to the old farmer, "Soon I will come to that village to make my home. I am going to live there. Farmer, you have lived there for many years. Please tell me what it is like. Is it a nice place to live?"

3.

Woman: The farmer looked at the young man. "So, you want to know what kind of place that village is?" he said. "First, let me ask you: What kind of place is it where you come from?" The young man said, "Where I come from, the houses are pretty, the people are all very nice, and life is good." The old farmer replied, "I'm happy to say that you will find my village is just the same. I'm sure you will enjoy your life there very much." "Oh, thank you, thank you," said the young man, and he continued walking.

4.

Woman: Later that same day, a rich man was walking to the village. He saw the old farmer and stopped. The rich man said, "Old man, I want to know about that village. I have to move there soon. Tell me, what is it like?"

5.

Woman: The farmer slowly turned to the rich man and said, "First, tell me what it is like in *your* hometown." The rich man answered, "Not good, not good at all. Where I come from is a boring place. The people are unfriendly, and life is very difficult." The farmer was quiet for a moment. Then he looked at the rich man and said sadly, "Sir, I'm very sorry to say that you will find my village is just the same. I'm sure you would not be very happy there."

Part B Listen again. Circle the correct answers.

[*Replay Quiz • Unit 16, Part A, track 17*]

Tests

Introduction

Testing, at its best, can be a great means of providing feedback to students, as well as a way of holding ourselves accountable as teachers for what we teach. To know that students have really understood material, you need to test them in the same way you teach them. It makes little sense to test students on tasks they have not done in the classroom. The *Active Listening* tests are designed as achievement tests – to measure how well students have mastered the material in Student's Book 1 of the *Active Listening, Second Edition* series. The tests reflect the material covered in Student's Book 1 and measure students' progress in the three listening skill areas introduced in the course: main idea, details, and inference.

Criterion-referenced tests, like the *Active Listening* tests, don't compare each student to other students. Instead, they assess how well students have done what they were supposed to do. In this case, the tests measure how well students have learned to listen. If you choose to give each test twice – once as a pre-test and once as a post-test – you can use it to measure the progress each student makes.

These tests, theoretically at least, allow all the students in a class to score 100 percent by the end of the course. They also allow teachers to evaluate students based on their progress, from starting point to finish. Of course, few classes are perfect, so your class's results are likely to look something like a bell curve. We hope, of course, that the bell is bigger on the right side. Most students should get a good score. However, if all your students get A's, pat them on the back; pat yourself on the back. They have reached the "criterion," the highest level. They have learned what you taught. That's not just OK! That's success!

As the tests are intended to gauge students' mastery of the vocabulary and skills presented in the Student's Book, and do not test material outside the course content, you should expect the majority of your students to do well. If many students perform poorly, consider moving through the material more slowly and reviewing material more often.

Purpose of the tests

It is important to discuss the purpose of the tests with your students. Explain to them that the tests are designed to show them (and you) how well they have learned to listen, and to measure their progress in your course.

About the tests

Test 1 covers the listening skills, topics, and language covered in Units 1–8. Test 2 covers the listening skills, topics, and language covered in Units 9–16.

Each test consists of fifty multiple-choice questions and is divided into five sections:
Section 1: picture questions (8 items)
Section 2: appropriate response (10 items)
Section 3: short conversation (10 items)
Section 4: short monolog (10 items)
Section 5: long conversation and monolog (12 items)

Test 1 and its corresponding test answer sheet can be found on pages 111–118 of this Teacher's Manual; Test 2 on pages 120–127.

The answer key for Test 1 is on page 119 of this Teacher's Manual; the answer key for Test 2 is on page 128.

The audio scripts start on page 129 of this Teacher's Manual for Test 1 and on page 131 for Test 2.

Administration and scoring guide

Using the tests
• You may wish to use Test 1 as a mid-term test and Test 2 as a final (end-of-course) test. You can still use the tests if you skipped one or two units. In this case, do not count students' answers to questions from the skipped units against their final score (but let them know whether or not they answered correctly).

• You could give the tests twice, once as a pre-test before you begin the relevant section of the Student's Book, and again as a post-test, after students complete the units. This way, students can see their own progress. Of course, if you do choose to give the test twice, the answers should not be discussed with students until after they complete the post-test.

• For students who have been absent from class, consider making the audio program available in a self-access (sign out and return) situation. This way, students can make up missed lessons and get the necessary practice before the test.

• Have students check their own test answers. In addition to saving you time, this provides students with specific feedback on areas where they need more practice.

• If you do not already do so, consider counting attendance, class participation, and homework as part of students' grades in addition to formal testing. A multifaceted approach to evaluation will fit well with the interactive nature of the *Active Listening, Second Edition* course.

Preparation
1. Photocopy pages 111–118 of this Teacher's Manual for Test 1. For Test 2, photocopy pages 120–127.

2. You may also wish to make transparencies of each answer sheet (page 118 for Test 1 and page 127 for Test 2) for clarifying instructions, and of each answer key (page 119 for Test 1 and page 128 for Test 2) for self-scoring.

Administering the tests
1. Have students sit apart from one another. Hand out the test pages and answer sheets separately.

2. Read the following instructions aloud to students:
Make sure that you have seven printed test pages and one answer sheet. Write your name on the answer

sheet. Please mark all of your answers on the answer sheet. Do not write on the test pages.

3. To demonstrate how to use the answer sheet, you can use a transparency and show students how to fill in the boxes with their answer choices.

4. Read the following instructions aloud:
This test has fifty questions. There are five sections. Each section is different. Listen carefully to the instructions at the beginning of each section.

Notes
Section 1: picture questions (see, for example, page 111 of this Teacher's Manual)

• This section has eight questions. The task requires students to select the picture that best matches what they hear.

• Read the instructions aloud. Give students time to look at the pictures.

• Make sure students understand the instructions. Then play the audio program.

• The instructions are repeated on the audio program. You should first read them aloud and check to make sure students understand them. Then, when students hear the instructions again on the audio program, it gives them a chance to "tune" their ears before beginning the test.

Section 2: appropriate response (see, for example, page 114 of this Teacher's Manual)

• This section has ten questions. The task requires students to select a suitable reply for a statement or question made by the speaker.

• Read the instructions aloud. Give students time to look at the answer choices.

• Make sure students understand the instructions. Then play the audio program.

Section 3: short conversation (see, for example, page 115 of this Teacher's Manual)

• This section has ten questions. The task requires students to listen to a short conversation and complete the sentences that follow.

• Read the instructions aloud. Give students time to look at the sentences and answer choices.

• Make sure students understand the instructions. Then play the audio program.

Section 4: short monolog (see, for example, page 116 of this Teacher's Manual)

• This section has ten questions. The task requires students to listen to a short monolog and complete the sentences that follow.

• Read the instructions aloud. Give students time to look at the sentences and answer choices.

• Make sure students understand the instructions. Then play the audio program.

Section 5: long conversation and monolog (see, for example, pages 117 and 126 of this Teacher's Manual)

• This section has twelve questions. The task requires students to listen to either a long conversation or monolog and complete the sentences that follow. There are two questions for each conversation or monolog.

• Read the instructions aloud. Give students time to look at the sentences and answer choices.

• Make sure students understand the instructions. Then play the audio program.

5. When students have finished, collect the tests and the answer sheets to check answers, or use a transparency of the answer key to have students check their own tests.

Scoring

Each correct answer is worth two points. Add the scores from each section to give a total score out of 100. Record students' scores on their test answer sheets, as well as on the Score Records Sheet (page 134 of this Teacher's Manual).

Test 1 • Units 1–8

Section 1

🎧 Listen. What are the people talking about? Choose the correct pictures.

1. **a**   **b**   **c**

2. **a**   **b**   **c**

3. **a**   **b**   **c**

Active Listening, Second Edition **Book 1**   **111**

4. **a**　　　**b**　　　**c**

5. **a**　　　**b**　　　**c**

6. **a**　　　**b**　　　**c**

Test 1 • Units 1–8

7. **a**    **b**    **c**

8. **a**    **b**    **c**

End of Section 1

Active Listening, Second Edition **Book 1**

Test 1 • Units 1–8

Section 2

Listen. Imagine the people are talking to you. What is your part of the conversation? Choose the best answers.

9. a. Hi. I'm (*your name*).
    b. No, I'm not.
    c. How about you?

10. a. The music was really good.
    b. Yes, I like it a lot.
    c. Do you think so?

11. a. Yes, they are.
    b. She's older.
    c. They're younger.

12. a. Yes, it is.
    b. No. It's 555-1213.
    c. Yes, please.

13. a. Let's watch TV.
    b. Yes, we do.
    c. OK. Where do you want to go?

14. a. I often play music.
    b. I never play basketball.
    c. I think so.

15. a. They watch TV or DVDs.
    b. I usually read newspapers.
    c. Because they like it.

16. a. I watch TV.
    b. Yes, I can.
    c. Hardly ever.

17. a. Yes, I'll wear my blue one.
    b. Yes, it's very hot.
    c. I often wear a tie.

18. a. That's a good idea.
    b. How about 6:30?
    c. It's a little late.

End of Section 2

Test 1 • Units 1–8

Section 3

🎧 **Listen. Choose the correct information.**

19. He needs to call
    a. 214-2961.
    b. 241-2961.
    c. 241-6291.

20. The number is
    a. (202) 555-2436.
    b. (212) 553-4326.
    c. (212) 555-4236.

21. They're talking about
    a. ice cream.
    b. coffee.
    c. pizza.

22. They're talking about
    a. a hamburger.
    b. salad.
    c. soup.

23. She goes out for dinner
    a. after work.
    b. during the week.
    c. on weekends.

24. He visits relatives
    a. on weekends.
    b. on vacation.
    c. on Sunday.

25. The man thinks the woman should buy
    a. a yellow sweater.
    b. a red sweater.
    c. an orange dress.

26. They're talking about
    a. a TV.
    b. a couch.
    c. a bookshelf.

27. The woman
    a. isn't hungry.
    b. is busy.
    c. is late.

28. Now, it's
    a. 7:00.
    b. 7:15.
    c. 8:15.

End of Section 3

Test 1 • Units 1–8

Section 4

🎧 Listen. Choose the correct information.

29. Sara and Tom have
    a. two children.
    b. three children.
    c. four children.

30. The final score was
    a. Bears 68, Tigers 48.
    b. Bears 88, Tigers 68.
    c. Bears 48, Tigers 68.

31. The woman wants soup and
    a. a sandwich.
    b. some bread.
    c. some dessert.

32. The man reads the newspaper
    a. once a week.
    b. on weekends.
    c. every day.

33. Jenny is wearing
    a. a red T-shirt.
    b. sneakers.
    c. socks.

34. Mike is wearing
    a. a plaid tie.
    b. white pants.
    c. a striped tie.

35. The woman is talking about
    a. a calendar.
    b. a clock.
    c. a desk.

36. The man is talking about
    a. a chair.
    b. a TV stand.
    c. a coffee table.

37. If an American invites you to dinner, you should come
    a. a little late.
    b. on time.
    c. very early.

38. If an American invites you to a party at 8:00, you should come around
    a. 7:45.
    b. 8:30.
    c. 9:30.

End of Section 4

Test 1 • Units 1–8

Section 5

🎧 **Listen. Choose the correct information.**

39. The man is talking about
    a. his friends.
    b. his students.
    c. his children.

40. Amy is
    a. eight years old.
    b. twelve years old.
    c. seventeen years old.

41. The winning teams were
    a. the Hawks and the Eagles.
    b. the Eagles and the Bears.
    c. the Hawks and the Panthers.

42. The Bears had
    a. 5 points.
    b. 65 points.
    c. 90 points.

43. The woman is
    a. at a restaurant.
    b. in her home.
    c. at a friend's house.

44. The pasta comes with
    a. fresh bread.
    b. cheese.
    c. vegetables.

45. The people are talking about
    a. playing music.
    b. going out.
    c. watching TV.

46. The woman
    a. often watches movies.
    b. never goes out.
    c. doesn't like movies.

47. A *corsi* is
    a. a heater.
    b. a blanket.
    c. a bed.

48. When people use a *corsi*, they
    a. stand in the middle of the room.
    b. lie down on couches.
    c. sit around a table.

49. The people are talking about
    a. eating breakfast.
    b. going to work.
    c. exercising.

50. The people will meet at
    a. 5:30.
    b. 6:00.
    c. 8:30.

End of Section 5

Test 1 answer sheet • Units 1–8

Name: _____   Date: _____

Teacher: _____   Class: _____

Section 1			
1	☐ a.	☐ b.	☐ c.
2	☐ a.	☐ b.	☐ c.
3	☐ a.	☐ b.	☐ c.
4	☐ a.	☐ b.	☐ c.
5	☐ a.	☐ b.	☐ c.
6	☐ a.	☐ b.	☐ c.
7	☐ a.	☐ b.	☐ c.
8	☐ a.	☐ b.	☐ c.

Section 2			
9	☐ a.	☐ b.	☐ c.
10	☐ a.	☐ b.	☐ c.
11	☐ a.	☐ b.	☐ c.
12	☐ a.	☐ b.	☐ c.
13	☐ a.	☐ b.	☐ c.
14	☐ a.	☐ b.	☐ c.
15	☐ a.	☐ b.	☐ c.
16	☐ a.	☐ b.	☐ c.
17	☐ a.	☐ b.	☐ c.
18	☐ a.	☐ b.	☐ c.

Section 3			
19	☐ a.	☐ b.	☐ c.
20	☐ a.	☐ b.	☐ c.
21	☐ a.	☐ b.	☐ c.
22	☐ a.	☐ b.	☐ c.
23	☐ a.	☐ b.	☐ c.
24	☐ a.	☐ b.	☐ c.
25	☐ a.	☐ b.	☐ c.
26	☐ a.	☐ b.	☐ c.
27	☐ a.	☐ b.	☐ c.
28	☐ a.	☐ b.	☐ c.

Section 4			
29	☐ a.	☐ b.	☐ c.
30	☐ a.	☐ b.	☐ c.
31	☐ a.	☐ b.	☐ c.
32	☐ a.	☐ b.	☐ c.
33	☐ a.	☐ b.	☐ c.
34	☐ a.	☐ b.	☐ c.
35	☐ a.	☐ b.	☐ c.
36	☐ a.	☐ b.	☐ c.
37	☐ a.	☐ b.	☐ c.
38	☐ a.	☐ b.	☐ c.

Section 5			
39	☐ a.	☐ b.	☐ c.
40	☐ a.	☐ b.	☐ c.
41	☐ a.	☐ b.	☐ c.
42	☐ a.	☐ b.	☐ c.
43	☐ a.	☐ b.	☐ c.
44	☐ a.	☐ b.	☐ c.
45	☐ a.	☐ b.	☐ c.
46	☐ a.	☐ b.	☐ c.
47	☐ a.	☐ b.	☐ c.
48	☐ a.	☐ b.	☐ c.
49	☐ a.	☐ b.	☐ c.
50	☐ a.	☐ b.	☐ c.

	Score
Section 1	
Section 2	
Section 3	
Section 4	
Section 5	
Total	

Test 1 answer key • Units 1–8

		a.	b.	c.
Section 1	1	○ a.	■ b.	○ c.
	2	○ a.	○ b.	■ c.
	3	■ a.	○ b.	○ c.
	4	○ a.	■ b.	○ c.
	5	■ a.	○ b.	○ c.
	6	○ a.	○ b.	■ c.
	7	○ a.	○ b.	■ c.
	8	■ a.	○ b.	○ c.
Section 2	9	■ a.	○ b.	○ c.
	10	○ a.	■ b.	○ c.
	11	○ a.	○ b.	■ c.
	12	○ a.	■ b.	○ c.
	13	○ a.	○ b.	■ c.
	14	○ a.	■ b.	○ c.
	15	■ a.	○ b.	○ c.
	16	○ a.	○ b.	■ c.
	17	■ a.	○ b.	○ c.
	18	○ a.	■ b.	○ c.
Section 3	19	○ a.	■ b.	○ c.
	20	○ a.	○ b.	■ c.
	21	■ a.	○ b.	○ c.
	22	■ a.	○ b.	○ c.
	23	○ a.	○ b.	■ c.
	24	○ a.	■ b.	○ c.
	25	■ a.	○ b.	○ c.
	26	○ a.	○ b.	■ c.
	27	○ a.	■ b.	○ c.
	28	○ a.	■ b.	○ c.

		a.	b.	c.
Section 4	29	○ a.	■ b.	○ c.
	30	■ a.	○ b.	○ c.
	31	○ a.	■ b.	○ c.
	32	○ a.	○ b.	■ c.
	33	○ a.	■ b.	○ c.
	34	○ a.	○ b.	■ c.
	35	■ a.	○ b.	○ c.
	36	○ a.	○ b.	■ c.
	37	○ a.	■ b.	○ c.
	38	○ a.	■ b.	○ c.
Section 5	39	○ a.	○ b.	■ c.
	40	■ a.	○ b.	○ c.
	41	○ a.	○ b.	■ c.
	42	○ a.	■ b.	○ c.
	43	■ a.	○ b.	○ c.
	44	○ a.	○ b.	■ c.
	45	○ a.	■ b.	○ c.
	46	○ a.	○ b.	■ c.
	47	■ a.	○ b.	○ c.
	48	○ a.	○ b.	■ c.
	49	○ a.	○ b.	■ c.
	50	○ a.	■ b.	○ c.

Test 2 • Units 9–16

Section 1

🎧 Listen. What are the people talking about? Choose the correct pictures.

1. **a** **b** **c**

2. **a** **b** **c**

3. **a**
Department Store | Pet Shop
Café | Grocery Store
Movie Theater | Jewelry Store

b
Pet Shop | Toy Store
Jewelry Store | Department Store
Grocery Store | Museum

c
Movie Theater | Pet Shop
Department Store | Grocery Store
Café | Jewelry Store

Test 2 • Units 9–16

4. **a** Chocolates **b** **c**

5. **a** **b** **c**

6. **a** **b** **c**

Test 2 • Units 9–16

7. **a**

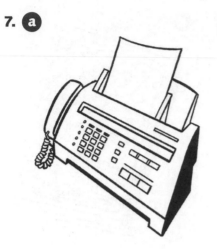

b

c

8. **a**

b

c

End of Section 1

Test 2 • Units 9–16

Section 2

🎧 Listen. Imagine the people are talking to you. What is your part of the conversation? Choose the best answers.

9. a. I like horror movies.
   b. I like silly situations.
   c. I don't have a favorite actor.

10. a. I like it a lot.
    b. He's great.
    c. They're not very good.

11. a. I have dinner at 7:00.
    b. I usually have pasta.
    c. I read or watch TV.

12. a. It's across from the aquarium.
    b. They're six and eight years old.
    c. It opens at 9:00.

13. a. There's a toy store near here.
    b. It's next to the museum.
    c. I'm going to buy some toys.

14. a. How about a DVD?
    b. It's on March 6.
    c. He doesn't like chocolate.

15. a. No, I don't like serving.
    b. I'd like a pizza, please.
    c. Yes, I worked in a café.

16. a. Yes, I want to make a lot of money.
    b. Yes, I need the experience.
    c. No, you don't have to volunteer.

17. a. We fly beautiful kites.
    b. I don't have any children.
    c. My favorite holiday is New Year.

18. a. Where is it?
    b. What's it for?
    c. Sure.

End of Section 2

Test 2 • Units 9–16

Section 3

🎧 Listen. Choose the correct information.

19. They're talking about
    a. a book.
    b. a newspaper.
    c. a movie.

20. The man likes
    a. to watch TV.
    b. to read.
    c. to listen to music.

21. The man drinks coffee. Next, he
    a. reads the newspaper.
    b. goes to work.
    c. eats breakfast.

22. The computer store is
    a. next to the movie theater.
    b. on the corner.
    c. around the corner from the movie theater.

23. The man thinks
    a. a sweater is too expensive.
    b. clothing is too personal.
    c. it's not polite to give her boss a birthday present.

24. In China, clocks
    a. are a popular gift.
    b. bring good luck.
    c. are an unlucky gift.

25. The woman wants a job as
    a. a childcare worker.
    b. a business intern.
    c. a tour guide.

26. During Carnaval, the man liked
    a. eating special food.
    b. watching fireworks.
    c. wearing special clothes.

27. The woman
    a. doesn't want the glasses.
    b. already has the glasses.
    c. wants the glasses.

28. The people are talking about
    a. their jobs.
    b. their families.
    c. a folktale.

End of Section 3

Test 2 • Units 9–16

Section 4

🎧 **Listen. Choose the correct information.**

29. The movie is
    a. science fiction.
    b. a horror movie.
    c. a romance.

30. Before she goes to bed, she
    a. takes a bath.
    b. listens to music.
    c. exercises.

31. The clothing store is
    a. next to the mall.
    b. across from the restaurant.
    c. next to the shoe store.

32. For his birthday, the man wants
    a. to go out.
    b. to stay home.
    c. some books and clothes.

33. In the U.S., a good wedding gift is
    a. a gift certificate.
    b. money.
    c. a gift for the house.

34. The woman is
    a. a childcare worker.
    b. a tour guide.
    c. a tutor.

35. The man is
    a. a porter.
    b. a business intern.
    c. a convenience store clerk.

36. On White Day,
    a. men give candy to women.
    b. women give white chocolate to men.
    c. men send white cards to women.

37. Chewing gum was invented
    a. in the U.S.
    b. in Greece.
    c. in Mexico.

38. The man invented sandwiches so
    he could
    a. sit in the kitchen.
    b. make his own meals.
    c. eat and play cards.

End of Section 4

Test 2 • Units 9–16

Section 5

🎧 **Listen. Choose the correct information.**

39. *On Again, Off Again* is
    a. a comedy.
    b. a romance.
    c. a musical.

40. The movie critic
    a. liked the movie.
    b. liked some things about the movie.
    c. didn't like the movie.

41. The woman wants
    a. to buy new shoes.
    b. to shop for clothing.
    c. to go to the mall.

42. The man says to
    a. turn right.
    b. go around the corner.
    c. turn left.

43. The man is giving directions to
    a. the gift shop.
    b. the Life Science Center.
    c. the bridge.

44. You will see the gift shop
    a. after the Life Science Center.
    b. before the bridge.
    c. after the bridge.

45. Labor Day is always
    a. the first day in September.
    b. the first Sunday in September.
    c. the first Monday in September.

46. On Labor Day, people
    a. work very hard.
    b. watch fireworks.
    c. take a break from work.

47. This inventor was
    a. Indian.
    b. Italian.
    c. American.

48. He started his own company in
    a. 1879.
    b. 1897.
    c. 1899.

49. The people are talking about
    a. the number *three.*
    b. three folktales they know.
    c. three friends.

50. The people
    a. don't think it means anything.
    b. think it symbolizes long life.
    c. don't know what it means.

End of Section 5

Test 2 answer sheet • Units 9–16

Name: _____   Date: _____

Teacher: _____   Class: _____

Section 1	1	○ a.	○ b.	○ c.
	2	○ a.	○ b.	○ c.
	3	○ a.	○ b.	○ c.
	4	○ a.	○ b.	○ c.
	5	○ a.	○ b.	○ c.
	6	○ a.	○ b.	○ c.
	7	○ a.	○ b.	○ c.
	8	○ a.	○ b.	○ c.

Section 2	9	○ a.	○ b.	○ c.
	10	○ a.	○ b.	○ c.
	11	○ a.	○ b.	○ c.
	12	○ a.	○ b.	○ c.
	13	○ a.	○ b.	○ c.
	14	○ a.	○ b.	○ c.
	15	○ a.	○ b.	○ c.
	16	○ a.	○ b.	○ c.
	17	○ a.	○ b.	○ c.
	18	○ a.	○ b.	○ c.

Section 3	19	○ a.	○ b.	○ c.
	20	○ a.	○ b.	○ c.
	21	○ a.	○ b.	○ c.
	22	○ a.	○ b.	○ c.
	23	○ a.	○ b.	○ c.
	24	○ a.	○ b.	○ c.
	25	○ a.	○ b.	○ c.
	26	○ a.	○ b.	○ c.
	27	○ a.	○ b.	○ c.
	28	○ a.	○ b.	○ c.

Section 4	29	○ a.	○ b.	○ c.
	30	○ a.	○ b.	○ c.
	31	○ a.	○ b.	○ c.
	32	○ a.	○ b.	○ c.
	33	○ a.	○ b.	○ c.
	34	○ a.	○ b.	○ c.
	35	○ a.	○ b.	○ c.
	36	○ a.	○ b.	○ c.
	37	○ a.	○ b.	○ c.
	38	○ a.	○ b.	○ c.

Section 5	39	○ a.	○ b.	○ c.
	40	○ a.	○ b.	○ c.
	41	○ a.	○ b.	○ c.
	42	○ a.	○ b.	○ c.
	43	○ a.	○ b.	○ c.
	44	○ a.	○ b.	○ c.
	45	○ a.	○ b.	○ c.
	46	○ a.	○ b.	○ c.
	47	○ a.	○ b.	○ c.
	48	○ a.	○ b.	○ c.
	49	○ a.	○ b.	○ c.
	50	○ a.	○ b.	○ c.

	Score
Section 1	
Section 2	
Section 3	
Section 4	
Section 5	
Total	

Test 2 answer key • Units 9–16

Section 1
1. ☐ a. ☐ b. ■ c.
2. ■ a. ☐ b. ☐ c.
3. ☐ a. ☐ b. ■ c.
4. ☐ a. ■ b. ☐ c.
5. ☐ a. ☐ b. ■ c.
6. ☐ a. ■ b. ☐ c.
7. ☐ a. ■ b. ☐ c.
8. ■ a. ☐ b. ☐ c.

Section 2
9. ☐ a. ■ b. ☐ c.
10. ☐ a. ☐ b. ■ c.
11. ☐ a. ☐ b. ■ c.
12. ■ a. ☐ b. ☐ c.
13. ☐ a. ■ b. ☐ c.
14. ■ a. ☐ b. ☐ c.
15. ☐ a. ☐ b. ■ c.
16. ☐ a. ■ b. ☐ c.
17. ■ a. ☐ b. ☐ c.
18. ☐ a. ■ b. ☐ c.

Section 3
19. ☐ a. ☐ b. ■ c.
20. ■ a. ☐ b. ☐ c.
21. ■ a. ☐ b. ☐ c.
22. ■ a. ☐ b. ☐ c.
23. ☐ a. ■ b. ☐ c.
24. ☐ a. ☐ b. ■ c.
25. ■ a. ☐ b. ☐ c.
26. ☐ a. ☐ b. ■ c.
27. ■ a. ☐ b. ☐ c.
28. ☐ a. ☐ b. ■ c.

Section 4
29. ☐ a. ■ b. ☐ c.
30. ☐ a. ■ b. ☐ c.
31. ☐ a. ☐ b. ■ c.
32. ■ a. ☐ b. ☐ c.
33. ☐ a. ☐ b. ■ c.
34. ☐ a. ■ b. ☐ c.
35. ☐ a. ☐ b. ■ c.
36. ■ a. ☐ b. ☐ c.
37. ☐ a. ■ b. ☐ c.
38. ☐ a. ☐ b. ■ c.

Section 5
39. ☐ a. ■ b. ☐ c.
40. ☐ a. ☐ b. ■ c.
41. ■ a. ☐ b. ☐ c.
42. ☐ a. ☐ b. ■ c.
43. ☐ a. ■ b. ☐ c.
44. ☐ a. ☐ b. ■ c.
45. ☐ a. ☐ b. ■ c.
46. ☐ a. ☐ b. ■ c.
47. ☐ a. ■ b. ☐ c.
48. ☐ a. ■ b. ☐ c.
49. ■ a. ☐ b. ☐ c.
50. ☐ a. ☐ b. ■ c.

Active Listening, Second Edition **Book 1**

Test audio scripts

Test 1 • Units 1–8

(TM 1 CD, track 18)

Section 1 Listen. What are the people talking about? Choose the correct pictures.

1.
Woman: In some cultures, when good friends meet, they often hug each other.

2.
Man: Here's a picture of me with my two sons. They're great kids.

3.
Woman: My parents have been married for forty-five years now. Forty-five years! Isn't that wonderful?

4.
Man: May I have some milk and sugar, please? Thank you.

5.
Woman: I like mine with extra cheese and mushrooms. Mmm! Delicious.

6.
Woman: I'm wearing a striped skirt today. It's one of my favorites.

7.
Man: It's very comfortable. Three people can sit on it. We sit there when we watch TV.

8.
Woman: It's small, but it's very bright. I bought it because I like to read in bed.

(TM 1 CD, track 19)

Section 2 Listen. Imagine the people are talking to you. What is your part of the conversation? Choose the best answers.

9.
Man: My name's Brian.

10.
Woman: I really like this music. Do you like jazz?

11.
Man: Are your sisters older or younger than you?

12.
Woman: I'm sorry. Did you say five-five-five, one-two-one-two?

13.
Man: I don't want to cook tonight. Let's go out for dinner.

14.
Woman: How often do you play basketball?

15.
Man: What do most people do in the evenings?

16.
Woman: Do you ever go to clubs?

17.
Man: It's pretty cold outside. Are you going to wear a jacket?

18.
Woman: Sure! I'd love to go to the movies. What time should we meet?

(TM 1 CD, track 20)

Section 3 Listen. Choose the correct information.

19.
Man: Excuse me, Maureen. Can you tell me the number of the Family Health Center?
Maureen: Sure. Just a minute. You need to call two-four-one, two-nine-six-one.

20.
Woman: I'd like the number of the Metropolitan Hotel in New York, please.
Man: OK. That's area code two-one-two, five-five-five, four-two-three-six.

21.
Server: What kind would you like?
Man: I'll take chocolate, please.

22.
Server: OK. And what do you want on it?
Woman: Let's see . . . Um, I'd like lettuce, onion, and ketchup, please.

23.
Man: Do you go out for dinner very often?
Woman: Yes, I do, but not during the week. I usually go out on Saturday or Sunday.

24.
Woman: Do you ever visit relatives on weekends?
Man: No. They live far away, so I only visit them on vacation.

25.

Woman: I think I'll buy a sweater for Alison's new baby.

Man: Oh, look. This little yellow one's nice.

26.

Man: I like it. It's big enough to hold all our books and magazines.

Woman: Yeah, I like it, too. We can put it in the living room, next to the TV stand.

27.

Woman: Hi, Andy? Listen, I can't come to lunch today. I have *so* much work to do . . .

Andy: That's OK. We'll do it another day.

28.

Man: I'm sorry I'm so late.

Woman: Oh, that's OK. It's 7:15. You're not too late.

(TM 1 CD, track 21)

Section 4 Listen. Choose the correct information.

29.

Woman: I'm Sara. My husband's name is Tom. We have three children – two sons and a daughter.

30.

Man: In this week's basketball news, the Bears won the game. They beat the Tigers sixty-eight to forty-eight. That score again: Bears sixty-eight, Tigers forty-eight.

31.

Woman: I'd like a bowl of French onion soup and some bread to go with that. Oh, and I'll have some hot tea to drink.

32.

Man: I'm very interested in the news. I always read the newspaper in the morning, and I sometimes watch the news on TV in the evening, too.

33.

Woman: Jenny's dressed comfortably today. She's wearing a white T-shirt, a red skirt, and sneakers, but no socks.

34.

Man: Mike's dressed for work. He's wearing a blue suit, a plain white shirt, and a striped tie.

35.

Woman: I have one on the wall in my office. I use it for appointments and to see what day it is. Every month has a different picture.

36.

Man: I have one in my living room, in front of the couch. I put books and magazines on it, and there are some flowers in a vase on it, too.

37.

Woman: In the U.S., if you're invited to a friend's house for dinner, you should try to arrive on time. If the invitation says seven o'clock, you should come at seven o'clock.

38.

Man: In the U.S., people usually come to parties a little late. If the invitation says eight o'clock, you should come at eight-thirty, or even eight forty-five.

(TM 1 CD, track 22)

Section 5 Listen. Choose the correct information.

39. and 40.

Man: This is a picture of my three kids. Kevin's the oldest. He's seventeen; he's finishing high school this year. My other son, Pete, is twelve, and my daughter Amy is eight. They all get along great.

41. and 42.

Man: Turning now to sports, and high school basketball . . . On Friday, the Hawks played the Eagles. The Hawks beat the Eagles one-oh-one to ninety. That score again: the Hawks were the winners – Hawks one hundred and one, Eagles ninety. And in Saturday's game, the Panthers beat the Bears, seventy to sixty-five. That score again: the Panthers won by five points – Panthers seventy, Bears sixty-five.

43. and 44.

Server: Hi, welcome to Gino's. Tonight's special is a pasta dish. It has a spicy tomato sauce and is served with fresh vegetables and a salad. I'll give you a few more minutes to look over the menu, and then I'll come back and take your order.

45. and 46.

Man: Do you want to do something tonight? Maybe go to the movies?

Woman: Hmm. I don't really like movies that much. I hardly ever go to the movies.

Man: Really? Well, let's go to a club. There's a good jazz band at Artie's.

Woman: That sounds good. I love music – especially jazz.

47. and 48.

Man: In some parts of Iran, people use a *corsi* to stay warm. A *corsi* is a small table that holds a pan of hot coals under it. Usually the *corsi* is placed in the middle of the room, and people put a big blanket over it. Then they get under the blanket and sit around the *corsi* to keep warm.

49. and 50.

Woman: I just joined a new gym.

Man: Really? When do you go – in the morning or in the evening?

Woman: I always exercise in the morning. Do you want to come with me tomorrow?

Man: Sure, that sounds great. What time do you usually go?

Woman: Well, I get up at five-thirty, and I'm ready to go to the gym by six o'clock.

Man: Wow, that's early.

Woman: Well, yes, but I have to be at work by eight-thirty.

Man: OK. I'll see you tomorrow at six A.M.!

Test 2 • Units 9–16

(TM 1 CD, track 23)

Section 1 Listen. What are the people talking about? Choose the correct pictures.

1.

Woman: Oh, that's one of my favorite movies. I love action movies. They're so exciting.

2.

Man: After I get to work, the first thing I do is check my e-mail.

3.

Woman: The department store? Yes, it's on the left, between the café and the movie theater.

4.

Man: For Mother's Day, I'm going to buy her a big bunch of flowers. Yellow roses are her favorite.

5.

Woman: I'm going to work as a lifeguard this summer.

6.

Man: Independence Day is my favorite holiday. I love watching fireworks.

7.

Woman: I use this invention every day. I like to watch the news and sports.

8.

Man: Once upon a time, an old farmer lived with his two daughters. They were very poor.

(TM 1 CD, track 24)

Section 2 Listen. Imagine the people are talking to you. What is your part of the conversation? Choose the best answers.

9.

Woman: Why do you like comedies so much?

10.

Man: What're the special effects like?

11.

Woman: What do you usually do after dinner?

12.

Man: Where is the Children's Zoo?

13.

Woman: Is the toy store next to the restaurant or the museum?

14.

Man: What should I give Tyler for his birthday?

15.

Woman: So, you'd like to be a server here. Do you have any experience?

16.

Man: This isn't a paid job. Do you want to be a volunteer?

17.

Woman: In your country, what do you do on Children's Day?

18.

Man: Look at this! It's a new invention. I just bought it yesterday.

(TM 1 CD, track 25)

Section 3 Listen. Choose the correct information.

19.

Woman: That was great. There were some really funny jokes.

Man: Yes, but the acting wasn't very good. And the music was terrible!

20.

Man: I like to watch TV before bed.

Woman: Not me. I love to read and listen to music.

21.

Woman: Do you drink coffee in the morning?

Man: Yes. I always have a cup before I read the newspaper. After that, I eat breakfast.

22.

Man: Excuse me. How do I get to Ace Computer Store?

Woman: Go straight down this street. Then, turn right at the corner. It's on the left, next to the movie theater.

23.

Woman: I'm thinking about giving my boss a sweater for his birthday.

Man: I don't know. Maybe clothing's too personal. I think candy would be better.

24.

Man: Why didn't your friend like the gift?

Woman: She's from China. The word for "clock" in Chinese sounds like the word for "death." It's bad luck.

25.

Man: Do you think you'd like to work with children?

Woman: Oh, yes. I love playing with kids.

26.

Woman: Did you have a favorite holiday when you were growing up in Brazil?

Man: Oh, yes. I loved Carnaval. I liked dressing up in fancy clothes and looking at everybody's costumes.

27.

Man: Look at these – night glasses! They're glasses that help you see in the dark. Aren't they great?

Woman: Well, I don't need them. At night, I go to bed!

28.

Woman: That was an interesting story. What does it mean?

Man: I think the message is this: Listen to people who are older than you because they have more experience.

(TM 1 CD, track 26)

Section 4   Listen. Choose the correct information.

29.

Man: Coming this summer: *The Vampire of Summer Camp*! Bring a good friend with you to this one – someone to hold on to during the scary scenes! Not recommended for teenagers and young children.

30.

Woman: In the evening, I watch the news before dinner. After dinner, I clean up. Then I listen to music or read before going to bed. I'm usually asleep by ten.

31.

Man: There's a great new clothing store at the mall. It's way down at the end, between the Mexican restaurant and the shoe store. They sell really nice jeans and jackets.

32.

Man: I don't want any birthday presents this year. I have a lot of books and clothes. I'd rather just spend the evening with friends, maybe go out for a nice dinner.

33.

Woman: In the U.S., you shouldn't give a gift certificate as a wedding gift. It's better to give a more personal gift. Something for the house is always nice.

34.

Woman: I drive a small bus. I take tourists to see things in the city. I walk a lot, too. I like telling people about our city.

35.

Man: I work from seven P.M. to midnight. I sell things like coffee and newspapers, snacks, and even some school supplies – you know, things like paper, pens, and pencils.

36.

Woman: My favorite holiday in Japan is White Day. It's on March fourteenth. On this day, men give candy – especially white chocolate – to women. On Valentine's Day, in February, women usually give chocolate to men.

37.

Man: Many Americans like chewing gum, but chewing gum wasn't invented in the United States. It was invented in Greece over two thousand years ago. The Maya in Mexico also chewed something like gum, and the first Europeans to come to the U.S. learned to chew gum from the Native Americans.

38.

Woman: The sandwich is named after a rich English lord, the fourth Earl of Sandwich. The Earl loved to play cards, so he had his servants fix a meal that he could sit and eat without stopping his game of cards.

Section 5   Listen. Choose the correct information.

39. and 40.

Man: Good evening. This is Peter Irving, the movie critic. Last night, I saw *On Again, Off Again* – a romance about a couple who can't seem to make up their minds about each other. First, they love each other. Then, they don't. Then, they fall in love again. It almost put me to sleep. I say, turn this movie off!

41. and 42.

Woman: Excuse me. Is there a shoe store near here?

Man: A shoe store? I don't think so. Why don't you try the department store?

Woman: That's a good idea. Uh, where is the department store?

Man: Go straight and turn left at the Internet café. It's right across the street. You can't miss it.

43. and 44.

Man: To get to the Life Science Center, follow the path around that corner until you come to a bridge. It's not very far away. After you cross the bridge, you'll see the gift shop. Just past that is the Life Science Center.

45. and 46.

Woman: What is Labor Day exactly?

Man: It's a day to celebrate hard work.

Woman: When is it?

Man: It's the first Monday in September.

Woman: How do people celebrate it?

Man: There are some parades and speeches. But mostly it's just a day off from work – a time to relax and enjoy the end of summer.

47. and 48.

Man: An Italian inventor, named Marconi, invented the telegraph. He invented it in Italy and then established his own company in eighteen ninety-seven. Two years later, in eighteen ninety-nine, Marconi sent the first telegraph signals across the English Channel to France.

49. and 50.

Woman: Have you ever noticed that the number *three* is very popular in folktales?

Man: Three? What do you mean?

Woman: You know . . . there are always *three* daughters, or *three* sons . . .

Man: The genie gives three wishes . . . Hey, you're right.

Woman: What do you think it means?

Man: Hmm. I'm not really sure.

Score records sheet

Students' names	Unit 1	Unit 2	Unit 3	Unit 4	Unit 5	Unit 6	Unit 7	Unit 8	Test 1	Unit 9	Unit 10	Unit 11	Unit 12	Unit 13	Unit 14	Unit 15	Unit 16	Test 2
1.																		
2.																		
3.																		
4.																		
5.																		
6.																		
7.																		
8.																		
9.																		
10.																		
11.																		
12.																		
13.																		
14.																		
15.																		
16.																		
17.																		
18.																		
19.																		
20.																		
21.																		
22.																		
23.																		
24.																		
25.																		
26.																		
27.																		
28.																		
29.																		
30.																		

Student's Book audio scripts

CD 1
Before you begin

page 3
Listening task 1 • Could you repeat that?

B Now listen. Were you correct? Write the sentences.

1. What do you say when you want someone to say something again?

Woman: Could you repeat that?
   Could you repeat that?

2. What do you say when you want to hear the recording again?

Woman: Once more, please.
   Once more, please.

3. What do you say when you don't know how to spell a word?

Woman: How do you spell that?
   How do you spell that?

4. What do you say when you want to know a word in English?

Woman: How do you say that in English?
   How do you say that in English?

page 4
Listening task 2 • Types of listening

There are many ways to listen. We listen differently for different reasons.

A Listen to the conversation. What is the most important idea? Check the correct answer.

Woman: We're going out for dinner after class. Do you want to come, too?
Man: Maybe. Where are you going?
Woman: Pizza King.
Man: Pizza? I love pizza!

The answer is "dinner." They're talking about dinner.

Sometimes you don't need to understand everything you hear. You just want the main idea, or general meaning.

page 4
B Listen again. What are they going to eat? Check the correct answer.

[*The conversation is repeated here.*]

The answer is "pizza." They're going to eat pizza.

Sometimes you only need to understand the details, or specific information. Ask yourself, "What am I listening for?"

page 4
C Listen again. Will they go together? Check *yes* or *no*.

[*The conversation is repeated here.*]

The answer is "yes." The man says he loves pizza. He doesn't say, "Yes, I will go with you," but you can understand his meaning.

Sometimes people don't say the exact words. You can still understand the meaning. This is called listening "between the lines," or listening and making inferences.

page 5
Listening task 2 • Types of listening

Try it again. Two friends are talking on the telephone. Each time you listen, think about the information you need.

D Listen. What is the most important idea? Check the correct answer.

[*cell phone rings*]
Paul: Hello?
Kate: Hi, Paul. This is Kate.
Paul: Oh, hi. How are you feeling? Are you still sick?
Kate: No, I feel better, thanks. I'm going to school tomorrow. What's the homework for English class?
Paul: The homework? Just a minute. OK, here it is. Read pages twenty-three and twenty-four.
Kate: Twenty-three and twenty-four. OK. Thanks. See you tomorrow.
Paul: Yeah, see you tomorrow. Bye.

The answer is "school." They're talking about school.

page 5
E Listen again. What pages should she read? Write the page numbers.

[*The conversation is repeated here.*]

The answer is "twenty-three and twenty-four." Pages twenty-three and twenty-four.

page 5

F Listen again. Did both students go to school today? Check *yes* or *no*.

[*The conversation is repeated here.*]

The answer is "no." Kate was sick today. She didn't go to school.

You heard the same conversation three times. Each time, you listened for different reasons. Always think about why you are listening.

Unit 1 • Meeting people

page 7

Listening task 1 • How about you?

A Listen. People are meeting at a party for the first time. What do they ask? Circle the correct answers.

Kent and Lisa

1.

Kent: This is a good party and the music's great. I really like jazz. How about you?

Lisa: Jazz is OK, but it's not my favorite.

2.

Kent: Oh, yeah? Well, what kind of music do you like?

Lisa: Well, rock's my favorite, but I like all kinds of music.

3.

Kent: By the way, my name's Kent Adams. I don't think we've met. What's your name?

Lisa: I'm Lisa. Lisa James. It's nice to meet you.

Kent: Nice to meet you, too.

Lisa and Carlos

1.

Lisa: This is a really nice party.

Carlos: Yeah, I'm enjoying it.

Lisa: By the way, my name's Lisa.

Carlos: Nice to meet you, Lisa. I'm Carlos.

Lisa: So, Carlos. Are you a student?

Carlos: Yes, I am. I'm studying English here.

2.

Carlos: How about you, Lisa? What do you do?

Lisa: I'm a student, too. I'm studying art.

3.

Lisa: This is a great place to study. Do you like living here?

Carlos: Oh, yes, I do. I love it! I'm from a small town, so I really like living in a city.

4.

Lisa: Oh, really? Where are you from?

Carlos: I'm from Spain.

Lisa: Oh! I visited Spain on a school trip once. What a beautiful country!

page 7

B Listen. Imagine you are talking to Lisa. What is your part of this conversation? Check your answers.

1.

Lisa: This party is a lot of fun. I'm having a great time. How about you?

2.

Lisa: By the way, I don't think we've met. My name's Lisa. Lisa James. What's your name?

3.

Lisa: I'm studying art here. I'm from Vancouver. How about you? Where are you from?

4.

Lisa: Oh, really? That's cool. So, what do you do? Do you work, or are you a student?

5.

Lisa: Oh! Just like me! Do you like living here?

6.

Lisa: Well, I guess the band is getting ready to play again. I really like their music. How about you? Do you like it?

page 8

Listening task 2 • Around the world

A Listen. There are many ways to greet people around the world. Match each greeting with two places.

1. a bow

Man: Bowing is the traditional way of greeting in Northeast Asian countries like Japan and Korea. This picture, for example, shows how Japanese women bow. In Japan, when you bow, you *don't* look directly at the other person's eyes. In both Japan and Korea, people bow to show respect.

2. a hug

Woman: When good friends meet in Russia, they often hug each other. This is true for both men and women. But Russia isn't the only place where friends hug. In Brazil, for example, friends also hug each other when they greet. In Brazil, a hug is called *abraço*. When you hug someone, you usually give the person a light kiss on the cheek, too.

3. the *salaam*

Man: The *salaam* is a greeting from the Middle East and is used in Jordan, Saudi Arabia, and other Arab countries. It is most popular with older people. To give a *salaam,* first touch your heart, then your forehead. Then move your hand up, away from your head. When people use this greeting, they say, "Peace be with you."

4. the *namaste* or *wai*

Woman: People in India and Thailand use a different kind of greeting. It is called the *namaste* in India, and in Thailand it is called the *wai.* To do the *wai,* you put your hands together high in front of your chest, and you bow slightly. It is a way of greeting. It also means "thank you" and "I'm sorry."

page 8

B Listen again. Are the statements true or false? Check the correct answers.

[*Replay Listening task 2 • Exercise A, track 7*]

page 9

Your turn to talk • Getting to know you

B

1. Listen and practice. Notice the rising intonation of the questions.

Woman: Are you a university student?
Are you from Canada?
Do you study English?
Do you live near here?

B

2. Listen. Do you hear *Do you* or *Are you*? Check the correct answers.

a.
Woman: Do you study here?

b.
Woman: Are you from a small town?

c.
Woman: Are you good at English?

d.
Woman: Do you like sports?

e.
Woman: Do you like jazz?

f.
Woman: Are you a baseball fan?

Unit 2 • Families

page 11

Listening task 1 • Family photos

A Listen. People are talking about their families. Who are they talking about? Check the correct pictures.

1.
Woman 1: Look at these two guys. Aren't they cute? They're my nephews, my brother's sons. I have a lot of fun with them. I like to take them out for pizza, and we go to baseball games sometimes, too. The boys are doing really well in school, and we're all really proud of them.

2.
Man 1: We took this picture last month in the park. My parents were visiting, and we took the kids out for a picnic. That's my mom on the left, with my wife and daughter. My father is next to me, and my son is hugging me. The kids really love Grandma and Grandpa. But we live so far away, they can't see them very often. We have to fly there, and it's a *long* plane ride.

3.
Woman 2: This is a picture we took at my mother's birthday party. That's her in the middle, and that's me on the right. My sister and niece are on the left. It was a great party with really good food! My sister made it all, and my niece helped her. My niece is a great kid. She's really into music and loves dancing.

4.
Man 2: This is a picture of me and my wife with our two grandchildren. My granddaughter loves school. She loves writing and drawing. My grandson likes video games. He beats me all the time. I think I'll e-mail this picture to them. It's one of my favorites.

page 11

B Listen again. Circle the correct information.

[*Replay Listening task 1 • Exercise A, track 10*]

page 12

Listening task 2 • Family ties

A Listen. Jason is talking about his family. Circle the correct information.

1.
Jason: Last week, my family went to the park. My wife and daughter and I went with my parents. My brother was there, too, with my nephew. It was a really nice day. I played some soccer with my daughter Morgan and my nephew. Morgan is on a soccer team at school. She's getting to be pretty good. Better than I am.

2.

Jason: My nephew Austin is a good player, too. He doesn't play on a team, but I think he might next year. Morgan and Austin go to the same school and they play together a lot. They're cousins, but they're also really good friends.

3.

Jason: While we played soccer, my brother Nick helped my father cook. Nick usually doesn't like to cook much, but he likes to barbecue outdoors. He makes great hamburgers. Nick says he's too busy to cook at home.

4.

Jason: I guess Nick learned to cook from my father. His name's Frank. My father loves to cook. He cooked all the time when we were growing up. I never learned much about cooking, though.

5.

Jason: My mother and Katherine, my wife, talked together. They always talk about books. Both of them read a lot. Katherine says I should read more, but I'd rather do something more active.

6.

Jason: My mother, her name is Janice, is great with her grandchildren. She sees them all the time. In fact, my parents are going to take the kids with them on a trip next year. I'm not sure where yet, maybe Disneyland.

page 12

B Listen again. Are the statements true or false? Check the correct answers.

[*Replay Listening task 2 • Exercise A, track 11*]

page 13

Your turn to talk • My family

B

1. Listen and practice. Notice the pronunciation of -*s* endings in verbs.

Woman: /s/, /z/, /ɪz/

/s/: like, likes, cook, cooks
/z/: go, goes, live, lives
/ɪz/: dance, dances, watch, watches

B

2. Write these words in the correct columns. Then listen and check your answers.

Woman: /s/ sleeps, works; /z/ plays, studies; /ɪz/ exercises, teaches

Unit 3 • Numbers

page 15

Listening task 1 • On the phone

A Listen. People are calling for information. What places do they ask about? Check the correct places.

1. Sydney, Australia

[*phone rings*]

Operator: Directory assistance.
Woman: Yes, I'd like the number of the Hyatt Hotel in Sydney, please.
Operator: The Park Hyatt, ma'am?
Woman: That's right, the Park Hyatt on Hickson Road.
Operator: The number is oh-two, nine-two-four-one, one-two-three-four.
Woman: Nine-two-four-one, one-two-three-four. Thank you. Oh, that's area code oh-two?
Operator: Yes, area code oh-two.

2. São Paulo, Brazil

[*phone rings*]

Hotel clerk: Front desk. How may I help you?
Woman: Yes, I need the phone number for the American Chamber of Commerce, please.
Hotel clerk: The American Chamber of Commerce. Just a minute, please. The city code of São Paulo is one-one. The Chamber of Commerce is five-one-eight-oh, three-eight-oh-four.
Woman: Um. City code one-one and then . . . I'm sorry, could you repeat that?
Hotel clerk: Sure, one-one, five-one-eight-oh, three-eight-oh-four.
Woman: So I dial one-one, five-one-eight-oh, three-eight-oh-four.
Hotel clerk: Yes, that's right.

3. Seoul, South Korea

[*phone rings*]

Hotel clerk: Good morning. Front desk. How may I help you?
Man: Hi. I need the phone number for the National Tourism Organization, please.
Hotel clerk: National Tourism Organization. Just a moment. Here it is. The number is seven-two-nine-nine, four-nine-six, four-nine-nine.
Man: I'm sorry. Did you say seven-nine-two-nine?
Hotel clerk: No. Seven-*two*-nine-nine. The number is seven-two-nine-nine, four-nine-six, four-nine-nine.
Man: OK. Great. Thanks.

4. Toronto, Canada.

[*phone rings*]

Operator: Directory assistance.

Man: Yes, the Toronto Blue Jays. I want to buy baseball tickets. So the Blue Jays . . . their ticket office, please.

Operator: The Blue Jays' Ticket office? Just a minute.

Automated voice: That number is one, eight-eight-eight, six-five-four, six-five-two-nine.

Man: One, eight-eight-eight, six-five-four, six-five-two-nine.

5. Tokyo, Japan

[*phone rings*]

Receptionist: United States Embassy.

Woman: Yes, what time does the American Center Library open tomorrow?

Receptionist: The American Center is in a different building, ma'am. The number for the library is oh-three, three-four-three-six, oh-nine-oh-one.

Woman: Let's see. Oh-three, three-four-three-six, oh-nine-oh-one?

Receptionist: That's right.

Woman: Thank you.

6. Mexico City, Mexico.

[*phone rings*]

Hotel clerk: Front desk.

Woman: Could I have the local number for Colombia Airlines, please?

Hotel clerk: Yes, just a minute. It's five-two-eight-three, five-five-oh-oh.

Woman: Five-two-eight-three, five-five-oh-oh. Thank you.

Hotel clerk: You're quite welcome.

page 15

B Listen again. Write the phone numbers for the places.

[*Replay Listening task 1 • Exercise A, track 14*]

page 16

Listening task 2 • Team scores

A Listen. These teams are in a basketball tournament. Which team wins each game? Write the first letter of the team's name in the circles.

Sportscaster: Hello, sports fans and welcome to *This Week in Sports*. The big news this week, of course, is the basketball championship. It started out with game one on Friday. The Lions won. The score: Lions, ninety-four, Hawks, sixty-eight. That score again, the Lions won. Lions ninety-four, Hawks sixty-eight.

The next game, game two, was between the Tigers and the Eagles. The Eagles won. But they won by just four points. The score: one-hundred three to ninety-nine. Again, the Eagles one-oh-three, the Tigers ninety-nine.

In game three, the Panthers played the Bears. The Panthers beat the Bears eighty-seven to seventy-three. Too bad, Bears fans. Your boys went down eighty-seven to seventy-three.

And in the last game on Friday, the Rockets beat the Comets. The Rockets won seventy-two to sixty-five. Rockets seventy-two, Comets sixty-five.

Then on Saturday, we saw some real action. In game one, it was the Lions against the Eagles. And the Lions won with ninety-two points. The Eagles had eighty points. The score: Lions ninety-two, Eagles eighty.

And in the other big game on Saturday, the Rockets beat the Panthers one-hundred seven to eighty-six. The Rockets over the Panthers by twenty-one points.

That brings us to the championship game today. It was the Lions against the Rockets. Both teams played well, but today, the Rockets were better. The final score: The Rockets one-oh-nine, the Lions ninety-eight. So the new champions are the Rockets. Rockets one-oh-nine, Lions ninety-eight.

That's it for basketball action. Turning to the excitement of professional bowling, it was a crazy day . . .

page 16

B Listen again. Write the score for each game in the chart.

[*Replay Listening task 2 • Exercise A, track 15*]

page 17

Your turn to talk • Numbers, numbers

B

1. Listen and practice. Notice the stress on the first syllable for numbers that end in T-Y. Numbers that end in T-E-E-N have the stress on the last syllable.

Woman: twenty, thirty, forty, fifty, sixty, seventy, eighty, ninety, thirteen, fourteen, fifteen, sixteen, seventeen, eighteen, nineteen

B

2. Listen. Which numbers are correct? Circle them.

a.

Man: Could you stop by after work? I'm at **Six**teen
thirteen Main Street.
Woman: Sixteen **thir**ty?
Man: No, one-three. Thir**teen**.

b.

Woman: Our basketball team won by
seven**teen** points!
Man: **Seven**ty points? That's amazing!
Woman: No, not **seven**ty. Seven**teen**.

c.

Woman: That's a great video game. How much does
it cost?
Man: Let's see. Wow, **for**ty dollars. That's a lot.
Woman: I don't know, four**teen** dollars sounds pretty
cheap to me.
Man: No, I said **for**ty dollars, four-zero.

d.

Man: Let's see, you're in Math one-oh-one. That's
room nine**teen**, with Mr. Lopez.
Woman: Excuse me. Did you say room nine**teen**?
Man: Yes, room nine**teen**. It's right over there.
Woman: OK. Thank you.

e.

Man: Hey, how did you do on the English test?
Woman: Oh, not too bad. I got an **eigh**ty.
Man: An eigh**teen**? I thought you did well!
Woman: What do you mean? An **eigh**ty's pretty good!
Man: Oh, an **eigh**ty. Yeah, that is pretty good.

f.

[*on the phone*]
Woman: Hello, how much are concert tickets?
Ticket agent: **Twen**ty dollars for adults and six**teen**
dollars for children under twelve.
Woman: Six**teen** dollars for children?
Ticket agent: Yes, that's right.

Unit 4 • Let's eat!

page 19

Listening task 1 • What would you like?

A Listen. People are ordering food in a restaurant.
Check their orders.

1. soup

Server: Have you decided?
Woman: Yes, I'd like some soup, please. What's the
soup of the day?

Server: Soup of the day? It's chicken vegetable.
Woman: Chicken vegetable? I don't think so. I don't
like vegetables very much. I guess I'll have the
French onion.
Server: French onion soup? Very good. And would
you like something to drink with that?

2. drink

Server: And what would you like to drink with that?
Man: Active Lemon. Large, please.
Server: OK. Would you like to try the new Active
Lemon Light? It's got no sugar or caffeine and just
one calorie.
Man: Hmm . . . I tried some the other day. No sugar
and *no* flavor. I'll go with the original one.
Server: One Active Lemon Original. You said large?
Man: Right.

3. toppings

Man: Let's see. Give me a . . . giant Monster Burger.
Server: One Monster Burger – giant size. And what
would you like on that?
Man: Pretty much everything. Ketchup, uh . . .
mustard, onions, lettuce, pickles, and, uh, tomatoes.
Server: Any mushrooms?
Man: Mushrooms? Yeah. They're good for me, right?
Server: How about cheese?
Man: No cheese. I'd better watch the fat.
Server: OK. One giant Monster Burger with
everything. Except . . . no cheese!
Man: Gotta start counting calories somewhere.
Server: Right.

4. salad

Server: And would you like a salad with that?
Woman: Yes, um, the garden salad. Are there
tomatoes in that?
Server: Yes ma'am. There are.
Woman: Oh, I don't like tomatoes much. How about
in the pasta salad?
Server: No tomatoes in that. There's broccoli and, uh,
mushrooms and onions, but no tomatoes.
Woman: Let me have the pasta salad then. And for
dessert, I'll have the chocolate cake.

page 19

B Listen again. Circle the correct information.

[*Replay Listening task 1 • Exercise A, track 18*]

page 20

Listening task 2 • This looks great!

A Listen. Which foods are the people talking about? Number the pictures from 1 to 6. There is one extra food item.

1.

Woman: Hey, this is a nice restaurant. Let's eat here.

Man: It *is* nice, and the food's great. I've eaten here before.

Woman: OK. Let's check out the menu board.

Man: Sure.

Woman: Well, I know what I'm having for dessert. Just look at this picture!

Man: You'll get chocolate, right? You always get chocolate.

Woman: I know, but maybe I'll have vanilla today for something different.

Man: Wow! Vanilla? That's a change.

2.

Man: OK. Now that you've decided on dessert, let's order the real food!

Woman: All right. Hey, look at all the toppings on that. Mushrooms, onions, black olives, green peppers, and extra cheese. It looks great.

Man: Yeah, it looks delicious. I'm going to order one. A big one.

Woman: Can I have a slice of yours?

3.

Woman: Or we could get some of this. It looks really good, too.

Man: It *does* look good, but I can make it at home now. I'm taking a cooking class at the Asia Center. You know, it's actually pretty easy to make.

Woman: Really? So how do you get the rice to stick together?

Man: Oh, it's the kind of rice. You need to use short-grain rice. It's kind of sticky. You just stick it together with your hands and put a piece of raw fish on it.

Woman: Hmm. It sounds easy enough. Will you teach me sometime?

4.

Woman: Gee, these look good, too. What's in them?

Man: Well, you can get chicken or beef, and they have onions, peppers, and tomatoes in them.

Woman: Maybe I'll try one with beef.

Man: I've had them here before, and they're really spicy. You don't need to put hot sauce, salsa, or anything on them.

Woman: Hmm. I'm not sure I want spicy food. Maybe I'll try them some other day.

5.

Woman: Oh, that looks delicious. Mmm, with some lemon. I think I'll have *that*. Yep. I've decided.

Man: Gee, maybe I will, too. But I hope there aren't a lot of bones.

Woman: Oh, don't be silly. They'll take the bones out for you, and I'm sure it's fresh from the ocean. It'll taste delicious.

Man: That's true. I guess I *will* order that. Let's hurry up and order. I'm starving.

6.

Woman: Oh, and one last thing. With my dessert, I'm going to order a whole pot of that! I'll be sleepy after all that food.

Man: And you'll add lots of cream and sugar, right?

Woman: No, no. Just black. I don't want to overdo it!

Man: I know what you mean. Well, are you ready to order?

page 20

B Listen again. How did you know? Write the words that gave you the hints.

[*Replay Listening task 2 • Exercise A, track 19*]

page 21

Your turn to talk • The Food Game

B

1. Listen and practice. Notice the intonation of *W-H* questions.

Woman: What's your favorite fast food?
What's a food you hate?
When do you eat dinner?
Where do you eat lunch?

B

2. Listen. Do you hear *What, When,* or *Where*? Check the correct answers.

a.

Woman: What would you like to order?

b.

Woman: Where are you going for dinner?

c.

Woman: What is your favorite snack?

d.

Woman: When do you eat breakfast?

e.

Woman: When do you eat special food?

f.

Woman: Where is your favorite restaurant?

Expansion 1 • Thailand

page 22

Listening task 1 • Information

A Listen. People are talking about Thailand. What are the topics? Circle the correct answers.

1.

Woman: Every year, people go to Thailand to visit the famous sites, the beautiful forests and beaches, and to learn about Thai culture. What do you know about Thai culture? In Thailand, people use the *wai* greeting when they meet friends and family. To do the *wai,* put your hands together in front of you and bow your head. When you greet friends, put your hands in front of your chest. For people who are older or more important, like parents or teachers, put your hands a little higher, in front of your head. This shows respect.

2.

Man: Who lives in Thailand? Thailand is made up of people from several different countries. About seventy-five percent of the people are Thai. About eleven percent are Chinese. Many years ago, their families came from China. And a few people are Malay. Their families were originally from Malaysia. About three-point-five percent of people living in Thailand are Malay. So the Thais are a mix of different people.

3.

Woman: You can't talk about Thai culture without talking about families. In the past, everyone in the family lived together, that is, with their grandparents, uncles and aunts, and cousins all in the same house. Today, more people live in smaller families. About fifty percent of Thais live just with their parents and brothers and sisters. But about thirty percent still live in bigger families.

4.

Man: Thais love food, and they love to talk about it. Food is always fresh. People usually buy fresh food every day, especially fruits and vegetables. And Thai food is quite spicy. Thais cook with a lot of different kinds of hot peppers. They don't eat a lot of meat, but there is usually a little beef, chicken, or fish in every dish. And, of course, rice. Most Thais eat rice every day.

page 22

B Listen again. Are the statements true or false? Check the correct answers.

[*Replay Listening task 1 • Exercise A, track 22*]

page 23

Listening task 2 • Food

A Listen. A woman is talking about two popular dishes in Thailand. What is in each dish? Check the things. There are two extra items for each dish.

1. Thai green curry

Interviewer: What are some of the most popular dishes in Thailand?

Woman: Well, one of the most popular dishes is definitely curry. Many Thais eat some kind of curry with rice every day. But actually, the most popular Thai dish is Thai green curry.

Interviewer: I see. What do you put in Thai green curry?

Woman: Well, let's see. We usually put coconut milk in it. And we put in garlic . . . lots of garlic, if you like it spicy. And, um, cut-up slices of chicken, and some basil leaves, . . . and something that I don't know the name of in English. They look like green beans, but they're very, very spicy.

Interviewer: Hot peppers?

Woman: Yes, peppers, that's it.

Interviewer: Sounds delicious.

2. pad Thai

Interviewer: So what's your favorite dish?

Woman: I love pad Thai. That's a popular dish in Thailand and in the U.S., too.

Interviewer: Yes, I've seen it on the menu at the Thai restaurant near my house. How do you make pad Thai?

Woman: Well, it's made with noodles and, um, it usually has some shrimp and bean sprouts. And some green onions and peanuts on top. But you know, the pad Thai in the U.S. is not the same as in Thailand. In Thailand it's sweet like it is here, but it's also very spicy – much spicier than it is here in the U.S. That's the way I like it – the real Thai way.

Interviewer: Mmm. I didn't know there was such a big difference. Are there any Thai dishes that aren't so spicy?

Woman: Oh, sure! Not all Thai dishes are spicy, you know. We have a lot of different kinds of salads, vegetables, rice and noodle dishes . . .

page 23

B Listen again. Circle the correct information.

[*Replay Listening task 2 • Exercise A, track 23*]

Unit 5 • Free time

page 25

Listening task 1 • How often?

A Listen. People are talking about their free-time activities. How often do they do them? Write *always, often, sometimes, hardly ever,* or *never.*

1.
Woman: Do you ever play sports in the afternoon?
Man: Me? Oh, hardly ever. I work from one to six during the week, so I can't play sports in the afternoon. Once a month, I have the afternoon off – then I go swimming.

2.
Man: How often do you go to the movies on weekends?
Woman: On weekends? Well, sometimes I go to the movies on weekends, and sometimes I go during the week, especially if there's a movie I really want to see. I like to watch movies on the big screen. They're just not as exciting at home on DVD.

3.
Woman: How often do you watch TV at night?
Man: At night? Well, I guess I always watch TV. I watch every night. I know I should study, but there are so many programs I like. So, I have to say I watch TV a lot. More than I should!

4.
Man: How often do you go to a club?
Woman: Me? Never! I went to a club once with some friends, but it wasn't my thing. I haven't gone back. I didn't enjoy it at all. I *hate* dancing in front of people. As a matter of fact, I never plan to go back again.

5.
Woman: Do you ever go out for lunch?
Man: Do you mean out to a restaurant? Yeah, I do. Often, actually.
Woman: How many times a week would you say?
Man: Oh . . . maybe three or four times. I like to eat lunch with my friends. Sometimes we go out to a fast food place; sometimes we go to the student union. Yeah, I'd say about three or four times a week.

6.
Man: Do you ever visit relatives on Sunday?
Woman: Yes, my cousins and I visit my grandparents every Sunday. My grandmother likes to make a big dinner for us, and we talk about the week. I love my grandmother's cooking, so I always visit my grandparents on Sunday.

page 25

B Listen again. Circle the reasons.
[*Replay Listening task 1 • Exercise A, track 24*]

page 26

Listening task 2 • What's popular?

A Listen. People in the U.S. spend their free time in the evening in different ways. Number the activities from 1 to 9.

1.
Husband: What do you want to do tonight?
Wife: Well, I'm not sure. I guess I was just planning to watch TV like we usually do.
Husband: Well, a lot of other people are doing the same thing.
Wife: What do you mean?
Husband: According to this survey in the newspaper, a lot of people in the U.S. choose to watch TV or DVDs in the evening.
Wife: Really?
Husband: Yeah. Twenty-six percent of the people say that's their favorite way to spend their free time in the evening.

2.
Wife: What else does the survey say? What's the second most popular activity?
Husband: Let's see here. Ah, it says the second most popular activity is staying home with family. Yeah. Twenty-five percent of the people in *this* survey think so.

3.
Wife: This is interesting. I mean, I like finding out what other people do in the evening. So, what's the third activity?
Husband: Number three on the list is . . . just resting or relaxing.
Wife: Hmm. That's what *I* really like doing after a long day at work.
Husband: Well, you're not alone. Nine percent of the people chose that one.

4.
Wife: OK. Keep going. What do other people do in their free time?
Husband: Let's see here. [*rustling of newspaper*] Aha! Here's *my* favorite way to spend an evening.
Wife: Wait – don't tell me . . . reading!
Husband: Yes! Reading is number four. And another nine percent of the people said they spend their evenings reading.

5.

Wife: Hey, all those activities are things people do at home. Doesn't anybody go out in the evening?

Husband: Yes, they do. In fact, the next most popular choice was getting together with friends.

Wife: How many people chose that?

Husband: Eight percent.

Wife: Eight percent, huh? You know, we should get together with our friends more often.

6.

Husband: You want to know where else people go in the evening?

Wife: Sure. Where else do they go?

Husband: Next on the list is going out to the movies or a play.

Wife: Oh, yeah? Do a lot of people do that?

Husband: Five percent of them do.

7.

Wife: Hey, I'm getting hungry. What should we have for dinner tonight?

Husband: Funny you should say that. The next thing on the survey is eating out. Five percent of the people in the U.S. chose that one.

8.

Wife: That seems like a lot of different activities. I can't imagine what else people do with their free time.

Husband: Well, some people say they spend the evening playing a sport or exercising.

Wife: That's a great idea. Let's get out there and join them!

Husband: Whoa, wait a minute. It's not *that* popular of an activity. Only three percent say they do that.

9.

Wife: OK, so what do all the rest of the people like to do?

Husband: That's a good question. It doesn't really say. Ten percent of the people chose "other." It could be anything, really. . . . So, honey, what do you want to do tonight? You name it!

page 26

B Listen again. What percent of the people do each activity? Write the percents in the chart.

[*Replay Listening task 2 • Exercise A, track 25*]

page 27
Your turn to talk • My free time

B

1. Listen and practice. Notice that the important words in the sentences are stressed.

Woman: I like **shopping** with **friends**.
You like **reading** on rainy **days**.
I don't like going to the **movies alone**.
Joe doesn't like staying **home** on **weekends**.

B

2. Circle the stressed words in the sentences. Then listen and check your answers.

a.
Woman: On rainy **days**, I like staying **home**.

b.
Woman: She likes playing **sports** with **friends**.

c.
Woman: I don't like **watching TV**.

d.
Woman: He doesn't like **visiting relatives**.

e.
Woman: I like **swimming** after **class**.

f.
Woman: You don't like **studying alone**.

CD 2
Unit 6 • Great outfit!

page 29
Listening task 1 • Choosing an outfit

A Listen. Megan is telling her friend Erica what she's planning to wear to a party. Number the items from 1 to 6. There are two extra items.

1.

[*cell phone rings*]
Megan: Hello?
Erica: Hi, Megan. What are you doing?
Megan: Oh, hi, Erica. I'm getting my clothes ready for the party tonight.
Erica: Oh, right, Josh's party! So, what are you wearing?
Megan: Well, I think I'm going to wear my blue dress.
Erica: What blue dress?
Megan: You know, the one with short sleeves and a white stripe across the top.
Erica: Oh, the summer one? No, Megan, uh-uh. It's going to be too cold for that.

2.

Megan: OK, maybe not. Maybe I'll wear a skirt.

Erica: Good idea. You've got some nice skirts.

Megan: Maybe the black one . . . or the plaid one.

Erica: Oh, the blue and green plaid one?

Megan: Yes. It's short, but it's not too short, and it looks good on me.

Erica: Yeah, and plaid is really in right now.

3.

Erica: And then you need a blouse, right?

Megan: Oh! I just remembered! I bought the cutest blouse last week! You haven't seen it yet.

Erica: What does it look like?

Megan: It's yellow – light yellow – with pink and blue flowers on it. It's *so* pretty.

Erica: Megan, flowers? With a plaid skirt? I don't think so.

4.

Megan: Oh, right. Well, I also have a white blouse. It isn't fancy, but it looks nice with the skirt.

Erica: It doesn't have any stripes or checks or flowers or anything like that, does it?

Megan: No, it's just white.

Erica: White? Great! That will match your skirt.

5.

Erica: The party's indoors, right?

Megan: Well, dinner is indoors, but I'm sure we'll be outside some of the time, too.

Erica: Oh, won't you be cold in just a skirt and blouse?

Megan: Well, I'll bring a sweater. I have one that matches my skirt perfectly.

Erica: You mean . . . a plaid sweater?

Megan: No, a blue sweater, the same blue that's in the skirt.

Erica: Oh, OK!

6.

Megan: OK. My plaid skirt, my white blouse, my blue sweater . . . and my favorite cap.

Erica: Wait a minute. I know that cap, and I know it's your favorite, but Megan, it's not the same plaid as your skirt. And you don't really need a cap. Well, Megan. I've got to get going. I have to figure out what *I'm* going to wear!

page 29

B Listen again. Does Erica like Megan's choices? Check the correct answers.

[*Replay Listening task 1 • Exercise A, track 1*]

page 30

Listening task 2 • The meaning of colors

A Listen. What do these colors mean for some people? Match the colors with the words.

1. red

Woman: Red is a powerful color and can be a symbol of strength. Wear something red when you feel good about yourself or want to attract attention. In many Asian countries, the color red brings luck, and in China, brides wear red wedding dresses.

2. green

Man: If you go to the hospital in the U.S., you might see the staff wearing green uniforms. Doctors often wear green pants and green shirts. That's because green relaxes people. It helps sick people feel better. Green is also associated with plants and nature.

3. yellow

Woman: People often associate this bright color with sunshine and happy feelings. Maybe that's why yellow is a popular color for babies' clothes. Yellow is also easy to see, so some sports teams have yellow uniforms, and many information signs are yellow.

4. black

Man: Advice from color experts can sometimes influence what people wear. For example, fashion experts recommend people wear black if they want to look thinner because dark colors make people look thinner. So, if you're trying to look thinner, solid colors might look better than stripes or checks.

5. blue

Woman: When you think of the police, what color clothes do you imagine? In many places, police uniforms are blue, a color that people associate with loyalty. Blue is also a good color to wear to a job interview. It can create good feelings. It can show you are a loyal worker who will work many years for the company.

6. white

Man: Brides in North America and Europe traditionally wear white dresses to symbolize purity. However, in some Asian countries, white is associated with death. In China, white gifts are brought to funerals when someone dies. In Nepal, the oldest son traditionally wears white clothing for one year after the death of a parent.

page 30

B Listen again. Circle the correct information.

[*Replay Listening task 2 • Exercise A, track 2*]

page 31

Your turn to talk • Find the differences

B

1. Listen and practice. Notice the contractions for *is* and *is not*.

Woman: He's wearing sandals.
She's wearing a black skirt.
He isn't wearing a hat.
She isn't wearing a flowered shirt.

B

2. Listen. Do you hear the contraction for *is* or *is not*? Check the correct answers.

a.
Woman: She isn't wearing a sweater.

b.
Woman: He's wearing a striped tie.

c.
Woman: She's wearing a flowered dress.

d.
Woman: He isn't wearing socks.

e.
Woman: He's wearing a T-shirt and blue jeans.

f.
Woman: She isn't wearing a jacket.

Unit 7 • In the house

page 33

Listening task 1 • Where does it go?

A Listen. Justin and Alex are roommates. Check the six things they are going to buy for their apartment.

1.
Justin: OK, let's get in and out of here. I hate shopping.
Alex: Well, we have to do it. Come on. This store is great, and it's not very expensive. The first thing we need is something else to sit on. Hey, how about this one?
Justin: I like it. It's really comfortable. Try it.
Alex: It does feel good. And three people can sit on it. It's big, though.
Justin: No problem. We can put it under the big window.
Alex: Yeah. I think it'll fit under the window.

2.
Justin: And speaking of the window, we need these.
Alex: Yeah, I suppose. But yellow?

Justin: What's wrong with yellow?
Alex: Oh, I don't know.
Justin: Well, then, how about these dark blue ones?
Alex: Those are better. But only on the big window, OK?

3.
Justin: Like it or not, we're going to be studying. This would be useful. It's really bright.
Alex: Really? I don't think we need it.
Justin: But I like to read at night. I can put it on the little table between the bookshelf and the chair.
Alex: OK. If you really think you need it, go ahead.

4.
Justin: Hey! Look over here. I love this! It has great purple flowers. And it looks so healthy!
Alex: Yeah, because it's not real. Are you sure you want an artificial one? And where are we going to put it?
Justin: Well, it's so small. We can put it next to the vase on the coffee table. And we won't have to water it!
Alex: OK. If you say so.

5.
Justin: Whoa, look at this. We need to watch some movies. We can't study *all* the time. We have to get this.
Alex: Are you crazy? That's pretty expensive! And we already have a TV.
Justin: Yeah, but don't you like to watch movies?
Alex: Where are we going to put it? We don't have enough room.
Justin: Yes, we do. We can put it right under the TV. Come on, if we each pay half . . .
Alex: Well, OK.

6.
Alex: Well, I think we have everything. Let's get out of here.
Justin: Wait, I'm just going to get this.
Alex: It's got a nice frame, but what's it supposed to be?
Justin: I don't know. But it looks cool. It's got great colors, and the price includes the frame. I'm going to put it on the wall next to the clock.
Alex: You know, for someone who doesn't like shopping, you're sure buying a lot!

page 33

B Listen again. Where are they going to put the things? Number the picture from 1 to 6. There is one extra space.

[Replay Listening task 1 • Exercise A, track 5]

Listening task 2 • Where's the heater?

A How do people keep their houses warm in different countries? Circle the heater in each room. Then listen and check your answers.

1. Syria

Woman: People think the Middle East is very warm, and it is. But it can get cold during the winter. I visited my grandparents in Syria last winter. Wow, it was really cold for about a week. Fortunately, they had a great heater. Some houses have a large heater that heats the whole house. My grandparents' house had a very big heater in the living room.

2. Germany

Man: When I visited my friend in Germany last year, she explained that some of the houses have a heater called a *kachelofen*. In her house, it's in the living room. It has a metal door. The front is covered with tiles. Wood burns inside it, and the tiles get very warm. After all the wood has burned, the *kachelofen* heats the house for two or three more days.

3. South Korea

Woman: I used to live in South Korea. It can get really cold during the winter, but the house I lived in had an *ondol* floor. That's a floor with pipes under it. The pipes carry hot water, and the hot pipes heat up the whole floor. The entire floor is a heater.

4. Japan

Man: I loved living in Japan. They have this kind of heater called a *kotatsu*. It's electric. It's in a low table, under the tabletop. When you sit at the table, the *kotatsu* keeps your legs warm. Of course, there are other ways to stay warm. Many homes have large electric heaters, too.

B Listen again. Did the people visit or live in the countries? Check the correct answers.

[*Replay Listening task 2 • Exercise A, track 6*]

Your turn to talk • My room

B

1. Listen and practice. Notice the pronunciation of plural *-s* endings.

Woman: /s/, /z/, /ɪz/

/s/: book, books, lamp, lamps
/z/: window, windows, chair, chairs
/ɪz/: vase, vases, brush, brushes

B

2. Write these words in the correct columns. Then listen and check your answers.

Woman: /s/ photographs, plants; /z/ bookshelves, curtains; /ɪz/ dishes, glasses

Unit 8 • Time

Listening task 1 • Changing plans

A Listen. Some people are changing plans. Cross out the old information. Write any new information.

1.

Woman: So we're meeting at seven-thirty in front of Hayes Hall, right?

Man: Well, how about a bit earlier? Would you like to get something to eat before the concert?

Woman: That'd be nice.

Man: OK. About six-thirty?

Woman: Ah, well, could we meet at a quarter after six? Give ourselves a little more time.

Man: Quarter after six, in front of Hayes Hall. Got it. No problem.

Woman: No, wait a minute. Let's meet at Museum Café instead. We can eat there.

Man: OK. Sure. Six-fifteen in front of Museum Café. See you there!

2.

Airport announcer: Attention passengers on China Pacific Airways flight C-A thirty-nine to Taipei. Due to poor weather conditions in the Taipei area, fight C-A thirty-nine has been delayed. The flight will now depart at eight o'clock. Flight C-A thirty-nine to Taipei will leave at eight o'clock from gate eleven.

Man: Oh no! Eight o'clock! We've got a long wait ahead of us. Why don't we go get something to eat.

3.

[*phone rings*]

Nicole: Hello.

Tony: Hi, Nicole. This is Tony.

Nicole: Oh, hi. Hey, I'm looking forward to our lunch tomorrow.

Tony: Uh, that's what I'm calling about. We were supposed to meet at noon, right?

Nicole: Yeah, noon at the Bangkok Café.

Tony: You know, that place gets really crowded around noon. We'll probably have to wait a long time for a table.

Nicole: OK. How about the Plaza then?

Tony: Good idea. The Plaza has great food. How about meeting at twelve-thirty so we miss the crowd there?

Nicole: Hmm. Is a quarter past OK?

Tony: Sure. Twelve-fifteen at the Plaza. I'll be there!

4.

[*phone rings*]

Secretary: English Department.

Daniel: Hi, uh, this is Daniel Smith. I'm in Professor Barton's Advanced English class.

Secretary: Yes, hello, Daniel.

Daniel: We have a test today, but I'm really sick. I don't know what to do. I don't want to miss the test.

Secretary: Don't worry. Professor Barton has a make-up day scheduled. I mean, if you're really sick, you can take the test on another day.

Daniel: Oh, great. When is the make-up day?

Secretary: It's on Wednesday morning at eight-fifteen.

Daniel: Wednesday at a quarter past eight? I'll be there. Thanks!

Secretary: Hope you feel better!

page 37

B Listen again. Circle the correct reason for each change.

[*Replay Listening task 1 • Exercise A, track 9*]

page 38

Listening task 2 • Time and cultures

A Listen. Some students are talking about time in different countries. Number the pictures from 1 to 4. There is one extra picture.

1.

Woman 1: I hear you just got back from Brazil, John. Did you enjoy yourself?

John: I had a wonderful time. Well, speaking of time, actually . . . I had a little problem with Brazilian time.

Woman 1: Really? What happened?

John: Well, I gave a dinner party one night. I invited everyone to come at seven-thirty, so I had dinner on the table by then, but I had no guests!

Woman 1: Ah, I bet they all came about nine-thirty, right?

John: Yeah. They came at nine-thirty, two hours late.

Woman 1: Two hours late? That's right on time in Brazil!

2.

Man 1: I had a similar problem here in the U.S. I was invited to my professor's house. He said to come at seven. I arrived at about seven-ten, but I guess it was a little early.

John: Why? What did your professor say?

Man 1: He didn't say anything. He was still in the shower. His wife opened the door.

John: So they were still getting ready? Well, Americans usually show up at a party about twenty or thirty minutes late. But you weren't *too* early.

Man 1: Really? I was very embarrassed.

John: Oh, don't worry about it. Your professor should have been ready to greet his guests!

3.

Woman 2: Time is really different in my country. I invited some American friends to my wedding in Morocco. The invitation said to come at nine P.M., but I told them to come much later than nine. Moroccan weddings last all night, you know. Well, anyway, they came at about ten-thirty.

Woman 1: Ten-thirty? Were they late then?

Woman 2: Late? No, I was still getting ready. The wedding actually started at midnight. I felt bad. I should have told them to come really, really late, for them.

4.

John: You know a country that's *really* on time? Switzerland.

Man 1: Did you have some trouble?

John: Well, I had to get used to some differences. You know how the buses *here* are always a little late.

Man 1: Yes.

John: Once I had to catch a bus to the airport. The schedule said the next bus was at ten-seventeen, so I arrived at the bus stop at ten-eighteen, but there was no bus. The bus had left at exactly ten-seventeen, so I missed it!

Man 1: Really? I think I'd like Switzerland!

page 38

B Listen again. Circle the correct times.

[*Replay Listening task 2 • Exercise A, track 10*]

page 39

Your turn to talk • Making plans

B

1. Listen and practice. Notice the pronunciation of *want to* /wɑnə/ and *have to* /hæftə/.

Woman: *want to* /wɑnə/, *have to* /hæftə/

Do you want to go to a movie on Saturday?

Man: Sure. I have to work until six P.M. How about seven?

Woman: Do you want to go out on Friday?

Man: I'm sorry. I can't. I have to work.

B

2. Listen. Do you hear *want to* /wɑnə/ or *have to* /hæftə/? Check the correct answers.

a.
Woman: I want to have a cup of coffee.

b.
Woman: I want to see a movie tonight.

c.
Woman: Do you have to call your friend?

d.
Woman: Do you want to play tennis this weekend?

e.
Woman: Do you have to go to class soon?

f.
Woman: I have to work this evening.

Expansion 2 • Kuwait

page 40

Listening task 1 • Information

A Listen. People are talking about Kuwait. What are they talking about? Number the pictures from 1 to 4. There is one extra picture.

1.
Woman: Kuwait is a country in the Middle East. It's located between Iraq and Saudi Arabia. Kuwait City is the capital of the country. It is very modern and busy, and it is the center of Kuwaiti business. Today, Kuwaiti life is an interesting mix of modern and traditional styles. Kuwaitis like their modern lifestyles, but they also still enjoy their old customs, too.

2.
Man: Kuwait City is always busy, especially the area of Salmiya, the place where young Kuwaitis go to find their favorite fashions. There you may see one of the old-style Kuwaiti covered markets between modern Western shops and restaurants. Shopping hours are Saturday through Thursday, nine A.M. to one P.M., and then again from four-thirty P.M. to nine P.M.

3.
Woman: In their free time, people often gather in coffee shops. In the morning and afternoon hours, they are filled with women visiting with each other while their children play together. But the coffee shops are the most popular with the older gentlemen, who gather in the evenings to drink tea or coffee, and to relax and talk with their friends.

4.
Man: Sports are an important part of Kuwaiti life. Since Kuwait is on the coast, people enjoy water sports like swimming, wind surfing, and water skiing. For many Kuwaitis, soccer is the most popular sport. There are over one hundred twenty soccer fields in the country, and Kuwaitis hardly ever miss a match when their team is playing. Traditional sports, such as horse racing, are also still popular in Kuwait.

page 40

B Listen again. Circle the correct answers.

[*Replay Listening task 1 • Exercise A, track 13*]

page 41

Listening task 2 • Clothing styles

A Listen. A woman is describing women's clothing styles in Kuwait. Which style is she talking about? Check *Islamic, Western,* or *both.*

1.
Interviewer: Hello, Fatema. Thank you for agreeing to speak with me about your country, Kuwait.
Fatema: My pleasure.
Interviewer: I'd like to ask you about the style of dress there, in particular for women. Could you tell me what kind of clothes typical Kuwaiti women wear?
Fatema: Typical Kuwaiti women? Well, Kuwait is really a mix of different cultures. Actually, only forty-five percent of the people who live in Kuwait are Kuwaiti. Fifty-five percent come from other countries. You can see the influence of these different cultures in women's clothing. There are two main styles of dress for Kuwaiti women: Islamic and Western dress. It's interesting. In a group of friends, it's possible to see both clothing styles at the same time; some women might wear Islamic dress and some Western.

2.
Interviewer: Oh, that's very interesting. Can you tell me some more about women's clothing styles?
Fatema: OK, sure. The Islamic style originally came from Saudi Arabia. Women usually cover their hair and their clothes when they are outside the house. The *hijab* is kind of a scarf that covers the head and hair, but not the face. With the *hijab,* women usually wear a long, black coat called an *abaya* over their clothes when they leave the house. The *abaya* is made of silk and has big, wide sleeves.

3.

Interviewer: This is so interesting, Fatema.

Fatema: Yes, and did you know that designer clothing is especially popular? Kuwaiti women can find many Western styles in expensive designer shops in Kuwait City. In their homes, some women wear fashionable designer clothes from Paris, London, and New York: dresses, suits, or skirts and blouses. Many women enjoy wearing scarves and fine jewelry, too.

4.

Interviewer: So if both styles are popular, how does a Kuwaiti woman decide which style to wear?

Fatema: You know, the style of dress a woman chooses really depends on what she likes. Some women wear Western clothing at home or at work, and then wear a *hijab* and the *abaya* for afternoon visits or trips to the mall. It is pretty common for a Kuwaiti woman to wear both Islamic and Western styles on the same day, depending on where she goes and what she does.

Interviewer: Thank you very much, Fatema. I've enjoyed learning a little bit about Kuwaiti culture.

Fatema: You're very welcome.

page 41

B Listen again. Circle the correct information.

[Replay Listening task 2 • Exercise A, track 14]

Unit 9 • Movies

page 43

Listening task 1 • What's playing?

A Listen. What kinds of movies do you hear? Number the signs from 1 to 5. There is one extra sign.

1.

Jessica: Don't go!

Chris: I have to go, Jessica.

Jessica: When will you be back, Chris?

Chris: Soon, don't worry. I love you, Jessica. I'll always love you.

Jessica: I love you, too, Chris. Wait! Before you go, there's something I have to tell you.

2.

[noise]

Man: What's that noise?

Woman: It's so scary. Stay here! It's dangerous. You'll get hurt.

Man: There's nothing to be afraid of. I'm just going to go outside and take a look.

Woman: I don't think that's a good idea. There might be a vampire or something out there.

Man: Don't worry. I'll be right back.

3.

Man 1: OK. We're ready to start. Hey, what are you doing? You're going to hurt yourself.

Man 2: I'm fine. *[crash]* Ouch!

Man 1: Now, let me have that.

Man 2: OK. Here it is. Oops. *[crash]* Ouch!

4.

Robot: Captain, look. Approaching starship.

Captain: Can you see where it's from, Zork? Are they friendly?

Robot: Looks like the enemy, Captain.

Captain: Wait. Let's make sure. *[weapons fire]*

Robot: It's definitely the enemy, Captain.

Captain: Turn around, quick! Go the other way!

Robot: Yes, captain. Turning around.

5.

Police officer 1: There they go! Let's get them. Quick! Follow them.

Police officer 2: Look, they're wearing masks.

Police officer 1: Of course they're wearing masks, rookie. They just robbed a bank.

Police officer 2: Watch out! *[tires screech]*

Police officer 1: *[into police radio]* Need assistance, south on Fifth Avenue, approaching Elm. Over.

page 43

B Listen again. What's going on? Circle the correct information.

[Replay Listening task 1 • Exercise A, track 15]

page 44

Listening task 2 • Film critics

A Listen. What kinds of movies are the film critics talking about? Check the correct answers.

1.

Mark: Good evening and welcome to *A Night at the Movies*. I'm Mark.

Anna: And I'm Anna. Tonight we're going to look at this week's new films, starting with *Beyond the Moon*.

Mark: *Beyond the Moon* – what a movie! It's the story of a flight to Mars that gets into trouble. A team of robots saves the astronauts aboard a spaceship. The movie is full of space travel and lots of special effects.

Anna: I liked it, too. The special effects are wonderful. Go see this movie.

2.

Mark: Next, we have *A Man's Best Friend*. This is the funniest movie you will see all year. It's about a cat that can talk. The cat causes problems for his owner.

If you like good jokes and silly situations, this is the movie for you. You'll laugh the whole time.

Anna: Oh, I don't know, Mark. There aren't many laughs, and the story is stupid. There is nothing new about talking animals – boring.

3.

Mark: Well, Anna, I think we will agree on *San Francisco*. It's one of the best in a long time. The songs are great, and the dancing's fantastic.

Anna: I liked *San Francisco* a lot. It's about a girl who comes from a poor family. She works hard and becomes a famous nightclub singer. I don't usually like this kind of movie, but this was different. As you said, excellent singing and dancing.

4.

Mark: OK. Now to the next movie: *Running*. Car chases, car crashes, fights – this is a noisy, violent movie. It's about two police officers who are old friends. They travel across the country trying to avoid bad guys. It's totally boring.

Anna: I agree, Mark. I thought this movie was much too violent. It's just too much. Skip this movie.

5.

Mark: Our last movie is called *You and Me Alone*. It's the same old story. Two teenagers meet at school. At first, they don't like each other. Then things change, and they fall in love. Her family doesn't like him, so they have to meet secretly. I thought the acting was awful and the dialog was even worse.

Anna: Really? Oh, no, no, no, Mark. These are teenagers and they act like teenagers do. This is like Romeo and Juliet in jeans and T-shirts. It's a good movie – with good, young actors.

page 44

B Listen again. Do Mark and Anna like or dislike the movies? Circle the smile or the frown.

[*Replay Listening task 2 • Exercise A, track 16*]

page 45

Your turn to talk • My favorite movie

B

1. Listen and practice. Notice the contractions for *is* and *are*.

Woman: What's your favorite movie?
How's the acting?
Who's in it?
What're the special effects like?
How're the actors?
Who're the stars?

B

2. Listen. Do you hear the contraction for *is* or *are*? Check the correct answers.

a.
Woman: Who's your favorite actress?

b.
Woman: What're your favorite kinds of movies?

c.
Woman: What's the music like?

d.
Woman: What're the new horror movies like?

e.
Woman: How're the other actors?

f.
Woman: What's that new comedy like?

Unit 10 • A typical day

page 47

Listening task 1 • What's your schedule?

A Listen. Anne is looking for a roommate. She's asking Heather about her schedule. What are they talking about? Check the correct answers.

1.

Heather: [*door closes*] Wow, this is a lovely apartment.
Anne: Thank you. I'm pretty happy living here. So, you're a student, right?
Heather: Yes, I started at the university last year. I'm studying economics, so I'm pretty busy. It feels as if I'm always studying!
Anne: How many classes are you taking?
Heather: Four. My first class is at nine o'clock in the morning, so I get up at eight.

2.

Anne: Really? Hmm. I don't get up until about nine o'clock.
Heather: Oh, I'm really quiet in the morning. I just get up and leave for class.
Anne: You don't eat anything before you go?
Heather: No, not before. I eat when I get to school. I eat breakfast around eight-thirty, and then I'm ready for class at nine.

3.

Anne: What do you do after class?
Heather: Well, I have classes until eleven-thirty. After that, I usually go to the sports center and work out for at least an hour.
Anne: Really? What kind of exercise do you do?

Heather: Well, three days a week I swim. The other days I lift weights.

Anne: That's really great.

4.

Anne: And . . . where do you do your homework? I always do mine at Rick's Restaurant.

Heather: I go to the library on campus. I like it because it's very quiet, and there are nice big desks where I can work. And there are computers, so I can check my e-mail occasionally.

5.

Anne: How about in the evening? Do you eat at school with friends?

Heather: No, I like to make my own dinner. I eat pretty early, around five-thirty or six o'clock.

Anne: Oh, I usually eat around then, too.

Heather: Then we could eat together, if you like. I'm a pretty good cook!

Anne: Really? What do you like to cook?

Heather: Well, lots of things, but Italian is my specialty.

Anne: Oh, I love pizza and pasta.

6.

Anne: What do you do after dinner?

Heather: Well, I either read or watch TV. I don't go out much. I just don't have the time or the energy in the evening. I'm usually in bed by ten.

Anne: Well, I can't see any problems with your schedule. And . . . [*dog barks*] Max likes you! So that settles it. The rent is . . .

page 47

B Listen again. Circle the correct answers.

[*Replay Listening task 1 • Exercise A, track 19*]

page 48

Listening task 2 • Daily schedules

A Listen. People are talking about their daily schedules. Check the three activities each person mentions.

1. Alex Chan, office worker, Taipei

Alex: I get up at five-thirty in the morning. It takes me two hours to get to work on the train, so I leave my house at six-fifteen. I start work at eight-thirty, but I usually read the newspaper and have a cup of green tea before I start work. Then I check my e-mail. I always have so many messages! I eat lunch from twelve-fifteen to one. Work ends at five-thirty.

2. Sophie Martin, student, Paris

Sophie: My favorite day of the week is Wednesday because there is no school on Wednesdays. We go on Saturday mornings instead. So on Wednesdays, I sleep late – until eight-thirty or nine. I eat a small breakfast, just some bread and jam. I have a piano lesson at ten-thirty. Then I usually meet some of my friends. I get home around four-thirty and do my homework until dinnertime. After dinner, I watch TV with my brother.

3. Hannah Williams, server, Vancouver

Hannah: I work evenings, so I have to go to work at four-thirty. Things are pretty quiet then, so I clean my area and get ready. The first customers come around five-thirty, and things get really busy from about six. I take a break after dinnertime when things are slow. That's usually around eight-thirty. I work until ten, and then I take the bus home.

4. Emilio Maisano, store clerk, Rome

Emilio: I usually eat breakfast in my favorite café at eight. The store opens at nine-thirty. I have to get ready before we open, so I go to work at nine. Lunch time is from twelve-thirty to three-thirty. I always go home and eat lunch with my family. Sometimes I take a nap after lunch, and sometimes I walk around the city a little. Then I go back to work. I leave work at seven-thirty. I usually meet some friends, and we eat dinner together in a restaurant. We stay out pretty late – sometimes until midnight.

page 48

B Listen again. Write the correct times.

[*Replay Listening task 2 • Exercise A, track 20*]

page 49

Your turn to talk • The perfect schedule

B

1. Listen and practice. Notice the linked sounds of consonants and vowels.

Woman: Mia gets up at eight. [*getsupateight*] Next, she exercises at [*exercisesat*] the sports center. Then she has a [*hasa*] cup of [*cupof*] coffee. Finally, she arrives at [*arrivesat*] work and [*workand*] checks e-mail [*checksemail*].

B

2. Draw lines for the linked sounds. Then listen and check your answers.

a.

Woman: John works until five.

b.

Woman: He sometimes goes out for dinner.

c.

Woman: Then he takes a bus home.

d.

Woman: Rita wakes up at eleven.

e.

Woman: Then she drinks a cup of tea.

f.

Woman: She uses a computer at work.

Unit 11 • Locations

page 51

Listening task 1 • Where is it?

A Listen. Where are the places? Number the map from 1 to 6. There is one extra place.

1. Monkey Mountain

Dad: OK, kids, here we are at Safari Park. Remember, we only have about two hours. Maybe we should decide first what we want to see.

Boy: Let's check out Monkey Mountain. That sounds cool!

Girl: Yeah, Dad, can you find Monkey Mountain on the map?

Dad: It looks like it's on the other side of the zoo from here. Let me see. Yes, Monkey Mountain is on the other side of the zoo. It's across from People Bridge, next to the elephants, on the right.

2. Lion Land

[lion roars]

Girl: Whoa! What was that? That wasn't a lion was it, Dad? You know, I'm afraid of lions.

Dad: Well, I think it *was* a lion, honey. But don't worry; they're in cages. Now, let me see. Yes, Lion Land is across Crocodile River from the elephants, next to the Garden of Eating. Well, that's convenient. So kids, should we go to Lion Land after Monkey Mountain?

Boy: Sure! I like wild animals – big, wild animals.

Girl: Oh, no!

3. Children's Zoo

Dad: How about the Children's Zoo, kids?

Boy: Uh, I don't know. What kind of animals are in the Children's Zoo?

Dad: Well, lots of animals – rabbits, sheep. They're all very friendly, and you can feed them and hold some of them, too. The Children's Zoo is between Bear Country and Monkey Mountain.

Boy: We can see rabbits and sheep anytime. I want to see some unusual animals.

Girl: Oh, come on! I want to hold some real animals. Let's go.

4. Ice House

Boy: After the Children's Zoo, let's go to Ice House. They have penguins there. Penguins are so fun to watch. They're always doing something interesting.

Girl: Yeah, penguins!

Dad: OK, penguins. Let's see. . . . It looks like they're between the Garden of Eating and Water House, where the dolphins are.

5. Brazilian Rain Forest

Boy: Is there anything you want to see, Dad?

Dad: Well, I vote for the Brazilian Rain Forest. It's on our way back. See People Bridge on the map? It's the walkway that goes from Crocodile River to the Reptile Ranch. The Brazilian Rain Forest is under People Bridge, right next to the reptiles. Does that sound OK, kids?

Boy: Yeah, that's great. We're studying insects of the rainforest in school now.

Girl: Insects? Yuck! I thought we came here to see animals!

6. Life Science Center

Dad: Hey, look! The new Life Science Center is finally open. It's right over there, around the corner from the film shop. There's an exhibit there about how people can protect the environment, and it has a souvenir shop, too.

Boy: Oh, Dad. Can I get a T-shirt? Or a toy, like a rubber snake or something? Please?

Girl: Hey, yeah! I want one of those, too, and then one of those things . . .

page 51

B Listen again. Who wants to see these things? Check *boy, girl,* or *both*.

[Replay Listening task 1 • Exercise A, track 23]

page 52

Listening task 2 • Find the treasure

A Listen. A boy is playing a video game. Where is he? Number the places from 1 to 6. There are three extra places.

1.

Girl: Oh, wow, you're playing Treasure Temple! I love that game.

Boy: Yeah, and I think I'm on the last level, but now I don't know what to do. I have to find the treasure somehow.

Girl: Do you want me to help you? I've played this lots of times.

Boy: Sure. Uh, do I go straight?

Girl: Yes, but now turn left, before that rock.

Boy: Why?

Girl: Because there's a snake on it. See? He's dangerous!

2.

Boy: OK. So I turn left. And then what?

Girl: Look, see that tree? Go to the tree. Do you see a bag? Pick it up.

Boy: OK . . . Oh! There's money inside!

Girl: Yes, you need that to buy things.

3.

Girl: Now go back to the path and go straight ahead. Then turn left into the café.

Boy: Which one is the café?

Girl: Oh, it's the little building between the store and the red house.

Boy: OK, I'm in the café.

Girl: Use your money to buy an ice cream cone. Trust me, you'll need it.

4.

Girl: Good. Now go out and turn left. Then turn right. Now you're walking to the boat. See?

Boy: Yes. OK, what do I do when I get to the boat?

Girl: Give the man the ice cream cone. Then he'll give you his boat. Get in the boat. There are some bananas in it. You need to go across the lake.

5.

Girl: Now go across the lake to the big tree. Take a banana from the boat.

Boy: How many?

Girl: Just one. Now, climb the tree. At the top, there's a monkey. Give him the banana . . . Great! Did he give you something?

Boy: Yes, he gave me a key. It looks like the key to a door.

6.

Girl: Now get back in the boat, but this time go toward that temple. Get out of the boat in front of the temple. Now go around the temple to the right side. Do you see a small door?

Boy: Yes, there it is.

Girl: OK. Use your key to open the door and go inside. What do you see?

Boy: Is it the treasure? Oh . . . it's a map. There's another level.

Girl: That's right. Do you want more help?

Boy: Yes, please!

page 52

B Listen again. Circle the correct information.

[Replay Listening task 2 • Exercise A, track 24]

page 53
Your turn to talk • Map it!

B

1. Listen and practice. Notice the stress for clarification.

Woman: Did you say turn **right** or **left**?
Man: Turn **right**.
Woman: Should I go **straight** or turn **left**?
Man: Go **straight**.
Woman: Is it **next** to the café or **behind** the café?
Man: It's **next** to the café.

B

2. Circle the stressed words in the sentences. Then listen and check your answers.

a.
Woman: Is the restroom **across** from the café or **next** to it?

b.
Woman: What's next to the movie theater, the **aquarium** or the **bank**?

c.
Woman: Do I go **straight** or turn **right** at the bridge?

d.
Woman: Is the restroom around the corner from the **café** or the **aquarium**?

e.
Woman: Is the entrance on the **left** or the **right** of the food court?

CD 3
Unit 12 • Gifts

page 55
Listening task 1 • Gift-giving occasions

A Listen. What are the gift-giving occasions? Number the occasions from 1 to 6. There are two extra occasions.

1.

Tyler: Hi, Vanessa! What are you doing here?

Vanessa: Hi, Tyler. I'm trying to choose a retirement gift for my mother. She's retiring next month.

Tyler: Really? I didn't know that. Good for her. What are you going to get her?

Vanessa: Well, a few years ago she got really interested in photography. I know she wants to spend more time taking pictures after she retires.

Tyler: I know the perfect thing, then. Look at this.

Vanessa: Wow! It's so small! And thin! It looks like a credit card.

Tyler: Isn't it amazing? But it takes great pictures. I know – I have one myself.

2.

Woman 1: Oh, a gift catalog! What are you looking for?

Woman 2: I need a gift for my niece. Her high school graduation is in June.

Woman 1: Oh, how nice. What kinds of things does she like?

Woman 2: Well, she wears a lot of jewelry – you know, necklaces, bracelets, earrings . . .

Woman 1: Hmm. Well, look at this. What do you think? It's a nice size, and she could put a lot of things in it. The wood looks pretty, too.

Woman 2: I think she'll like it a lot. I think I'll get it!

3.

Greg: Hey, Steve! What are you up to?

Steve: Oh, hi, Greg. I'm looking for something for Father's Day.

Greg: Well, any of these would be great. Does your dad play a lot?

Steve: Yes, he's out on the court almost every weekend. He loves to be outside, and he loves to exercise.

4.

Woman: Excuse me. I'm looking for a birthday gift for my grandson. He really loves music. Could you recommend something?

Store clerk: Sure. What kind of music does he like?

Woman: Uh, I'm not really sure.

Store clerk: Well, uh, who are his favorite singers?

Woman: Oh, I can't remember. He's sixteen. Just give me something that kids that age like to listen to.

Store clerk: Well, why don't you get him one of these? Then he can choose his own music.

Woman: That's a great idea. I'll take one for fifty dollars.

5.

Man: I can't believe classes are almost over.

Woman: Yeah, I know. I think I'm going to get something for Professor Wang. She's been so helpful to me this year, and I just want to thank her.

Man: Well, why don't you get her one of these?

Woman: I'm sure she has one already – or several. But she's always drinking tea before class. I'm going to get her one of these.

Man: Good idea. Better get a large one!

6.

Store clerk: How can I help you, sir?

Man: Well, it's our anniversary today.

Store clerk: Congratulations. How many years have you been married?

Man: Just one.

Store clerk: Well, in that case, you'll want to get something special. How about some of these?

Man: Those are beautiful. And pink's her favorite color.

Store clerk: Would you like twelve, a dozen?

Man: Yes, please.

page 55

B Listen again. Which gifts are the people going to buy? Check the correct pictures.

[Replay Listening task 1 • Exercise A, track 1]

page 56

Listening task 2 • Gifts and cultures

A Listen. Sometimes the meanings of gifts are different among cultures. Cross out the items that are not good gifts.

1. China

Woman: Did I tell you I'm going to China on business? I have to buy some gifts before I leave.

Man: Good idea. What are you going to bring?

Woman: I was thinking of bringing some handkerchiefs. They're colorful, beautiful . . . also lightweight. I don't want to carry anything heavy.

Man: Uh, I don't think you should give handkerchiefs. They aren't good gifts in Chinese culture.

Woman: Why not?

Man: A handkerchief is a symbol of saying good-bye or ending a relationship.

Woman: Saying good-bye?

Man: Yeah, like when you're going away, and people are crying, so they need a handkerchief. Actually, I've heard that one of the best things to give is a dinner – not a present, but a big dinner. It's good for business.

2. Argentina

Woman: I'm going to Argentina to do a homestay and I need to bring some gifts for my family. Did you know that in Argentina you should never give clothes unless you know the person really well?

Man: Don't give clothes? Why not?

Woman: Clothes – even things like neckties – are too personal. Only good friends give clothes.

Man: Huh? I never thought of a tie as being personal, just uncomfortable. So what are you going to bring?

Woman: I don't know. Maybe a plant or something for the house.

3. Italy

Woman: [*shop door closes*] Hello. I'd like to buy some flowers. I want to give them to a friend who's from Italy. How about those? About ten, I guess, please.

Store clerk: Ma'am, I don't think you should give ten flowers. In Italy, even numbers – two, four, six, and so on – are bad luck.

Woman: Even numbers are bad luck? OK, I'll take nine flowers then.

4. Japan

Store clerk: May I help you?

Man: I'm going to stay with a family in Japan. I need to get something for them.

Store clerk: Pen sets are always a good gift.

Man: Oh, that's a good idea. Let's see. . . . Here are some sets with a pen and pencil and bigger sets with four pens.

Store clerk: You said you're going to Japan?

Man: Yeah.

Store clerk: Don't give a set of four pens, then. In fact, don't give four of anything.

Man: Why not?

Store clerk: The Japanese word for "four" sounds like the word for "death." It's bad luck.

Man: Thanks for telling me. I'll take the pen and pencil set, then.

Store clerk: Good choice. These sets make very good gifts. After all, pens write in any language!

Man: Uh . . . yeah. Right.

page 56

B Listen again. Why are the items not good gifts? Circle the correct answers.

[*Replay Listening task 2 • Exercise A, track 2*]

page 57

Your turn to talk • Gift exchange

B

1. Listen and practice. Notice the intonation and pause before names.

Woman 1: These flowers are for you, Maria.

Woman 2: Oh, thanks, Mieko. They're beautiful.

Man 1: Congratulations on your new job, Susan.

Woman 3: Oh, this is lovely, John! Thank you so much!

B

2. Listen. Does the speaker say the person's name? Check *yes* or *no*.

a.

Woman: Oh, thanks for the book. I love this writer.

b.

Woman: Thank you so much for remembering my birthday, Kent.

c.

Woman: A scarf! Just what I need, Tom!

d.

Woman: Wow. You got this in France? Thanks.

e.

Woman: Oh, today's Valentine's Day. Thanks for the chocolates.

f.

Woman: This is really beautiful, Dennis. Did you make it yourself?

Expansion 3 • Italy

page 58

Listening task 1 • Information

A Listen. People are talking about Italy. Which cities are they talking about? Number the pictures from 1 to 4. There is one extra picture.

1.

Woman: The capital of Italy is a very old and very famous city. Did you know that many movies are made in Italy? In fact, over one hundred movies a year are filmed in this old capital. Italian film is most famous for its romances and comedies. This city is a popular city for international films, too. Famous sites, such as the Coliseum and the Trevi Fountain, are favorite movie locations. One of the most popular films was the American hit *Roman Holiday,* made in nineteen fifty-three.

2.

Man: Every year, people travel to Italy to see the latest in clothing design. Italian designers are known around the world. In Italy, this city is the best place to see the newest fashion designs. Each year, more and more people visit the city as fashion tourists. Tourists often buy expensive scarves, gloves, or ties for themselves and as gifts.

3.

Woman: If you're interested in art, Italy is the place to go. Some of the most famous art museums in the world are located in Italy. This city has many museums where you can see famous paintings and sculptures. There are several famous art museums on the north side of the river Arno, and you'll find the Pitti Palace just across the river. Also, don't miss the Boboli Gardens, located behind the Pitti Palace.

4.

Man: Another great thing about Italy is, of course, the food. If you're traveling in Italy, be sure to take a break often and try some of the delicious dishes. This city in particular has good food. It is famous for its pasta and its ice cream. The pasta sauce from this city – made with ground meat and tomatoes – is probably the most famous pasta sauce in the world.

page 58

B Listen again. There is one mistake in each sentence. Cross out the incorrect words. Then write the correct information.

[*Replay Listening task 1 • Exercise A, track 5*]

page 59
Listening task 2 • University life

A Listen. An Italian student is talking about university life in the U.S. and Italy. What is he talking about? Check the topics. There are two extra topics.

1.

Interviewer: You're from Italy, and you're here in the U.S. now as an international student at Youngstown State. I'd like to ask you a few questions about the differences between university life in Italy and in the U.S.

Student: OK, sure.

Interviewer: All right. First, let me ask about the school schedule in Italy. Is it the same as in the U.S.? I mean, here in the U.S., a school year begins in September and ends in May.

Student: Well, it's not quite the same in Italy. Our lessons begin in October and they finish in July.

Interviewer: I see. How long is the summer vacation, then? Two months?

Student: Yes, that's right. We just have a two-month summer vacation in Italy. American students are so lucky, they get three whole months for summer vacation.

2.

Interviewer: OK, next question. What's a typical school day like in Italy?

Student: For me, well, I usually get to school around seven-thirty if I have a class at eight. Then, if I have time, I check e-mail or read the newspaper before class. I usually have one or two classes in the

morning and one in the afternoon. For lunch, it's the same as it is here in the U.S. Students usually eat together with their friends in the university cafeteria. That's where I eat every day when I'm in Italy and when I am in the U.S.

3.

Interviewer: OK. Next, I'd like to ask you about your free time. When you aren't in class, what do you like to do? What kind of activities do you like?

Student: Usually I meet with my friends after class, or on weekends. We go to the café, take breaks – coffee breaks. I'm happy my American friends like to meet for coffee, too. There is a good café very close by, just around the corner from my university – just like in Italy, so I feel at home.

4.

Interviewer: That's great. OK, finally, I have a question about university housing in Italy. A lot of students in the U.S. live in dorms or apartments and travel home to see their families during vacations. Is this the same in Italy?

Student: No. In Italy every city has a university, so Italian students don't have to move far away to attend university. Besides, I think it's easier to live with my family. You know, I can eat with my family, do my laundry . . . I don't know, it's just easier. I can study better if I live at home.

Interviewer: OK. That was my last question. I'd love to have a cup of coffee. Can you tell me where that café is?

page 59

B Listen again. Where are these statements true? Check *in Italy, in the U.S.,* or *in both.*

[*Replay Listening Task 2 • Exercise A, track 6*]

Unit 13 • Part-time jobs

page 61
Listening task 1 • What's the job?

A Listen. Who are the people below talking to? Write the other people's jobs. There is one extra job.

1.

Man: OK. Here's what we've been doing in English class. We're supposed to write a five-page paper, but I don't have any ideas at all. Can you help me understand the assignment?

2.

Woman: Yes, I think we're ready now. I'm going to have a small green salad and a hamburger, and she's going to have the soup of the day and the fish. And we'll have tea to drink. Thanks.

3.

Woman: Hi, I'm ready to pay now. I've got a sandwich, a pack of gum, and this magazine. Oh, wait, I'm going to grab a cup of coffee, too. Large, please. Thanks.

4.

Woman: Oh, yes, that's our luggage over there – the black suitcase with the silver handles and also the small brown bag. We're in room seven-twenty-six. Thanks. Oh, and could you show me where the business center is? I need to photocopy some papers later.

5.

Man: Wow! What a beautiful old castle. You said it was built five hundred years ago? This was definitely worth the long bus ride! Oh, speaking of the bus, what time should we be back at the bus? Oh, and one more thing. Could you take a picture of me in front of the castle? I want to send it to my cousin.

6.

Man: Hi, this is my little brother Michael. Can you say hello, Michael? Well, he's a little shy at first. Um, he hasn't had a nap yet today, so I think he's a little tired. Do you have some toys or games that he could just play with quietly?

page 61

B Listen again. Circle the correct information.
[*Replay Listening task 1 • Exercise A, track 7*]

page 62
Listening task 2 • Job interviews

A Listen. People are interviewing for jobs. Check the correct information about each job below.

1. park ranger

Interviewer: OK, I see you have experience working outdoors. We need people with experience to explain our park and take people on nature walks. Do you enjoy talking to large groups of people?

Woman: Yes, I've given talks before about nature. You'll tell me the information I need to explain, right?

Interviewer: That's right. Now, this is a part-time job, only five hours a day on weekends.

Woman: OK.

Interviewer: And I'm afraid our paying jobs are all taken. We can offer you a volunteer internship,

though. You won't be paid, but you'll learn lots of things.

Woman: Not paid? Oh, I really need to make some money this summer.

2. camp counselor

Interviewer: So, I see you've been a camp counselor before. Great. We're looking for people with experience this summer.

Man: Yes, I love working with kids, teaching them how to swim and doing different outdoor activities. I hear you'll have campers from China this year.

Interviewer: That's right. We have campers from eleven countries now. Well, let me tell you about the job. It's full-time – more than full-time, actually: twenty-four hours a day, seven days a week, for a month. But we pay quite well.

Man: Great. It sounds like a job I'd like.

3. business intern

Interviewer: So what are you studying in college?

Man: Business. That's why I'm interested in this internship. I'd like to get an MBA after I graduate.

Interviewer: I see. How much experience do you have working with computers?

Man: Actually, I don't have any. But I'm willing to learn.

Interviewer: Well, that's good to know. We don't require experience. We'll be glad to train you. Now, this is full-time, but you understand this is a volunteer position.

Man: Oh, I know I won't get paid. And I understand I'll be working full-time. I just want to get some background in business.

Interviewer: Would you be able to start on June first?

Man: Yes, that's no problem. I finish my classes the third week of May.

Interviewer: Great. We need someone for June, July, and August.

Man: August? Oh, no, I have to be back at school on August first.

4. tennis instructor

Interviewer: Well, looks like you have the experience we require. It's great you've taught tennis for four years. We'd like to offer you the job. As you know, it's part-time.

Woman: That's perfect. I have a research paper for college that I'm working on this summer.

Interviewer: We have Internet access, so you can even do research on-line if you need to.

Woman: Great. Well, I'm really looking forward to this summer. And getting paid to play tennis is a dream job for me.

page 62

B Listen again. Will the people accept the jobs? Check *yes* or *no*.

[*Replay Listening task 2 • Exercise A, track 8*]

page 63
Your turn to talk • My ideal job

B

1. Listen and practice. Notice the stressed syllables.

Woman: life**guard**, **u**niform, as**sis**tant, ex**pe**rience, volun**teer**, rou**tine**

B

2. Listen. Circle the stressed syllables.

a.
Woman: in**tern**

b.
Woman: in**struc**tor

c.
Woman: **sal**ary

d.
Woman: **out**doors

e.
Woman: con**ve**nience

f.
Woman: a**lone**

Unit 14 • Celebrations

page 65
Listening task 1 • Fireworks, food, and fun

A Listen. When are these celebrations? Write the celebrations in the correct months.

1. St. Patrick's Day

Man: St. Patrick's Day is March seventeenth. It's named for a man who lived in Ireland. Of course, Irish people celebrate the day, but it's an even bigger festival in the United States. In Chicago, they even make the river green. People also have parties, and in large cities like New York and Chicago, there are big parades.

2. Moon Festival

Woman: The Moon Festival is a Chinese holiday. The holiday is often in September because the Chinese believe that September is the month of the moon's birthday. People eat cakes that are round like the moon. September is also the time for the harvest, when the food that was grown during the summer is gathered. Families get together and have big dinners.

3. Bob Marley Day

Man: February sixth is Bob Marley Day. Bob Marley was a famous musician. He introduced reggae music – the music of Jamaica – to the world. People in Jamaica loved Bob Marley. When Marley died, Jamaica made his birthday a national holiday. On February sixth, Jamaicans remember Marley through special events, especially concerts. There are concerts everywhere.

4. Day of the Dead

Man: The Day of the Dead in November is a very important holiday in Mexico. People believe that the dead come back to visit family members on this day. Mexicans go to visit graves – where the dead are buried. They have picnics near these graves. They bring food and flowers for the dead. The Day of the Dead in November is a time for remembering.

5. Kartini Day

Woman: Indonesia celebrates Kartini Day in April. Kartini was a princess who wanted girls to have better education in her country. She started a special school for girls. Kartini died when she was very young – only twenty-five. Her birthday, April twenty-first, is now a national holiday in Indonesia. Teachers and students share special lunches at school to honor Princess Kartini.

6. St. Lucia's Day

Woman: St. Lucia's Day is a holiday in Sweden. It's in December. St. Lucia's Day is a day to bring light into the house. Young girls wear special clothes: a white dress and a crown of candles. In December, towns all over Sweden choose their Queen of Light. Homes and shops all burn candles throughout the day.

page 65

B Listen again. What do people do to celebrate? Match each celebration with an activity.

[*Replay Listening task 1 • Exercise A, track 11*]

page 66
Listening task 2 • Celebration time

A Listen. People are describing celebrations around the world. Number the pictures from 1 to 4.

1.

Man: In many countries, this sport is popular. In Korea it has a special meaning. In the first half of January, many Korean boys fly kites. On January fifteenth, they write "No bad luck" on their kites and fly them very high in the sky. Then they cut the strings. The kites fly away. They believe this takes the bad luck away for the year.

2.

Woman: Many countries have holidays to bring good luck. In Thailand, people hold this festival. The festival takes place everywhere in Thailand, but is especially popular in the north. Water Festival takes place in the middle of April. It is part of the Thai New Year. People throw buckets of water on each other. There are even parades where people throw water. It's especially important to pour water on older people. It shows respect.

3.

Woman: Brazil is famous for this huge festival, with lots of music and dancing. The festival is called Carnaval. The most famous Carnaval parties are in Rio de Janeiro. In Rio, bands travel through the streets in parades. People enjoy dancing and dressing up in fancy clothes. The Brazilian samba dance contests are famous around the world. Carnaval is a festival for people to celebrate and have a good time.

4.

Man: This holiday is celebrated in many countries all over the world. It is a happy time in the Chinese calendar. There are parades in the streets, and families gather for big dinners. At these dinners, children get "lucky money" in red envelopes. Before the New Year, Chinese people always clean their houses to clean out bad luck. Everything must be fresh and clean. People also make sure they have paid all their bills. It is important to start the New Year without owing anyone money.

page 66

B Listen again. Circle the correct information.
[*Replay Listening task 2 • Exercise A, track 12*]

page 67
Your turn to talk • Holiday memories
B
1. Listen and practice. Notice the pronunciation of *Did you* [/dɪdʒə/] and *What did you* [/wʌt dɪdʒə/].

Woman: Did you /dɪdʒə/, What did you /wʌt dɪdʒə/
Did you give presents?
What did you buy?
Did you wear special clothes?
What did you do?

B

2. Listen. Do you hear *Did you* [/dɪdʒə/] or *What did you* [/wʌt dɪdʒə/]? Check the correct answers.

a.
Woman: What did you eat?

b.
Woman: What did you bring back?

c.
Woman: Did you travel somewhere?

d.
Woman: Did you have a good time?

e.
Woman: What did you see?

f.
Woman: Did you visit relatives?

Unit 15 • Inventions

page 69
Listening task 1 • What's the invention?

A Listen. What are the people talking about? Number the pictures from 1 to 6. There are two extra pictures.

1.

Woman: This is a game played by two people. You can play it inside or outside. The game was first played in ancient Iraq. It was a kind of fortune-telling game, a way to predict the future. Two people hit a small object like a ball back and forth for as long as they could. Why? Because if they hit the object back and forth for a long time, it meant that they would live a long time.

2.

Man: These were first made in the summer of eighteen fifty-three in New York. A customer ordered fried potatoes in a restaurant, but he didn't like the potatoes the cook made for him because they were too thick. He wanted thinner potatoes. The cook decided to play a joke on the customer, so he made the customer more potatoes, but he made them very, very thin. But to the cook's surprise, the customer loved them! And so did other people! They became the specialty of the restaurant.

3.

Woman: The first one of these wasn't made for tall buildings, and it wasn't electric. It was made for the king of France in the seventeen fifties. It went up one floor, from the first floor to the second. People called it the Flying Chair. The Flying Chair was on the outside of the building. Men pulled it up and down when the king wanted to change floors.

4.

Man: It was a very hot summer in nineteen oh four when the first one of these was invented. At a fair, a salesman didn't have any more cups for his ice-cold treats. He asked all the other salespeople if they had any extra cups, but nobody did. Then, he saw a stand with a kind of cookie. He bought all the cookies and put his ice cream into them. Today they are still made of thin cookies.

5.

Woman: The first one was made only about a hundred years ago. In those days, everybody drank water from the same place, so when people were sick, other people got sick, too. A rich man didn't want to get sick, so he had an inventor make one of these. Today, you can find these everywhere – we use them to drink water, coffee, and soft drinks.

6.

Man: The first one was made over three hundred and fifty years ago in France. A young man made it to help his father, who was a store clerk and had to work with numbers all day. He needed to add and subtract numbers quickly, so his son made a wooden box with sixteen dials. By turning the dials, his father could add and subtract quickly.

page 69

B Listen again. Circle the reasons for the inventions.
[*Replay Listening task 1 • Exercise A, track 15*]

page 70
Listening task 2 • What's it for?

A Listen. What are these things used for? Circle the correct information.

1.

Store clerk: Good afternoon. May I help you?
Woman: Yes, I'm going camping and I need something to keep the insects away.
Store clerk: How about these? They're new. They're insect guards.
Woman: Really? I've never seen anything like them before.
Store clerk: You can use them to keep insects off you – flies, mosquitoes, any insect.
Woman: These will keep insects off me? How?
Store clerk: They cover you, you know, like a net. They're very light and easy to use. You put one on each hand, each foot, and over your head. The insects can't bite you.

Woman: Right. Actually, I think I just want some bug spray.

2.

Man: What's this?
Woman: It's an electric spaghetti fork.
Man: An electric spaghetti fork?
Woman: Yes, you use it to eat spaghetti. You just put it in the spaghetti. Then you turn it on. [*motor buzzes*]
Woman: See how the fork moves in a circle. It pulls the spaghetti around the fork.
Man: Does this really help you eat spaghetti?
Woman: Yes, it does. And it's fun. You should buy one.
Man: Well, thanks anyway, but I don't think I need any help eating spaghetti.

3.

Store clerk: OK. You've got cat food and a brush. Anything else for your cat?
Man: I don't think so.
Store clerk: Have you seen our new cat mop?
Man: Uh . . . no.
Store clerk: Oh, it's the cutest thing. You can use it to have your cat clean the floor.
Man: I don't think my cat wants to clean the floor.
Store clerk: Oh, he has no choice. You put these shoes on the cat. On the bottom of each one, there's a little mop. As the cat runs, he cleans the floor.
Man: Well, I *could* use some help. Why not?

4.

Woman: Look at what I bought!
Man: It looks like a child's swing. What's it for?
Woman: You know how crowded the train is in the morning?
Man: Sure.
Woman: Well, you use this to sit on the train.
Man: Use it to sit on the train? How?
Woman: When you can't find a seat, you just hang it on those luggage bars above the seats. It's made of cloth so it's easy to carry.
Man: I don't get it.
Woman: When there are no seats on the train, you can sit on this. Put the hooks over the luggage bars. It makes a little seat.
Man: Ah, I get it! Hey, that sounds great. Where did you buy it?

5.

Man: Do you want to see something?
Woman: Sure. What?
Man: Look at this.
Woman: What is it?
Man: It's an electric letter opener. I can use it to open letters!

Woman: What?

Man: An electric letter opener. Watch. [*motor buzzes*] It only takes two seconds.

Woman: Well, how long does it take you with a knife?

Man: Yeah, but *this* is electric.

Woman: Hmm . . . I think I'll keep using a regular knife.

6.

Man: Excuse me, do you have umbrellas?

Store clerk: It's started to rain, hasn't it?

Man: Yes, it's really pouring out there.

Store clerk: How about this model? It's not just an umbrella. It also holds your camera so you can take pictures.

Man: Holds my camera?

Store clerk: Yes, you open the umbrella and put it on the ground. It has a special place that holds your camera, you know, so you can take your own picture, or be in pictures with friends.

Man: Wow, that's cool. I take lots of pictures. What a great idea!

page 70

B Listen again. Will the people buy the products? Check *yes* or *no*.

[*Replay Listening task 2 • Exercise A, track 16*]

page 71

Your turn to talk • Thank you, Mr. Robot!

B

1. Listen and practice. Notice the pronunciation of *can* /kən/ and *can't* /kænt/.

Woman: can /kən/, can't /kænt/

Man: My robot can vacuum.

Woman: My robot can't vacuum, but it can dust.

Woman: Can your robot do the dishes?

Man: No, it can't. It can't do the dishes.

B

2. Listen. Do you hear *can* /kən/ or *can't* /kænt/? Check the correct answers.

a.

Woman: Our robot can clean the bathroom.

b.

Woman: Our robot can't do the laundry.

c.

Woman: Can your robot do your homework?

d.

Woman: Our robot can cook.

e.

Woman: Our robot can't water the plants.

f.

Woman: Our robot can't make the bed.

Unit 16 • Folktales

page 73

Listening task 1 • The farmer and his sons

A Listen. You will hear a traditional folktale. Number the pictures from 1 to 6.

1.

Woman: Once upon a time, a farmer and his three sons lived on a farm. The farmer always worked very hard in his fields. But his sons did not like to work. They were very lazy and only wanted to sleep and play cards all day.

2.

Woman: One day, the farmer called his sons to him. He said, "Sons, I am old. I will soon die. I won't be able to take care of you anymore, so I am leaving you a treasure in the fields. There's a treasure in the fields."
The oldest son said, "A treasure? Is it gold?"
"Diamonds?" asked another son.
"Money?" asked the third son.
But the old farmer just smiled and said, "A treasure. You will find a treasure in the fields."

3.

Woman: The old farmer died. His sons ran to the fields. They began digging and digging, dreaming of the treasure they would find. Soon, they dug up the whole field. But they didn't find any treasure. They found no treasure at all.

4.

Woman: The sons decided to plant some wheat, and soon the fields were full of tall wheat plants. Now, the three young sons worked long, hard days in the hot fields to cut and harvest all of the wheat.

5.

Woman: When the sons finished harvesting the wheat, they drove to town and sold it to the rich townspeople. They did this year after year after year. And they made a lot of money.

6.

Woman: The three sons grew old together on the farm. After many years, they began to enjoy working hard in the fields. Selling the wheat gave them plenty of money, and they were happy. They finally understood that the land was their father's treasure. The land itself and the wheat in their fields brought them a good life.

page 73

B Listen again. Circle the correct answers.

[Replay Listening task 1 • Exercise A, track 19]

page 74

Listening task 2 • The stonecutter

A Listen to the story of the stonecutter. What is the main idea of each part of the story? Number the statements from 1 to 4.

1.

Man: Once upon a time, there was a stonecutter, a man who cut stones from the mountains to make people's houses. He was very good at his job, and he loved his work. The stonecutter lived in a tiny little house with his wife. The stonecutter and his wife didn't have much money, but they were happy just to be together.

2.

Man: One day, while he was working, the stonecutter found a dirty, old magic lamp. When the stonecutter rubbed the lamp to clean it, a genie appeared, and said, "I will grant you a wish! You can have anything you want."
The stonecutter thought for a moment. Just then, he looked out the window and saw the prince going by. "The prince is rich and powerful. I am just a poor stonecutter. Genie, can I become a prince?"
The genie said, "Your wish is granted," and he turned the stonecutter into a prince.

3.

Man: That night, when the stonecutter went home, he saw that his little house was now a beautiful prince's palace. His new life as a prince was very busy. People from the village came to his palace every day to ask the prince to help them with their problems and for favors of all kinds. The stonecutter prince and his wife were never alone, and soon they grew tired of so many people around them all the time. The stonecutter called the genie. He said, "Genie, a prince's life is too busy. I am tired. Can I become a rich man instead of a prince?"
The genie said, "Your wish is granted," and he turned the stonecutter into a rich man.

4.

Man: The stonecutter was now a rich man with a big house and servants to cook, clean, and give the rich man and his wife anything they wanted.
But something was still missing.
One day, the rich man was walking in the village and he saw another man building a stone house. He watched as the man worked, cutting the pieces of stone and putting them one on top of another to build a beautiful house. Suddenly, the rich man said "That is what I want to do! I want to be a stonecutter again!"
So the genie said, "Your wish is granted," and he turned him back into a poor stonecutter. And the stonecutter and his wife lived happily ever after.

page 74

B Listen again. Which statements are probably true? Check the correct answers.

[Replay Listening task 2 • Exercise A, track 20]

page 75

Your turn to talk • Once upon a time . . .

B

1. Listen and practice. Notice the pause after a comma when telling a story.

Woman: Once upon a time, there was a young boy.
One day, the boy met a princess.
He said, "I want to be a prince."
When the princess smiled, he became a prince.

B

2. Add a comma to show the pause in each sentence. Then listen and check your answers.

a.

Woman: One day, a young boy was working in the field.

b.

Woman: The boy was poor, so he worked very hard.

c.

Woman: When the boy finished working, a genie came and spoke to him.

d.

Woman: Because the boy worked so hard, the genie gave him three wishes.

Expansion 4 • India

page 76
Listening task 1 • Information

A Listen. People are talking about India. What are the topics? Check the correct answers.

1.

Woman: India is the sixth largest country in the world. It is located in South Asia. India is home to many people from different cultures, and they speak many languages. In fact, India has twenty-two different national languages in addition to the official language, Hindi. English is also used for official purposes.

2.

Man: India is famous for its food, especially its spicy dishes. Curry dishes with chicken, lamb, or vegetables are very popular. Beef is not served often because many Indians don't eat beef for religious reasons. India is also known for tropical fruits. There is even a national fruit – the mango. Indians drink many fruit juices, and Indian tea is famous all over the world.

3.

Woman: It was an Indian scientist named Aryabhatta who invented the number zero more than two thousand years ago. Aryabhatta may also have been the first person to say that the earth is round, like a ball. His work helped Indians invent some of their first calendars. Today, math and science, and especially computer science, are popular subjects for Indian students.

4.

Man: India is well known for its movie industry. Unlike Western movies, Indian movies with action, fighting, and violence may also include romantic scenes with music, singing, and dancing. Indian films are known for their beautiful colors and clothing. People around the world are watching more and more Indian movies in theaters and at home.

page 76

B Listen again. Circle the correct answers.

[*Replay Listening task 1 • Exercise A, track 23*]

page 77
Listening task 2 • A festival

A Listen. A woman is telling the story of the Indian festival Diwali. Number the sentences in the correct order from 1 to 7.

Interviewer: Can you tell me about one of your favorite Indian festivals?

Woman: Sure. One of my favorite Indian festivals is called Diwali. It is the festival of lights, celebrated all over India. It's something that I used to look forward to very much as a child. There are a lot of legends about this festival. My favorite one tells how the lights of Diwali became so important.

Interviewer: Oh, I'd love to hear it.

Woman: All right. I'll tell you the seven parts of the story.

1.

Woman: Once there was a woman who tried to save her husband's life by keeping away the lord of death.

2.

Woman: One night, the wife didn't let her husband go to sleep. She kept him awake all night.

3.

Woman: The woman did something very clever. She put her jewelry all over the house, along with her gold money and any other shiny things she could find.

4.

Woman: She went around the whole house, and she lit many candles and lights. You see, the lights were reflected in the woman's jewelry and all the shiny objects, and the whole house became very, very bright.

5.

Woman: When the lord of death came to take the woman's husband, the lord was blinded by all of the lights. It was too bright, and he couldn't see.

6.

Woman: The woman's husband was saved. The lord of death gave up and went away.

7.

Woman: The story explains the significance of the lights and the reason why this festival is celebrated.

page 77

B Listen. How do people celebrate Diwali today? Check five things they do.

Interviewer: So, what are some of the things that people do today to celebrate Diwali?

Woman: Well, today for Diwali people use many different kinds of lights in their homes. The most traditional ones are oil lamps made of brass. And outside they set off lots and lots of fireworks.

Interviewer: Sounds beautiful.

Woman: Yes, it is. Diwali starts with a lot of joy, a lot of happiness in everybody's life. There's a school vacation for kids. People buy new clothes and cook a lot of special foods and eat them. Basically it's a time for family togetherness – to meet relatives and enjoy spending time together.

Interviewer: You mentioned special clothes. Can you tell me about some of the clothes that people wear?

Woman: Oh, Diwali is one of the times when you buy new clothes and wear them, so kids look forward to this. Usually, adults wear traditional Indian clothes, whereas kids mostly wear whatever is popular, what is fashionable.

Interviewer: And what kinds of special foods do you eat?

Woman: Oh, there are all kinds of things. There are many sweets; there are many different dishes for lunch and dinner. Special foods, which last for longer than a day, are made and exchanged between friends and relatives.

Interviewer: Do people also exchange other kinds of gifts or presents?

Woman: Yeah, sure. In fact, one of the special days of Diwali is to welcome the goddess of wealth. This day, we display our important or expensive items like gold, jewelry, diamonds, and money. Anything precious we have in the house, we put out and show. Gifts are also exchanged; we give presents to kids especially.

Interviewer: OK, well, thank you very much. It sounds like a great festival. I hope I can see it someday.

Self-study audio scripts

Self-study • Unit 1

page 84

A

1. Listen to the conversation.

Man 1: Luis, I'd like you to meet my friend Emi.
Luis: Hi, Emi. Nice to meet you.
Emi: Nice to meet you, Luis. Are you a student?
Luis: Yes. I'm studying English.
Emi: Oh! Do you enjoy it?
Luis: Yeah, it's really fun. So, how about you? Are you a student, too?
Emi: Yes. I'm studying music.
Luis: Really? What kind of music do you like?
Emi: Oh, I like all kinds of music, but I'm studying classical music. I play the piano. How about you? What kind of music do you listen to?
Luis: I'm afraid I don't like classical music. Pop music's my favorite.
Man 1: Hey, we were just on our way to get some coffee. Do you want to join us, Emi?
Emi: Sure. That sounds good.

2. Listen again. Circle the correct answers.

[*The conversation is repeated here.*]

page 84

B Listen. Check *yes* or *no*. Then write your answers.

1. Are you a student? Do you go to school? Check *yes* or *no*. If you checked *yes,* write what subject you study. If you checked *no,* write your job.

2. Do you like where you live? Do you like the place you live? Check *yes* or *no*. If you checked *yes,* write the name of your hometown. If you checked *no,* write the name of another city or town near your hometown.

3. Do you like music? Do you like to listen to music? Check *yes* or *no*. If you checked *yes,* write your favorite kind of music on the line. If you checked *no,* write the name of a music group you know.

4. Do you like sports? Do you watch or play sports? Check *yes* or *no*. If you checked *yes,* write your favorite sport on the line. If you checked *no,* write something you like to do in your free time.

5. Do people in your culture bow when they meet? Do you usually bow when you first meet someone? Check *yes* or *no*. If you checked *yes,* write

something you say in your language when you first meet someone. If you checked *no,* write one way that people in your culture greet each other.

Self-study • Unit 2

page 85

A

1. Listen to the conversation.

Woman: So, Andy, tell me about your family.
Andy: My family? Well, let's see. Uh, there's my mother and father, and I have one sister and one brother, and then, of course, there's me.
Woman: Is your sister older than you, or younger?
Andy: My sister Lisa is the oldest. She's twenty-five. She doesn't live with my parents. She lives in another town and has a good job.
Woman: How about your brother?
Andy: Sam's also older than I am. He's in his last year at the university. He's studying to be a doctor.
Woman: Wow. That's great.
Andy: So, how about you? Do you have any brothers or sisters?
Woman: No, I don't. It's just my parents and me.

2. Listen again. Circle the correct answers.

[*The conversation is repeated here.*]

page 85

B Listen. Write your answers. You need to know these shapes: circle, diamond, square, star.

1. Find the star. Do you see the star? Write your family name in the star. How many people are there in your family? Write the number of family members you have in the star under your name.

2. Find the square. Did you find the square? Write your father's first name in the square. Does your father like sports? If your father likes sports, write *yes* in the square. If your father doesn't like sports, write *no* in the square.

3. Find the diamond. Do you see the diamond? Write your mother's first name in the diamond. Where is your mother from? What is her hometown? Write your mother's hometown in the diamond.

4. Find the circle. Do you see the circle? Do you have any brothers and sisters? Write the first names of your brothers and sisters in the circle. How old are they? Write your brothers' and sisters' ages next to their names. If you don't have any brothers or sisters, write *none*, N-O-N-E, in the circle.

Self-study • Unit 3

page 86

A

1. Listen to the conversation.

Sales clerk: All right, sir. I just need some information before I can start your new service.

Victor: Sure.

Sales clerk: Name and date of birth, please.

Victor: Yes, it's Victor Morales, and my birthday is eleven, twenty, eighty-seven.

Sales clerk: OK. And what's your *current* number?

Victor: It's eight-oh-two, five-five-five, two-six-four-six.

Sales clerk: OK. I think that's all the information we need. All right, I have the number for your new cell phone. I'll write it down here. It's four-one-five, five-five-five, nine-eight-three-five. If you could just sign here, we can give you your new phone.

Victor: Great. I can't wait to use it. I've wanted one for a long time.

2. Listen again. Circle the correct answers.

[*The conversation is repeated here.*]

page 86

B Listen. Write your answers.

1. What is your phone number? Write your telephone number in box number one.

2. What is today's date? In box number two, write today's date in numbers. Write the month first, then the day, then the year.

3. When is your mother's birthday? In numbers, write the date of your mother's birthday in box number three.

4. What is your best friend's phone number? Write the phone number of your best friend in box number four.

5. When were you born? In numbers, write the month and day you were born in box number five. You don't have to write the year.

6. What is a number that is important for you? Write an important number in box number six. Then, under the number, write how to say it in words.

Self-study • Unit 4

page 87

A

1. Listen to the conversation.

Husband: I'm going to the store. What do we need?

Wife: Um, what do you want for dinner tonight?

Husband: How about chicken?

Wife: We had chicken last night.

Husband: Yeah, that was really good. I wanted some more of that.

Wife: I'll make more next week. How about pasta for tonight?

Husband: Sure, I'd like that. I'll get some pasta and some mushrooms and onions.

Wife: Sounds good. Oh, and get some lettuce and tomatoes for a salad.

Husband: Do we have dessert?

Wife: No, we don't. Why don't you get a melon?

2. Listen again. Circle the correct answers.

[*The conversation is repeated here.*]

page 87

B Listen. A server is taking your order. What is she asking about? Write the food. Then check your order.

1. Good evening. My name is Michelle, and I'll be your server tonight. Would you like something to drink? What would you like to drink? What kind of drink would you like?

2. Would you like a salad? What kind of salad would you like? We have three kinds of salad. Which one would you like?

3. OK, and how about some soup? Would you like a bowl of soup? What kind of soup would you like?

4. All right. And you're having pizza for dinner. Good choice. What topping would you like on your pizza? You can choose one pizza topping.

5. Very good. And finally, would you like something for dessert? Would you like some dessert? We have some delicious cakes. What kind of cake would you like?

Self-study • Unit 5

page 88

A

1. Listen to the information.

Man: I had a great time last weekend. My friend Jack came to visit me for three days. He's never been here before, so I showed him around the city. He got here on Thursday. I never go out on Thursday nights because I have to be at work early on Fridays. So the first night we just stayed home and relaxed. On Friday, we went to a club. I hardly ever go to clubs. I don't really like dancing, but Jack loves it. He's a great dancer. Saturday, we took a tour of the city. I showed him some of my favorite places. Then we played basketball in the afternoon. On Sunday, we met some other friends and went out for lunch at this Italian place I often go to. And then Jack left in the afternoon. It was good seeing him.

2. Listen again. Circle the correct answers.

[*The conversation is repeated here.*]

page 88

B Listen. Check *yes* or *no*. Then write your answers.

1. Do you watch TV? Do you like watching TV in your free time? Check *yes* or *no*. If you checked *yes,* write how often you watch TV. Write *sometimes, hardly ever,* or *never.* If you checked *no,* write the name of a popular TV show you know.

2. Do you go to clubs? Do you enjoy clubs? Check *yes* or *no*. If you checked *yes,* write the name of a person you go to clubs with. If you checked *no,* write something else you like doing in the evening.

3. Do you eat dinner in restaurants? Do you eat out sometimes? Check *yes* or *no*. If you checked *yes,* write something you like to order at a restaurant. If you checked *no,* write any food you like.

4. Do you ever play sports on weekends? Do you play a sport on weekends? Check *yes* or *no*. If you checked *yes,* write a sport you like to play. If you checked *no,* write something else you like to do on weekends.

5. Do you visit relatives often? Do you often visit relatives? Check *yes* or *no*. If you checked *yes,* write the name of a relative you often visit. If you checked *no,* write the name of the relative who lives closest to you.

Self-study • Unit 6

page 89

A

1. Listen to the conversation.

Wife: Is that all you're taking? That little bag?
Husband: What do you mean? That's everything I need.
Wife: It's going to be cold in the mountains.

Husband: I know, but I don't want to bring too much. We still have to pack the skis and all the other stuff, too.
Wife: The car's big. Aren't you going to need some more clothes?
Husband: I've got a sweater, a jacket, a cap, pants, and a couple of shirts.
Wife: That's only enough for one day.
Husband: Come on – this trip is supposed to be relaxing. Whoa! You're not going to take *all* those bags, are you?

2. Listen again. Circle the correct answers.

[*The conversation is repeated here.*]

page 89

B Listen. Check *yes* or *no*. Then write your answers.

1. Look at what you are wearing now. Are you wearing a sweater? Check *yes* or *no*. If you checked *yes,* write the color of your sweater. If you checked *no,* write something else you are wearing.

2. Do you like jeans? Do you like wearing jeans? Check *yes* or *no*. If you checked *yes,* write how many pairs of jeans you own. If you checked *no,* write the name of a person you know who often wears jeans.

3. Are you wearing a T-shirt now? Do you have a T-shirt on? Check *yes* or *no*. If you checked *yes,* write the color of your T-shirt. If you checked *no,* write the kind of top you are wearing now. Is it long-sleeved, short-sleeved, or sleeveless? Write *long-sleeved, short-sleeved,* or *sleeveless.*

4. Are you wearing sandals today? Do you have sandals on? Check *yes* or *no*. If you checked *yes,* write the color of your sandals. If you checked *no,* write your shoe size. Write the shoe size you wear.

5. Do you have a favorite outfit for parties? Do you have favorite party clothes? Check *yes* or *no*. If you checked *yes,* write something you like to wear to parties. If you checked *no,* write something you like to wear on weekends.

Self-study • Unit 7

page 90

A

1. Listen to the conversation.

Man: How do you like your new apartment?
Woman: It's nice. It's bigger than my old place.
Man: Bigger? Did you have to buy new furniture?
Woman: Yeah, a lot.

Man: What did you get?

Woman: Well, for the living room, a new couch – a really nice blue one.

Man: What did you do with your old couch?

Woman: I still have it. Hey, do you want it?

Man: Really? That would be great.

Woman: I also got a new coffee table.

Man: Uh-huh. Anything else?

Woman: Oh, yeah, a new rug and curtains.

Man: What was wrong with your old rug?

Woman: Well, it didn't really match the couch very well.

2. Listen again. Circle the correct answers.

[*The conversation is repeated here.*]

page 90

B Listen. You are going to draw things in a room. Follow the instructions.

1. You are looking at a room. In the middle of the room there is a big table. Draw a big table in the middle of the room.

2. Behind the table, there is a chair. Draw a chair behind the table.

3. On the left wall, draw a small window. There's a small window on the left wall.

4. Draw a plant on the floor under the window. There's a plant under the window on the floor.

5. On the table, there's a lamp. Draw a lamp on the table.

6. There's a bookshelf on the right wall. Draw a bookshelf on the right wall.

7. There's a dog in the room. Where is the dog? Draw the dog anywhere you like. You choose where the dog is. Now, under the picture of the room, write a sentence that tells where the dog is. Write a sentence about the dog.

Self-study • Unit 8

page 91

A

1. Listen to the conversation.

Woman: Do you have any time to get together this week? We need to meet and plan John's birthday party.

Man: Sure. Let's see. . . . I have to work until five P.M.

Woman: Really? I finish work at five-thirty.

Man: OK. How about next Wednesday at six? Oh, next Wednesday's no good. I'm going to dinner at a friend's house. Can you meet Thursday at six?

Woman: Uh-uh. I'm going to get my hair cut then.

Man: Hmm. What about the mornings? Are you free then?

Woman: Next Tuesday is the only morning that's good for me.

Man: Oh. No, Tuesday won't work for me.

Woman: All right then, how about now? I have about twenty minutes before my next class.

Man: OK. Let's get started.

2. Listen again. Circle the correct answers.

[*The conversation is repeated here.*]

page 91

B Listen. Check *yes* or *no*. Then write your answers.

1. Do you wake up early in the morning? Do you get up early? Check *yes* or *no*. If you checked *yes*, write what time you usually wake up. If you checked *no*, write what time you usually go to bed at night.

2. Did you eat breakfast this morning? Did you eat something for breakfast? Check *yes* or *no*. If you checked *yes*, write what time you ate breakfast. If you checked *no*, write what time you usually eat lunch.

3. Do you have English class in the morning? Do you go to English class in the morning? Check *yes* or *no*. If you checked *yes*, write what time your English class begins. If you checked *no*, write how many days a week you study English.

4. Do you sometimes meet friends for dinner? Do you ever go out to dinner with friends? Check *yes* or *no*. If you checked *yes*, write what time you usually meet them. If you checked *no*, write what time you ate dinner last night.

5. Do you go to parties often? Do you often go to parties? Check *yes* or *no*. Imagine this: You are invited to your friend's party tonight. The party invitation says to come at eight. What time will you arrive? Write the time you will arrive at the party.

Self-study • Unit 9

page 92

A

1. Listen to the conversation.

Man: There're some great movies playing downtown. Want to go see one?

Woman: OK, that sounds good. Which movie do you want to see? Not some loud action movie with car chases, I hope.

Man: No, I was thinking of that new horror movie – you know, the one with the vampires and lots of scary scenes. I love those movies, don't you?

Woman: No, I don't. Come on, let's find a movie we both like. How about one with singing, dancing, and romance?

Man: Are you kidding?

Woman: Yes, I'm joking. I know you don't like those kinds of movies.

Man: How about a comedy – good jokes, silly situations? It'll be fun!

Woman: That sounds good. Let's see, what time is *Laughing in Las Vegas* playing? How about the seven-thirty show?

Man: When's the next show? Nine-thirty?

Woman: Yes. That's too late.

Man: Yeah.

2. Listen again. Circle the correct answers.

[*The conversation is repeated here.*]

page 92

B Listen. Check *yes* or *no*. Then write your answers.

1. Do you have a favorite movie? Is there one movie that you like best? Check *yes* or *no*. If you checked *yes,* write the name of your favorite movie. If you checked *no,* write the name of any movie you've seen recently.

2. Think about the last movie you saw. Did you like it? Did you like the last movie you saw? Check *yes* or *no*. If you checked *yes,* write the name of the last movie you saw. If you checked *no,* write where you saw the movie.

3. Do you often watch movies? For example, do you watch action, comedy, romance, or horror movies? Check *yes* or *no*. If you checked *yes,* write your favorite kind of movie. If you checked *no,* write the name of any popular movie you know.

4. Do you ever watch movies in English? Do you watch movies in English? Check *yes* or *no*. If you checked *yes,* write the name of a movie you watched in English. If you checked *no,* write the name of a movie you want to watch in English.

5. Do you like musicals? Do you enjoy watching musicals? Check *yes* or *no*. If you checked *yes,* write one reason why you like musicals. If you checked *no,* write one reason why you don't like musicals.

Self-study • Unit 10

page 93

A

1. Listen to the conversation.

Man: I am so busy! I can't get any studying done.

Woman: Really? Why are you so busy? What do you do all day?

Man: Well, I get up at eight o'clock. Then I have a cup of coffee and read the newspaper. After I finish my coffee, I check my e-mail and surf the Internet.

Woman: And how long does that take you?

Man: Oh, I don't know, about an hour. Then I have another cup of coffee and watch the nine A.M. sports show while I'm eating breakfast.

Woman: So, what time do you leave home?

Man: Well, my first class doesn't start until noon. So, I leave at eleven-thirty. After class, I take a break and meet some friends for coffee.

Woman: And you have no time at all to study?

Man: No, it's crazy.

Woman: You know, maybe you shouldn't take so many breaks.

Man: Hmm.

2. Listen again. Circle the correct answers.

[*The conversation is repeated here.*]

page 93

B Listen. Check *yes* or *no*. Then write your answers.

1. Do you drink coffee or tea in the morning? Check *yes* or *no*. If you checked *yes,* write how many cups of coffee or tea you usually drink. If you checked *no,* write the first thing you usually do after you wake up.

2. Do you check your e-mail every day? Check *yes* or *no*. If you checked *yes,* write what time you check your e-mail. If you checked *no,* write how often you check your e-mail.

3. Do you exercise every day? Check *yes* or *no*. If you checked *yes,* write what kinds of exercise you like to do. If you checked *no,* write the name of a person you know who exercises often.

4. Do you watch TV after dinner? Check *yes* or *no*. If you checked *yes,* write the name of a TV show that you watch after dinner. If you checked *no,* write what you usually do after dinner.

5. Do you take a bath or shower before you go to bed? Check *yes* or *no*. If you checked *yes,* write what time you usually take a bath or shower. If you checked *no,* write what you usually do just before you go to bed.

Self-study • Unit 11

page 94

A

1. Listen to the conversation.

Woman: My friend and I had a really nice time last night.

Man: Oh, yeah? What did you do?

Woman: We went out to the new Thai restaurant downtown.

Man: Really? That sounds good. Where is it?

Woman: It's right in the center of the city. Do you know where the art museum is?

Man: Yes.

Woman: Across from the art museum, there's a big bank. You go straight up that street.

Man: OK.

Woman: Look for the big coffee shop. The coffee shop is right across the street from the Thai restaurant.

Man: OK, I know where that is.

Woman: The Thai place is between a clothing store and a bookstore.

Man: Great! Maybe I'll go there tonight.

2. Listen again. Circle the correct answers.

[*The conversation is repeated here.*]

page 94

B Listen. Complete the sentences with your answers.

1. Imagine you are at school. You are leaving your English classroom to go home. You walk out the door. Do you turn right, turn left, or go straight? Write *turn right, turn left,* or *go straight.*

2. Imagine you are standing in the doorway of your school. You are looking out of the doorway. What is across from the school? Write what you see across from the school.

3. Now imagine you are going out of the school building. To go home, do you turn right, turn left, or go straight? Write *turn right, turn left,* or *go straight.*

4. Imagine you are at home. You want to go to the store to buy a snack. You go out the door. To go to the store, do you turn right, turn left, or go straight? Write *turn right, turn left,* or *go straight.*

5. You are leaving your house. You walk out your door and you turn right. What do you see on your left? Write what you see on your left.

Self-study • Unit 12

page 95

A

1. Listen to the conversation.

Man: My friends are getting married next month.

Woman: Oh, that's great. Are you going to the wedding?

Man: No, I can't go. I'm going to send them a wedding gift, but I just don't know what to get.

Woman: How about something for their kitchen, something they can use to cook with.

Man: I don't think they cook much. They're both really busy. I think they eat out a lot.

Woman: Well, how about something for their house, maybe a nice picture? Do they like art?

Man: Maybe, but I haven't seen their new house, and I don't know what would look good. It's hard to choose art for someone else.

Woman: That's true. Well, if you really don't have any ideas, why don't you give them money. They could probably use it.

Man: Hmm, that's a good idea. I guess I could do that.

2. Listen again. Circle the correct answers.

[*The conversation is repeated here.*]

page 95

B Listen. Follow the instructions.

1. Imagine it's your best friend's birthday. What kind of present will you give to your friend? Will you make something or buy something? Check *make something* or *buy something.*

2. Imagine you're going to another country to stay with your friend's family. What kind of gift are you going to bring? Will you buy something from your country or something from another country? Check *something from my country* or *something from another country.*

3. What is a good gift to give someone you love? Do you give someone you love flowers, chocolate, or something else? Check your answer. If you checked *something else,* write the gift on the line.

4. Imagine your friend is graduating from college. It's your friend's graduation. What's a good gift to give your friend: some money, some CDs, or something else? Check your answer. If you checked *something else,* write the gift on the line.

5. What's a number or color of gift that is unlucky in your culture? On the line, write a number or color that is unlucky. If there aren't any unlucky numbers or colors, write *none,* N-O-N-E.

Self-study • Unit 13

page 96

A

1. Listen to the conversation.

Man: So, do you know what kind of job you're going to get this summer?

Woman: Not yet. I can't decide. How about you?

Man: I want to work in the mountains, at a tourist hotel.

Woman: Oh, yeah! You could be a porter or a server in the restaurant, or you could be a tour guide.

Man: I definitely wouldn't want to be a server. I was a server last summer. I hated it. It was much too busy.

Woman: I know what you mean. I was a server, too. It was hard work, and it wasn't much fun. What about being a porter? Too boring?

Man: No, that'd be OK, I guess. Or maybe I could be a clerk in one of the gift shops.

Woman: That's not a bad idea. And it would be good experience for the future.

Man: Yeah. I think I'll try to find something like that.

2. Listen again. Circle the correct answers.

[*The conversation is repeated here.*]

page 96

B Listen. Answer the job interview questions. Check *yes* or *no*.

1. This job requires you to work with children. Do you like children? Do you want to work with children?

2. This is a summer job. This job will end in the fall. Do you want a summer job?

3. This is a full-time job. It's not a part-time job. Do you want to work full-time?

4. You need to speak some English for this job. Do you like English? Do you want a job that requires you to speak English?

5. This is not a volunteer job, but it doesn't pay much money. Is a high salary important to you? Do you need to make a lot of money?

Self-study • Unit 14

page 97

A

1. Listen to the conversation.

Woman: I can't wait for Thanksgiving.

Man: I can't either. What are you going to do?

Woman: Well, I'm going to visit my relatives.

Man: Oh, that sounds like a great way to spend your vacation.

Woman: Yeah, it'll be fun. My uncle's really funny, and my aunt's a great cook. She always makes special food for the holidays.

Man: I'm sure you'll have a good time. You know what I'm going to do? I'm going to see the parade in New York.

Woman: Really? That sounds like fun. I've seen that parade on TV. It's really big.

Man: Yeah, huge. I can't wait to see it in person.

Woman: Well, I guess before Thanksgiving comes, we need to get some work done. I'm going back to my desk.

Man: Yeah, I should, too. See you.

Woman: Bye.

2. Listen again. Circle the correct answers.

[*The conversation is repeated here.*]

page 97

B Listen. Follow the instructions.

1. Think of a holiday you really like. What holiday is it? Write the name of the holiday. Write the name of a holiday you really like.

2. Do you wear special clothes on your favorite holiday? Do you wear something special? Check *yes* or *no.* If you checked *yes,* write one thing that you wear. If you checked *no,* write another holiday when people wear special clothes.

3. How about food? Do you eat any special food on your favorite holiday? Check *yes* or *no.* If you checked *yes,* write one kind of food you eat. If you checked *no,* write another holiday when people eat special food.

4. Do you give presents on this holiday? Do you give presents to your family or friends? Check *yes* or *no.* If you checked *yes,* write someone you give a present to. If you checked *no,* write another holiday when people give presents.

5. Do you go anywhere on your favorite holiday? Do you go somewhere on this day? If you checked *yes,* write where you go. If you checked *no,* write something you usually do.

Self-study • Unit 15

page 98

A

1. Listen to the conversation.

Woman: What's wrong? You don't look very happy.

Man: Oh, I have to write a paper about the most important invention ever made. It's for my history class.

Woman: That's not too hard. There are lots of good inventions.

Man: Yeah, but it's due tomorrow.

Woman: Well, what invention are you going to write about?

Man: Hmm, the computer, I guess.

Woman: Hmm. Isn't everybody going to write about that? Maybe you should choose something older, like clocks or calendars.

Man: No, I can't. I don't know anything about them, and I don't have much time to do research.

Woman: OK. Well, I'm sure you'll come up with something good.

Man: Hey! What do *you* think is the most important invention ever?

Woman: Me? Let's see. . . . Uh, chocolate!

2. Listen again. Circle the correct answers.

[*The conversation is repeated here.*]

page 98

B Listen. Check your guesses to the Inventions Quiz. Then listen to the correct answers. Did you guess correctly?

1. When were the first tea bags sold? When was tea first put into little bags for people to use to make a cup of tea?

2. The first photograph was taken in eighteen twenty-seven. Where was the first photograph taken? In what country did that happen?

3. When was the first English dictionary written? What was the first year that you could buy an English dictionary?

4. What was invented first: eyeglasses to help people see, bicycles for people to ride, or telephones? What came first: eyeglasses, bicycles, or telephones?

5. Where were cell phones invented? In what country was the first cell phone used?

Listen to the correct answers.

1. The first teabags were sold in nineteen oh four by Thomas Sullivan of New York. The answer to number one is *nineteen oh four.*

2. The first photograph was taken in France in eighteen twenty-seven. The answer to number two is *France.*

3. The first English dictionary was finished in seventeen fifty-five. It took nine years to write! The answer to number three is *seventeen fifty-five.*

4. Alexander Graham Bell invented the telephone in eighteen seventy-six. Bicycles were invented in the eighteen sixties. But the first eyeglasses were invented in Italy long before that – around twelve eighty-four! The answer to number four is *eyeglasses.*

5. The first call on a cell phone was made in the U.S. in nineteen seventy-three. Cell phones didn't become popular there until much later, though. The answer to number five is *the U.S.*

Self-study • Unit 16

page 99

A

1. Listen to the conversation.

Man: What are you guys doing?

Woman: Oh, we're making a movie for English class. It's going to be a traditional story, you know, like a fairy tale or a folktale.

Man: Cool! Who's going to be in the movie?

Woman: Well, I'm going to be a princess, and Adam is going to be a prince.

Man: That's a good choice. Adam looks like a good prince. Who else will be in the movie?

Woman: Let's see . . . Jason is going to be a poor farmer . . .

Man: A farmer? Jason? I don't know. Don't you think he's a little too young?

Woman: Well, we don't really have a choice. We don't have any other men. Hey, unless you . . . Would *you* like to be in this movie?

Man: Wow! Could I? That would be great!

2. Listen again. Circle the correct answers.

[*The conversation is repeated here.*]

page 99

B Listen to the story. Imagine the scene. Then listen again. Write the missing words on the lines.

A road went through a forest. A woman was walking down the road. Suddenly, she saw a man. He was wearing a shirt, pants, and a hat. He smiled and said something. A road went through a forest. A woman was walking down the road. Suddenly, she saw a man. He was wearing a shirt, pants, and a hat. He smiled and said something.

page 99

C Listen again. When you hear the bell [*bell*], write any word in the circle that makes sense. You can choose any word you want.

A [*bell*] road went through a [*bell*] forest. A [*bell*] road went through a [*bell*] forest.

A [*bell*] woman was walking down the road. A [*bell*] woman was walking down the road.

Suddenly, she saw a [*bell*] man. Suddenly, she saw a [*bell*] man.

He was wearing a [*bell*] shirt, [*bell*] pants, and a [*bell*] hat. He was wearing a [*bell*] shirt, [*bell*] pants, and a [*bell*] hat.

He smiled and said, [*bell*]. He smiled and said, [*bell*].

Quizzes and tests track listing

The audio CD contains the audio quizzes and tests from Teacher's Manual 1.

Quizzes

Track	Unit	Page
Track 2	Unit 1	Page 82
Track 3	Unit 2	Page 83
Track 4	Unit 3	Page 84
Track 5	Unit 4	Page 85
Track 6	Unit 5	Page 86
Track 7	Unit 6	Page 87
Track 8	Unit 7	Page 88
Track 9	Unit 8	Page 89
Track 10	Unit 9	Page 90
Track 11	Unit 10	Page 91
Track 12	Unit 11	Page 92
Track 13	Unit 12	Page 93
Track 14	Unit 13	Page 94
Track 15	Unit 14	Page 95
Track 16	Unit 15	Page 96
Track 17	Unit 16	Page 97

Test 1

Track	Section	Pages
Track 18	Section 1	111–113
Track 19	Section 2	114
Track 20	Section 3	115
Track 21	Section 4	116
Track 22	Section 5	117

Test 2

Track	Section	Pages
Track 23	Section 1	120–122
Track 24	Section 2	123
Track 25	Section 3	124
Track 26	Section 4	125
Track 27	Section 5	126

Active Listening 1, 2nd ed.
Teacher's Manual + Test CD
Brown & Smith
Cambridge
9-780-521-678-1110